CATHOLIC DAILY AND SUNDAY MISSAL FOR 2025

Mass Reflections and prayers for your Spiritual Journey

Vol. 1

JANANUARY-JUNE

Copyright©2025 Dorothy B. Neal

All Rights Reserved.

No part of this book may be reproduced, distributed, or transmitted in any form or by any means, including photocopying, recording, or other electronic or mechanical methods, without the prior written permission of the publisher, except in the case of brief quotations embodied in critical reviews and certain other non-commercial uses permitted by copyright law.

Thank You

Dear Readers,

With heartfelt gratitude, I extend my deepest thanks to you for choosing to make **CATHOLIC DAILY AND SUNDAY MISSAL FOR 2025** a part of your spiritual journey. Your trust and dedication to deepening your faith and connecting with God through His Word is both inspiring and humbling. It is my sincere hope that this book has been a source of light, guidance, and comfort in your daily walk with Christ.

Each page of this book was crafted with prayerful reflection, and prayer with the aim of bringing the richness of the Scriptures into your everyday life. Whether you have turned to these pages in times of joy, seeking wisdom, or finding solace in difficult moments, know that you are part of a community of believers united in faith and love.

Your commitment to embracing the daily and Sunday readings not only strengthens your own spiritual life but also enriches the Church as a whole. It is through our shared reflection on the Word of God that we grow closer to one another and to our Lord.

As you continue on your faith journey, may the words within this book inspire you to live with greater compassion, hope, and love. Remember that you are never alone; God walks with you, and the entire community of believers surrounds you in prayer.

Thank you for allowing this book to accompany you throughout the year. May God's grace fill your heart and guide your steps, now and always.

With gratitude and blessings,

Dorothy B. Neal

Dorothy B. Neal

Dorothy B. Neal is a devoted Catholic and passionate author who finds deep joy in sharing the transformative power of the Word of God. Her love for Scripture and dedication to her faith have led her to create **CATHOLIC DAILY AND SUNDAY MISSAL FOR 2025**, aiming to provide a meaningful spiritual companion for readers.

With a background in theology and years of active involvement in various ministries, Dorothy offers guidance and insight to those seeking a closer relationship with God. Her writings are marked by a deep reverence for Catholic traditions, making the daily and Sunday Mass readings accessible and relevant to modern believers.

Dorothy lives her faith daily, cherishing time with her family and community, and continues to inspire others through her teaching and writing. She invites you to join her on a journey through the liturgical year, deepening your connection with God and finding inspiration in the living words of Scripture.

CONTENT

JANUARY 2025 14

WEDNESDAY, JANUARY 1 15
- *Mary, Mother of God - Solemnity - * Holy Day of Obligation ** 15

THURSDAY, JANUARY 2 17
- *Saints Basil the Great and Gregory Nazianzen, bishops and doctors – Memorial* 17

FRIDAY, JANUARY 3 18
- *First Friday* 18
- *Friday of the First week of Christmas* 18
- *Most Holy Name of Jesus - Optional Memorial* 18

SATURDAY, JANUARY 4 20
- *First Saturday* 20
- *Saturday of the First week of Christmas* 20
- *Saint Elizabeth Ann Seton, Religious - Memorial (United States)* 20

SUNDAY, JANUARY 5 21
- *Second Sunday of Christmas* 21
- *Epiphany of the Lord - Solemnity (United States)* 21

MONDAY, JANUARY 6 23
- *Epiphany of the Lord - Solemnity* 23
- *In the United States Monday after Epiphany* 23

TUESDAY, JANUARY 7 25
- *Tuesday after Epiphany* 25
- *Saint Raymond of Peñafort, priest - Optional Memorial* 25

WEDNESDAY, JANUARY 8 26
- *Wednesday after Epiphany* 26

THURSDAY, JANUARY 9 28
- *Thursday after Epiphany* 28

FRIDAY, JANUARY 10 29
- *Friday after Epiphany* 29

SATURDAY, JANUARY 11 31
- *Saturday after Epiphany* 31

SUNDAY, JANUARY 12 32
- *Baptism of the Lord - Feast* 32

MONDAY, JANUARY 13 34
- *Monday of the First week in Ordinary Time* 34
- *Saint Hilary, bishop and doctor - Optional Memorial* 34

TUESDAY, JANUARY 14 36
- *Tuesday of the First week in Ordinary Time* 36

WEDNESDAY, JANUARY 15 37
- *Wednesday of the First week in Ordinary Time* 37

THURSDAY, JANUARY 16 39
- *Thursday of the First week in Ordinary Time* 39

FRIDAY, JANUARY 17 40
- *Saint Anthony, abbot - Memorial* 40

SATURDAY, JANUARY 18 42

- ❖ Saturday of the First week in Ordinary Time 42
- ❖ Blessed Virgin Mary - Optional Memorial 42

SUNDAY, JANUARY 19 43
- ❖ Second Sunday in Ordinary Time 43

MONDAY, JANUARY 20 45
- ❖ Monday of the Second week in Ordinary Time 45
- ❖ Saint Fabian, pope and martyr - Optional Memorial 45
- ❖ Saint Sebastian, martyr - Optional Memorial 45

TUESDAY, JANUARY 21 47
- ❖ Saint Agnes, virgin and martyr - Memorial 47

WEDNESDAY, JANUARY 22 48
- ❖ Wednesday of the Second week in Ordinary Time 48
- ❖ Saint Vincent, deacon and martyr - Optional Memorial 48
- ❖ In the United States-Day of Prayer for the Legal Protection of Unborn Children 48

THURSDAY, JANUARY 23 50
- ❖ Thursday of the Second week in Ordinary Time 50
- ❖ In the United States- Thursday of the Second week in Ordinary Time 50
- ❖ Saint Vincent, deacon and martyr - Optional Memorial 50
- ❖ Saint Marianne Cope, Virgin - Optional Memorial 50

FRIDAY, JANUARY 24 52
- ❖ Saint Francis de Sales, bishop and doctor - Memorial 52

SATURDAY, JANUARY 25 53
- ❖ Conversion of Saint Paul, apostle - Feast 53

SUNDAY, JANUARY 26 55
- ❖ Third Sunday in Ordinary Time 55

MONDAY, JANUARY 27 57
- ❖ Monday of the Third week in Ordinary Time 57
- ❖ Saint Angela Merici, virgin - Optional Memorial 57

TUESDAY, JANUARY 28 59
- ❖ Saint Thomas Aquinas, priest and doctor - Memorial 59

WEDNESDAY, JANUARY 29 60
- ❖ Wednesday of the Third week in Ordinary Time 60

THURSDAY, JANUARY 30 62
- ❖ Thursday of the Third week in Ordinary Time 62

FRIDAY, JANUARY 31 63
- ❖ Saint John Bosco, priest - Memorial 63

FEBRUARY 2025 65

SATURDAY, FEBRUARY 1 66
- ❖ First Saturday 66
- ❖ Saturday of the Third week in Ordinary Time 66
- ❖ Blessed Virgin Mary - Optional Memorial 66

SUNDAY, FEBRUARY 2 67
- ❖ Presentation of the Lord - Feast 67

MONDAY, FEBRUARY 3 69
- ❖ Monday of the Fourth week in Ordinary Time 69
- ❖ Saint Blase, bishop and martyr - Optional Memorial 69
- ❖ Saint Ansgar, bishop - Optional Memorial 69

TUESDAY, FEBRUARY 4 71

- Tuesday of the Fourth week in Ordinary Time 71

WEDNESDAY, FEBRUARY 5 72
- *Saint Agatha, virgin and martyr - Memorial* 72

THURSDAY, FEBRUARY 6 74
- *Saint Paul Miki and companions, martyrs - Memorial* 74

FRIDAY, FEBRUARY 7 75
- *First Friday* 75
- *Friday of the Fourth week in Ordinary Time* 75

SATURDAY, FEBRUARY 8 77
- *Saturday of the Fourth week in Ordinary Time* 77
- *Saint Jerome Emiliani - Optional Memorial* 77
- *Saint Josephine Bakhita - Optional Memorial* 77
- *Blessed Virgin Mary - Optional Memorial* 77

SUNDAY, FEBRUARY 9 78
- *Fifth Sunday in Ordinary Time* 78

MONDAY, FEBRUARY 10 80
- *Saint Scholastica, virgin - Memorial* 80

TUESDAY, FEBRUARY 11 82
- *Tuesday of the Fifth week in Ordinary Time* 82
- *Our Lady of Lourdes - Optional Memorial* 82

WEDNESDAY, FEBRUARY 12 83
- *Wednesday of the Fifth week in Ordinary Time* 83

THURSDAY, FEBRUARY 13 85
- *Thursday of the Fifth week in Ordinary Time* 85

FRIDAY, FEBRUARY 14 86
- *Saint Cyril, monk, and Methodius, bishop - Memorial* 86

SATURDAY, FEBRUARY 15 88
- *Saturday of the Fifth week in Ordinary Time* 88
- *Blessed Virgin Mary - Optional Memorial* 88

SUNDAY, FEBRUARY 16 90
- *Sixth Sunday in Ordinary Time* 90

MONDAY, FEBRUARY 17 92
- *Monday of the Sixth week in Ordinary Time* 92
- *Seven Founders of the Order of Servites - Optional Memorial* 92

TUESDAY, FEBRUARY 18 93
- *Tuesday of the Sixth week in Ordinary Time* 93

WEDNESDAY, FEBRUARY 19 95
- *Wednesday of the Sixth week in Ordinary Time* 95

THURSDAY, FEBRUARY 20 96
- *Thursday of the Sixth week in Ordinary Time* 96

FRIDAY, FEBRUARY 21 98
- *Friday of the Sixth week in Ordinary Time* 98
- *Saint Peter Damian, bishop and doctor - Optional Memorial* 98

SATURDAY, FEBRUARY 22 99
- *Chair of Saint Peter, apostle - Feast* 99

SUNDAY, FEBRUARY 23 101
- *Seventh Sunday in Ordinary Time* 101

MONDAY, FEBRUARY 24 103
- *Monday of the Seventh week in Ordinary Time* 103

TUESDAY, FEBRUARY 25 104
- *Tuesday of the Seventh week in Ordinary Time* 104

WEDNESDAY, FEBRUARY 26 106
- *Wednesday of the Seventh week in Ordinary Time* 106

THURSDAY, FEBRUARY 27 107
- *Thursday of the Seventh week in Ordinary Time* 107

FRIDAY, FEBRUARY 28 108
- *Friday of the Seventh week in Ordinary Time* 108

MARCH 2025 111

SATURDAY, MARCH 1 112
- *First Saturday* 112
- *Saturday of the Seventh week in Ordinary Time* 112
- *Blessed Virgin Mary - Optional Memorial* 112

SUNDAY, MARCH 2 113
- *Eighth Sunday in Ordinary Time* 113

MONDAY, MARCH 3 115
- *Monday of the Eighth week in Ordinary Time* 115
- *In the United States- Monday of the Eighth week in Ordinary Time* 115
- *Saint Katharine Drexel, virgin - Optional Memorial* 115

TUESDAY, MARCH 4 117
- *Tuesday of the Eighth week in Ordinary Time* 117
- *Saint Casimir - Optional Memorial* 117

WEDNESDAY, MARCH 5 118
- *Day of Fast and Abstinance* 118
- *Ash Wednesday* 118

THURSDAY, MARCH 6 120
- *Thursday after Ash Wednesday* 120

FRIDAY, MARCH 7 122
- *First Friday* 122
- *Day of Abstinance* 122
- *Saints Perpetua and Felicity, martyrs - Commemoration* 122

SATURDAY, MARCH 8 123
- *Saturday after Ash Wednesday* 123
- *Saint John of God, religious - Commemoration* 123

SUNDAY, MARCH 9 125
- *First Sunday of Lent* 125

MONDAY, MARCH 10 127
- *Monday of the First week of Lent* 127

TUESDAY, MARCH 11 128
- *Tuesday of the First week of Lent* 128

WEDNESDAY, MARCH 12 129
- *Wednesday of the First week of Lent* 129

THURSDAY, MARCH 13 131
- *Thursday of the First week of Lent* 131

FRIDAY, MARCH 14 132
- *Day of Abstinance* 132
- *Friday of the First week of Lent* 132

SATURDAY, MARCH 15 134

	❖ Saturday of the First week of Lent	*134*
SUNDAY, MARCH 16		135
	❖ Second Sunday of Lent	*135*
MONDAY, MARCH 17		137
	❖ Monday of the Second week of Lent	*137*
	❖ Saint Patrick, bishop - Commemoration	*137*
TUESDAY, MARCH 18		139
	❖ Tuesday of the Second week of Lent	*139*
	❖ Saint Cyril of Jerusalem, bishop and doctor - Commemoration	*139*
WEDNESDAY, MARCH 19		140
	❖ Saint Joseph, Husband of Mary - Solemnity	*140*
THURSDAY, MARCH 20		142
	❖ Thursday of the Second week of Lent	*142*
FRIDAY, MARCH 21		143
	❖ Day of Abstinance	*143*
	❖ Friday of the Second week of Lent	*143*
SATURDAY, MARCH 22		145
	❖ Saturday of the Second week of Lent	*145*
SUNDAY, MARCH 23		146
	❖ Third Sunday of Lent	*146*
MONDAY, MARCH 24		148
	❖ Monday of the Third week of Lent	*148*
TUESDAY, MARCH 25		149
	❖ Annunciation of the Lord - Solemnity	*149*
WEDNESDAY, MARCH 26		151
	❖ Wednesday of the Third week of Lent	*151*
THURSDAY, MARCH 27		152
	❖ Thursday of the Third week of Lent	*152*
FRIDAY, MARCH 28		154
	❖ Day of Abstinance	*154*
	❖ Friday of the Third week of Lent	*154*
SATURDAY, MARCH 29		155
	❖ Saturday of the Third week of Lent	*155*
SUNDAY, MARCH 30		156
	❖ Fourth Sunday of Lent	*156*
MONDAY, MARCH 31		158
	❖ Monday of the Fourth week of Lent	*158*
APRIL 2025		**160**
TUESDAY, APRIL 1		161
	❖ Tuesday of the Fourth week of Lent	*161*
WEDNESDAY, APRIL 2		162
	❖ Wednesday of the Fourth week of Lent	*162*
	❖ Saint Francis of Paola, hermit - Commemoration	*162*
THURSDAY, APRIL 3		163
	❖ Thursday of the Fourth week of Lent	*163*
FRIDAY, APRIL 4		165
	❖ First Friday	*165*
	❖ Day of Abstinance	*165*

- ❖ Friday of the Fourth week of Lent 165
- ❖ Saint Isidore, bishop and doctor - Commemoration 165

SATURDAY, APRIL 5 166
- ❖ First Saturday 166
- ❖ Saturday of the Fourth week of Lent 166
- ❖ Saint Vincent Ferrer, priest - Commemoration 166

SUNDAY, APRIL 6 168
- ❖ Fifth Sunday of Lent 168

MONDAY, APRIL 7 170
- ❖ Saint John Baptist de la Salle, priest - Commemoration 170

TUESDAY, APRIL 8 171
- ❖ Tuesday of the Fifth week of Lent 171

WEDNESDAY, APRIL 9 172
- ❖ Wednesday of the Fifth week of Lent 172

THURSDAY, APRIL 10 174
- ❖ Thursday of the Fifth week of Lent 174

FRIDAY, APRIL 11 175
- ❖ Day of Abstinance 175
- ❖ Friday of the Fifth week of Lent 175
- ❖ Saint Stanislaus, Bishop and martyr - Commemoration 175

SATURDAY, APRIL 12 176
- ❖ Saturday of the Fifth week of Lent 176

SUNDAY, APRIL 13 178
- ❖ Passion (Palm) Sunday 178

MONDAY, APRIL 14 180
- ❖ Monday of Holy Week 180

TUESDAY, APRIL 15 181
- ❖ Tuesday of Holy Week 181

WEDNESDAY, APRIL 16 182
- ❖ Wednesday of Holy Week 182

THURSDAY, APRIL 17 184
- ❖ Holy Thursday 184

FRIDAY, APRIL 18 186
- ❖ Day of Fast and Abstinance 186
- ❖ Good Friday 186

SATURDAY, APRIL 19 188
- ❖ Holy Saturday 188

SUNDAY, APRIL 20 192
- ❖ Easter Sunday - Solemnity 192

MONDAY, APRIL 21 195
- ❖ Monday of Easter Week 195

TUESDAY, APRIL 22 196
- ❖ Tuesday of Easter Week 196

WEDNESDAY, APRIL 23 198
- ❖ Wednesday of Easter Week 198

THURSDAY, APRIL 24 199
- ❖ Thursday of Easter Week 199

FRIDAY, APRIL 25 201
- ❖ Saint Mark, evangelist - Feast 201

SATURDAY, APRIL 26	202
❖ Saturday of Easter Week	202
SUNDAY, APRIL 27	204
❖ Second Sunday of Easter	204
MONDAY, APRIL 28	206
❖ Monday of the Second week of Easter	206
❖ Saint Peter Chanel, priest and martyr - Optional Memorial	206
❖ Saint Louis Mary de Montfort, priest - Optional Memorial	206
TUESDAY, APRIL 29	207
❖ Saint Catherine of Siena, virgin and doctor - Memorial	207
WEDNESDAY, APRIL 30	208
❖ Wednesday of the Second week of Easter	208
❖ Saint Pius V, pope - Optional Memorial	208
MAY 2025	**210**
THURSDAY, MAY 1	211
❖ Thursday of the Second week of Easter	211
❖ Saint Joseph the Worker - Optional Memorial	211
FRIDAY, MAY 2	213
❖ First Friday	213
❖ Saint Athanasius, bishop and doctor - Memorial	213
SATURDAY, MAY 3	214
❖ First Saturday	214
❖ Saints Philip and James, apostles - Feast	214
SUNDAY, MAY 4	216
❖ Third Sunday of Easter	216
MONDAY, MAY 5	218
❖ Monday of the Third week of Easter	218
TUESDAY, MAY 6	219
❖ Tuesday of the Third week of Easter	219
WEDNESDAY, MAY 7	220
❖ Wednesday of the Third week of Easter	220
THURSDAY, MAY 8	222
❖ Thursday of the Third week of Easter	222
FRIDAY, MAY 9	223
❖ Friday of the Third week of Easter	223
SATURDAY, MAY 10	225
❖ Saturday of the Third week of Easter	225
❖ In the United States	225
❖ Saturday of the Third week of Easter	225
❖ Saint Damien de Veuster, Priest - Optional Memorial	225
SUNDAY, MAY 11	227
❖ Fourth Sunday of Easter	227
MONDAY, MAY 12	229
❖ Monday of the Fourth week of Easter	229
❖ Saints Nereus and Achilleus, martyrs - Optional Memorial	229
❖ Saint Pancras, martyr - Optional Memorial	229
TUESDAY, MAY 13	230
❖ Tuesday of the Fourth week of Easter	230

- ❖ Our Lady of Fatima - Optional Memorial 230

WEDNESDAY, MAY 14 232
- ❖ Saint Matthias, apostle - Feast 232

THURSDAY, MAY 15 233
- ❖ Thursday of the Fourth week of Easter 233
- ❖ In the United States 233
- ❖ Thursday of the Fourth week of Easter 233
- ❖ Saint Isidore the Farmer - Optional Memorial 233

FRIDAY, MAY 16 235
- ❖ Friday of the Fourth week of Easter 235

SATURDAY, MAY 17 236
- ❖ Saturday of the Fourth week of Easter 236

SUNDAY, MAY 18 237
- ❖ Fifth Sunday of Easter 237

MONDAY, MAY 19 239
- ❖ Monday of the Fifth week of Easter 239

TUESDAY, MAY 20 240
- ❖ Tuesday of the Fifth week of Easter 240
- ❖ Saint Bernardine of Siena, priest - Optional Memorial 240

WEDNESDAY, MAY 21 242
- ❖ Wednesday of the Fifth week of Easter 242
- ❖ Saints Christopher Magallanes, priest and martyr, and Companions, martyrs - Optional Memorial 242

THURSDAY, MAY 22 243
- ❖ Thursday of the Fifth week of Easter 243
- ❖ Saint Rita of Cascia, religious - Optional Memorial 243

FRIDAY, MAY 23 245
- ❖ Friday of the Fifth week of Easter 245

SATURDAY, MAY 24 246
- ❖ Saturday of the Fifth week of Easter 246

SUNDAY, MAY 25 247
- ❖ Sixth Sunday of Easter 247

MONDAY, MAY 26 249
- ❖ Saint Philip Neri, priest - Memorial 249

TUESDAY, MAY 27 250
- ❖ Tuesday of the Sixth week of Easter 250
- ❖ Saint Augustine of Canterbury, bishop - Optional Memorial 250

WEDNESDAY, MAY 28 252
- ❖ Wednesday of the Sixth week of Easter 252

THURSDAY, MAY 29 253
- ❖ Ascension of the Lord - Solemnity - * Holy Day of Obligation * 253
- ❖ In the archdioceses and dioceses of the US states of Alaska, California, Hawaii, Idaho, Montana, Nevada, Oregon, Utah, and Washington only 253
- ❖ Thursday of the Sixth week of Easter 253

FRIDAY, MAY 30 254
- ❖ Friday of the Sixth week of Easter 254

SATURDAY, MAY 31 255
- ❖ Visitation of the Virgin Mary to Elizabeth - Feast 255

JUNE 2025 257

- SUNDAY, JUNE 1 258
  - ❖ Seventh Sunday of Easter 258
  - ❖ In the archdioceses and dioceses of the US states of Alaska, California, Hawaii, Idaho, Montana, Nevada, Oregon, Utah, and Washington only 258
  - ❖ Ascension of the Lord - Solemnity 258
- MONDAY, JUNE 2 260
  - ❖ Monday of the Seventh week of Easter 260
  - ❖ Saints Marcellinus and Peter, martyrs - Optional Memorial 260
- TUESDAY, JUNE 3 261
  - ❖ Saints Charles Lwanga and companions, martyrs - Memorial 261
- WEDNESDAY, JUNE 4 262
  - ❖ Wednesday of the Seventh week of Easter 262
- THURSDAY, JUNE 5 263
  - ❖ Saint Boniface, bishop and martyr - Memorial 263
- FRIDAY, JUNE 6 264
  - ❖ First Friday 264
  - ❖ Friday of the Seventh week of Easter 264
  - ❖ Saint Norbert, bishop - Optional Memorial 264
- SATURDAY, JUNE 7 266
  - ❖ First Saturday 266
  - ❖ Saturday of the Seventh week of Easter 266
- SUNDAY, JUNE 8 267
  - ❖ Pentecost - Solemnity 267
- MONDAY, JUNE 9 269
  - ❖ Monday of the Tenth week in Ordinary Time 269
  - ❖ Saint Ephrem, deacon and doctor - Optional Memorial 269
- TUESDAY, JUNE 10 270
  - ❖ Tuesday of the Tenth week in Ordinary Time 270
- WEDNESDAY, JUNE 11 271
  - ❖ Saint Barnabas, apostle - Memorial 271
- THURSDAY, JUNE 12 273
  - ❖ Thursday of the Tenth week in Ordinary Time 273
- FRIDAY, JUNE 13 274
  - ❖ Saint Anthony of Padua, priest and doctor - Memorial 274
- SATURDAY, JUNE 14 275
  - ❖ Saturday of the Tenth week in Ordinary Time 275
  - ❖ Blessed Virgin Mary - Optional Memorial 275
- SUNDAY, JUNE 15 277
  - ❖ The Holy Trinity - Solemnity 277
- MONDAY, JUNE 16 279
  - ❖ Monday of the Eleventh week in Ordinary Time 279
- TUESDAY, JUNE 17 280
  - ❖ Tuesday of the Eleventh week in Ordinary Time 280
- WEDNESDAY, JUNE 18 281
  - ❖ Wednesday of the Eleventh week in Ordinary Time 281
- THURSDAY, JUNE 19 283
  - ❖ The Body and Blood of Christ (Corpus Christi) - Solemnity 283

- In the United States- Thursday of the Eleventh week in Ordinary Time 283

FRIDAY, JUNE 20 284
- Friday of the Eleventh week in Ordinary Time 284

SATURDAY, JUNE 21 285
- Saint Aloysius Gonzaga, religious - Memorial 285

SUNDAY, JUNE 22 287
- Twelfth Sunday in Ordinary Time 287
- In the United States 287
- The Body and Blood of Christ (Corpus Christi) - Solemnity 287

MONDAY, JUNE 23 289
- Monday of the Twelfth week in Ordinary Time 289

TUESDAY, JUNE 24 290
- Birth of Saint John the Baptist - Solemnity 290

WEDNESDAY, JUNE 25 292
- Wednesday of the Twelfth week in Ordinary Time 292

THURSDAY, JUNE 26 293
- Thursday of the Twelfth week in Ordinary Time 293

FRIDAY, JUNE 27 294
- Sacred Heart of Jesus - Solemnity 294

SATURDAY, JUNE 28 296
- Saint Irenaeus, bishop and martyr - Memorial 296

SUNDAY, JUNE 29 297
- Saints Peter and Paul, apostles - Solemnity 297

MONDAY, JUNE 30 299
- Monday of the Thirteenth week in Ordinary Time 299
- First Martyrs of the Church of Rome - Optional Memorial 299

January 2025

Wednesday, January 1

❖ Mary, Mother of God - Solemnity - * Holy Day of Obligation *

- ➢ First Reading: Numbers 6: 22-27
- ➢ Responsorial Psalm: Psalms 67: 2-3, 5, 6, 8
- ➢ Second Reading: Galatians 4: 4-7
- ➢ Alleluia: Hebrews 1: 1-2
- ➢ Gospel: Luke 2: 16-21
- ➢ Lectionary: 18

On this first day of the year, the Church celebrates the Solemnity of Mary, Mother of God. This feast not only honors Mary's unique role in salvation history but also reflects on her maternal care for the Church and all humanity. As we begin a new year, we seek her intercession, asking for her guidance and protection. Today's readings draw us into the mystery of God's love and the fulfillment of His promises through Mary's "yes."

➢ First Reading: Numbers 6: 22-27

In this passage from the Book of Numbers, God instructs Moses to teach Aaron and his sons the priestly blessing to bestow upon the Israelites. This blessing is a powerful reminder of God's protection, grace, and peace. As we start the new year, we are invited to receive this blessing with open hearts, trusting in God's providence and care.

Reflection:
God's blessing is a gift of His presence in our lives. As we reflect on this passage, let us consider the ways in which we can be open to His grace in the coming year. Just as the Israelites were blessed by God through Aaron, we, too, are blessed daily by God's love and mercy. This blessing is not just for protection, but for a deeper relationship with the Divine, one that brings peace to our hearts and minds.

Prayer:
Heavenly Father, as we begin this new year, may Your blessing be upon us. Fill our hearts with Your peace, and guide us with Your grace. Help us to trust in Your protection and to seek Your presence in all that we do. Amen.

➢ Second Reading: Galatians 4: 4-7

In his letter to the Galatians, St. Paul speaks of the fullness of time when God sent His Son, born of a woman, to redeem those under the law. Through Jesus, we have received adoption as children of God and can now call Him "Abba, Father." This passage reminds us of the great gift of our salvation and our new identity in Christ.

Reflection:
Our identity as children of God is a profound truth that shapes our lives. As we meditate on this passage, let us remember that through Mary, the Mother of God, we have been brought into the family of God. This relationship with God is not distant or formal; it is intimate and personal. Let us embrace our identity as God's children and live out this truth in our daily lives.

Prayer:
Loving God, thank You for the gift of Your Son, through whom we have become Your children. Help us to live each day in the light of this truth, knowing that we are loved and cherished by You. May we always seek to grow in our relationship with You and share Your love with others. Amen.

➢ Gospel: Luke 2: 16-21

The Gospel of Luke recounts the visit of the shepherds to the newborn Jesus, Mary, and Joseph. After the shepherds share what the angels had told them about the child, Mary treasures all these things in her heart. On this day, we also hear about the circumcision of Jesus, where He is officially named as the angel Gabriel had instructed: "Jesus."

Reflection:
Mary's role as the Mother of God is beautifully illustrated in this Gospel passage. She is a model of contemplation, treasuring the mysteries of her Son in her heart. As we reflect on this reading, let us follow Mary's example by pondering the events of our own lives with faith and trust in God's plan. The name "Jesus" means "God saves," reminding us of the purpose of His coming into the world. May we carry His name in our hearts and lives throughout this year.

Prayer:
Holy Mary, Mother of God, guide us as we seek to follow your Son more closely. Help us to treasure His words and actions in our hearts, and lead us to a deeper understanding of His love. May we honor His holy name in all that we do, and may His presence be with us throughout the year. Amen.

Thursday, January 2

❖ Saints Basil the Great and Gregory Nazianzen, bishops and doctors – Memorial

➢ First Reading: First John 2: 22-28
➢ Responsorial Psalm: Psalms 98: 1, 2-3ab, 3cd-4
➢ Alleluia: Hebrews 1: 1-2
➢ Gospel: John 1: 19-28
➢ Lectionary: 205

Today, the Church commemorates Saints Basil the Great and Gregory Nazianzen, two of the most prominent figures in early Christianity. Both were bishops, theologians, and doctors of the Church, known for their profound teachings and deep friendship. Their contributions to the development of Christian doctrine, particularly regarding the Holy Trinity, have left a lasting legacy. As we reflect on their lives, we are called to deepen our understanding of the faith and to pursue wisdom and holiness.

➢ First Reading: 1 John 2: 22-28

In this passage from the First Letter of John, the apostle warns against false teachers and urges believers to remain faithful to the truth of Christ. He reminds us that those who deny that Jesus is the Christ are antichrists, and he encourages the faithful to abide in what they have been taught. By holding fast to the truth, we are assured of eternal life.

Reflection:
Staying true to the teachings of Christ is essential for our spiritual journey. Saints Basil and Gregory were steadfast defenders of the faith, standing firm against heresies that threatened to distort the truth. As we reflect on this passage, let us be inspired by their courage and dedication. In our own lives, we are called to discern truth from falsehood and to remain grounded in the teachings of the Church. By doing so, we preserve our relationship with Christ and the promise of eternal life.

Prayer:
Heavenly Father, grant us the wisdom and courage to remain faithful to Your truth. Help us to recognize and reject false teachings, and to hold fast to the faith that has been handed down to us. May the example of Saints Basil and Gregory inspire us to seek knowledge and live in the light of Your Word. Amen.

➢ **Gospel: John 1: 19-28**

The Gospel reading presents the testimony of John the Baptist as he prepares the way for the coming of Christ. When questioned by the priests and Levites, John humbly denies being the Messiah, Elijah, or the Prophet. Instead, he identifies himself as "the voice of one crying out in the wilderness," fulfilling the prophecy of Isaiah. John's role is to point others to Christ, the one who is greater and who will baptize with the Holy Spirit.

Reflection:

John the Baptist's humility and clarity of purpose are exemplary for all who seek to follow Christ. Like John, Saints Basil and Gregory devoted their lives to pointing others to the truth of Christ. They understood their roles as servants of a greater mission, one that transcends personal glory. As we reflect on this Gospel, we are called to consider how we, too, can be voices in the wilderness, preparing the way for the Lord in our own contexts. Let us embrace humility and strive to lead others to Christ through our words and actions.

Prayer:

Lord Jesus, help us to follow the example of John the Baptist in humility and purpose. May we always seek to glorify You and lead others to Your saving grace. Grant us the courage to be witnesses to Your truth, and may the lives of Saints Basil and Gregory inspire us to remain faithful and steadfast in our mission. Amen.

Friday, January 3

- ❖ First Friday
- ❖ Friday of the First week of Christmas
- ❖ Most Holy Name of Jesus - Optional Memorial

➢ First Reading: First John 2: 29 – 3: 6
➢ Responsorial Psalm: Psalms 98: 1, 3cd-4, 5-6
➢ Alleluia: John 1: 14a, 12a
➢ Gospel: John 1: 29-34
➢ Lectionary: 206

On this day, we honor the Most Holy Name of Jesus, a name that carries immense power, love, and salvation. The name of Jesus, which means "God saves," reminds us of the purpose of His incarnation and His mission to redeem humanity. This day also marks the First Friday of the month, a time traditionally dedicated to the Sacred Heart of Jesus, inviting us to reflect on His boundless love and mercy. As we continue in the Christmas season, today's readings deepen our understanding of who Jesus is and what His name signifies.

➢ First Reading: 1 John 2: 29 – 3: 6

In this passage, John speaks about the transformative power of being children of God. He emphasizes the importance of righteousness and living in a way that reflects our true identity in Christ. John reminds us that when Christ appears, we shall be like Him, for we shall see Him as He is. He also calls us to purity and cautions against sin, which is incompatible with our new life in Christ.

Reflection:

Being called children of God is both a privilege and a responsibility. As we meditate on this passage, we are encouraged to live in a manner worthy of our identity. The name of Jesus, which we honor today, is the foundation of this new life. It is through Him that we are reborn and called to reflect His purity and righteousness. Let us examine our lives and ask ourselves if we are living in a way that honors the name of Jesus. Are we striving to embody the virtues that come with being God's children?

Prayer:

Heavenly Father, thank You for the gift of being called Your children. Help us to live in a way that honors the name of Jesus, reflecting His purity and righteousness. May we always strive to grow in holiness and to live out our identity as Your beloved sons and daughters. Amen.

➢ Gospel: John 1: 29-34

In this Gospel passage, John the Baptist sees Jesus approaching and declares, "Behold, the Lamb of God, who takes away the sin of the world!" John testifies that Jesus is the one who will baptize with the Holy Spirit and that he has seen and borne witness that Jesus is the Son of God. This powerful moment reveals Jesus' identity and His mission to take away the sins of the world.

Reflection:

John the Baptist's proclamation of Jesus as the Lamb of God is central to our faith. It is a reminder of the sacrificial love of Jesus, who came to take away the sins of the world. The name of Jesus embodies this mission of salvation. As we reflect on this Gospel, we are invited to contemplate the profound significance of Jesus' name and His role as our Savior. Let us recognize the power of His name in our lives, and like John, bear witness to His saving grace.

Prayer:

Lord Jesus, we praise Your holy name, the name that brings salvation to the world. Help us to bear witness to Your love and mercy in our lives. May we always honor Your name by living according to Your will, and may we share the good news of Your salvation with others. Amen.

Saturday, January 4

- ❖ First Saturday
- ❖ Saturday of the First week of Christmas
- ❖ Saint Elizabeth Ann Seton, Religious - Memorial (United States)

> - First Reading: First John 3: 7-10
> - Responsorial Psalm: Psalms 98: 1, 7-8, 9
> - Alleluia: Hebrews 1: 1-2
> - Gospel: John 1: 35-42
> - Lectionary: 207

Today, we honor Saint Elizabeth Ann Seton, the first native-born citizen of the United States to be canonized a saint. A woman of deep faith, courage, and resilience, Elizabeth Ann Seton founded the first Catholic school in America and established the Sisters of Charity. Her life exemplifies trust in God amidst trials and a commitment to serving others. As we observe the First Saturday and continue in the Christmas season, we are invited to reflect on the transformative power of God's grace in our lives and the call to live out our faith through service and love.

> - First Reading: 1 John 3: 7-10

In this passage, John draws a clear distinction between those who live righteously and those who practice sin. He emphasizes that those who are born of God do not continue to sin, for they have God's seed abiding in them. John urges believers to live as children of God, rejecting sin and embracing righteousness. He reminds us that our actions reveal our true identity—whether we belong to God or the devil.

Reflection:
John's message is a powerful reminder of the seriousness of sin and the importance of living a life that reflects our identity as children of God. Saint Elizabeth Ann Seton's life is a testament to this call to righteousness. Despite the challenges and hardships she faced, she remained faithful to God, allowing His grace to guide her actions and decisions. As we reflect on this passage, let us consider how we are living out our faith. Are we choosing righteousness and striving to grow in holiness, or are we allowing sin to take root in our lives? Let us ask for the grace to live as true children of God, following the example of the saints.

Prayer:
Loving Father, help us to live as Your children, rejecting sin and embracing the righteousness that comes from following Your will. May we be inspired by the example of Saint Elizabeth Ann Seton, who lived a life

of faith and service. Strengthen us to choose righteousness in our daily lives and to grow in holiness. Amen.

➤ Gospel: John 1: 35-42

In this Gospel passage, John the Baptist again points to Jesus, saying, "Behold, the Lamb of God!" Two of John's disciples, hearing this, follow Jesus. When Jesus turns and asks them what they are seeking, they respond with a desire to know where He is staying. Jesus invites them to "come and see," leading to their encounter with the Messiah. One of these disciples, Andrew, then brings his brother Simon to Jesus, who gives him the name Peter.

Reflection:
This Gospel highlights the beginning of the disciples' journey with Jesus. Their willingness to follow Him after hearing John's testimony and their desire to know Him more deeply is a model for all who seek a relationship with Christ. Saint Elizabeth Ann Seton's life was marked by a similar desire to follow Jesus, leading her to profound personal transformation and a life of service. As we reflect on this passage, we are invited to respond to Jesus' call to "come and see." How do we seek to know Jesus more deeply? Are we open to the transformation He offers? Let us, like Andrew, bring others to Jesus, sharing the joy of our encounter with Him.

Prayer:
Lord Jesus, thank You for calling us to follow You. Help us to respond with a willing heart, eager to know You more deeply. May we, like the first disciples, be transformed by our encounter with You and share the joy of knowing You with others. Inspired by Saint Elizabeth Ann Seton, may we dedicate our lives to Your service and lead others to You. Amen.

Sunday, January 5

- ❖ Second Sunday of Christmas
- ❖ Epiphany of the Lord - Solemnity (United States)

- ➤ First Reading: Isaiah 60: 1-6
- ➤ Responsorial Psalm: Psalms 72: 1-2, 7-8, 10-11, 12-13
- ➤ Second Reading: Ephesians 3: 2-3a, 5-6
- ➤ Alleluia: Matthew 2: 2
- ➤ Gospel: Matthew 2: 1-12
- ➤ Lectionary: 20

On this feast of the Epiphany, we celebrate the manifestation of Christ to the Gentiles, symbolized by the visit of the Magi. This Solemnity reveals that Jesus is not only the Savior of the Jews but of all nations. The arrival of the Magi highlights the universal scope of Christ's mission and invites us to reflect on the light that Jesus brings to our lives. As we continue in the Christmas season, the Epiphany reminds us of the revelation of God's grace to all peoples and calls us to recognize and honor Christ in our own lives.

➢ First Reading: Isaiah 60: 1-6

The prophet Isaiah speaks of a future time of glory when the light of God will shine upon Jerusalem, attracting nations and kings. This passage foresees a time when the radiance of God's presence will gather people from afar, bringing them to worship and honor Him. The imagery of light and the gathering of riches symbolize the fulfillment of God's promises and the universal recognition of His sovereignty.

Reflection:

Isaiah's vision of light and gathering is fulfilled in the Epiphany, when the Magi come to adore the newborn King. This reading invites us to reflect on how the light of Christ illuminates our own lives and draws us to Him. As we meditate on this passage, let us consider how we are responding to the light of Christ in our own journey. Are we open to the transformative power of His presence, and do we allow His light to guide our paths? The Magi's journey teaches us to seek and recognize the divine light in our lives and to bring our gifts in humble adoration.

Prayer:

Lord God, Your light has come into the world through Your Son, Jesus Christ. Help us to recognize and follow this light in our lives, and may we be drawn closer to You. As we celebrate the Epiphany, fill our hearts with Your radiant love and guide us in our journey to honor and serve You. Amen.

➢ Second Reading: Ephesians 3: 2-3a, 5-6

In this reading, St. Paul reveals the mystery of Christ, which was made known to him by revelation. He explains that this mystery is that the Gentiles are coheirs with the Jews, members of the same body, and sharers in the promise of Christ Jesus. This passage highlights the inclusive nature of the Gospel and the unity that all believers share in Christ.

Reflection:

St. Paul's message emphasizes the universal scope of the Gospel, a truth that is beautifully illustrated by the Epiphany. The revelation of Christ to the Magi signifies that salvation through Jesus is for all people, breaking down barriers and uniting all believers. As we reflect on this reading, let us rejoice in our shared inheritance in Christ and strive to live out the unity that His Gospel brings. How can we foster this sense of unity and inclusivity in our communities and in our relationships with others?

Prayer:

Gracious Lord, thank You for revealing the mystery of Your salvation to all nations. Help us to live in the unity of the Spirit and to embrace the inclusive nature of Your love. May we recognize and celebrate our shared inheritance in Christ, and may our lives reflect the unity and grace You offer to all people. Amen.

> Gospel: Matthew 2: 1-12

The Gospel of Matthew recounts the visit of the Magi from the East, who follow a star to find the newborn King of the Jews. They come bearing gifts of gold, frankincense, and myrrh, and worship Him. Their journey signifies the recognition of Jesus as the Savior of all people and the fulfillment of Old Testament prophecies. The Magi's story highlights the theme of revelation and the response of adoration to Christ's presence.

Reflection:

The visit of the Magi is a powerful symbol of the universal recognition of Christ's kingship. Their journey, guided by the star, reflects the search for truth and the response of worship to the divine revelation. As we reflect on this Gospel passage, let us consider how we respond to Christ's presence in our lives. Are we, like the Magi, willing to journey in faith, bringing our gifts and offering our worship? The Epiphany challenges us to recognize and honor Christ as the light and King of our lives, and to respond with the same reverence and joy shown by the Magi.

Prayer:

Lord Jesus, You are the light of the world and the King of all nations. We thank You for revealing Yourself to us and for guiding us on our journey of faith. Like the Magi, may we come to You with open hearts, bringing our gifts and worshiping You with joy. Help us to follow Your light and to share the good news of Your love with others. Amen.

Monday, January 6

❖ Epiphany of the Lord - Solemnity
❖ In the United States Monday after Epiphany

> First Reading: First John 3: 22 – 4: 6
> Responsorial Psalm: Psalms 2: 7bc-8, 10-11
> Alleluia: Matthew 4: 23
> Gospel: Matthew 4: 12-17, 23-25
> Lectionary: 212

Today, we continue celebrating the Solemnity of the Epiphany, reflecting on the manifestation of Christ to the world. The Epiphany reveals Jesus as the light and Savior for all nations, and today's readings deepen our understanding of His mission and the nature of our response to His call. As we reflect on this feast, we are reminded of the call to recognize and follow Christ, who brings light and healing to all.

➤ First Reading: 1 John 3: 22 – 4: 6

In this passage, St. John discusses the importance of remaining in God and His love. He emphasizes that those who live according to God's commandments and love one another are truly of God. John also warns about false prophets, encouraging believers to test the spirits to see whether they are from God. The true spirit of God acknowledges Jesus Christ come in the flesh.

Reflection:
John's exhortation to live in love and to test the spirits reflects the central message of the Epiphany: recognizing Christ's presence and responding with authentic faith. The love of God is evident in those who follow His commandments and who love others. As we celebrate the Epiphany, we are called to examine our own faith and actions. Are we living out the love of God in our lives? Do we discern the true spirit of Christ in our interactions with others? Let us strive to embody the love and truth that God reveals to us.

Prayer:
Lord God, help us to remain in Your love and to live according to Your commandments. Give us the wisdom to discern Your true spirit and to recognize the signs of Your presence in our lives. May we reflect Your love to others and grow in our understanding of Your truth. Amen.

➤ Gospel: Matthew 4: 12-17, 23-25

This Gospel passage describes the beginning of Jesus' public ministry in Galilee. Upon hearing of John the Baptist's arrest, Jesus withdraws to Galilee, fulfilling the prophecy of Isaiah that speaks of a great light shining in the darkness. He begins preaching, "Repent, for the kingdom of heaven has come near," and performs many miracles, healing the sick and afflicted. The news of His works spreads, attracting great crowds.

Reflection:
Matthew's account of Jesus' ministry highlights the fulfillment of Old Testament prophecies and the dawning of a new era with Jesus as the light of the world. His call to repentance and the healing miracles signify the arrival of God's kingdom. As we reflect on this Gospel, we are invited to consider how we respond to Jesus' call. Are we attentive to His message of repentance and the presence of His kingdom in our lives? The Epiphany calls us to recognize and embrace Jesus as the light that dispels darkness and to respond to His invitation with faith and action.

Prayer:
Lord Jesus, You are the light that shines in our darkness. As we celebrate the Epiphany, help us to heed Your call to repentance and to embrace the kingdom of heaven You bring. May we follow Your example in spreading Your light and love to those around us. Strengthen us in our faith and guide us in Your truth. Amen.

Tuesday, January 7

- ❖ Tuesday after Epiphany
- ❖ Saint Raymond of Peñafort, priest - Optional Memorial

> First Reading: First John 4: 7-10

> Responsorial Psalm: Psalms 72: 1-2, 3-4, 7-8

> Alleluia: Luke 4: 18

> Gospel: Mark 6: 34-44

> Lectionary: 213

Today, we commemorate Saint Raymond of Peñafort, a priest known for his significant contributions to canon law and his dedication to preaching and pastoral care. His life is a testament to the power of love and service in advancing the mission of the Church. The readings for today focus on the profound nature of God's love and the miraculous provision of Jesus, reminding us of the centrality of love and compassion in our Christian calling.

> First Reading: 1 John 4: 7-10

In this passage, St. John emphasizes the importance of love as the core of the Christian faith. He asserts that love comes from God and that those who love are born of God and know God. John reveals that God's love is manifest in the sending of His Son, Jesus Christ, to be the atonement for our sins. Love is not just a feeling but a divine action that demonstrates God's commitment to humanity.

Reflection:
The essence of Christian life is love, which is rooted in God's own nature. Saint Raymond of Peñafort exemplified this love through his work in canon law and his dedication to serving others. As we reflect on this passage, let us consider how we are living out this divine love in our own lives. Are our actions and relationships characterized by the love that comes from God? Let us strive to embody this love in our interactions with others, following the example of Christ and the saints.

Prayer:
Heavenly Father, we thank You for Your boundless love revealed through Your Son, Jesus Christ. Help us to live in Your love and to reflect it in all our relationships. May we, like Saint Raymond, serve others with a heart full of compassion and commitment. Strengthen us to love as You love and to be a witness to Your grace in the world. Amen.

> Gospel: Mark 6: 34-44

In this Gospel passage, Jesus sees the large crowd and has compassion for them, as they are like sheep without a shepherd. He begins teaching them and, as it grows late, the disciples suggest sending the people away to find food. Instead, Jesus performs a miracle by multiplying five loaves and two fish to feed the crowd of five thousand men, besides women and children. This act of provision reveals Jesus' care and His ability to meet our needs abundantly.

Reflection:
Jesus' miracle of feeding the multitude illustrates His deep compassion and ability to provide for our needs beyond our expectations. It also points to the Eucharistic theme of Christ being the Bread of Life, satisfying our spiritual hunger. As we reflect on this passage, let us recognize Jesus' ongoing provision in our lives and His call to share His abundance with others. Saint Raymond of Peñafort, through his commitment to teaching and service, also exemplified this spirit of generosity and care. How can we respond to Jesus' compassion by meeting the needs of those around us?

Prayer:
Lord Jesus, we thank You for Your miraculous provision and Your compassion for us. Help us to trust in Your ability to meet our needs and to share Your blessings with others. Inspire us to act with love and generosity, following the example of Saint Raymond. May we always be attentive to the needs of others and reflect Your caring presence in our lives. Amen.

Wednesday, January 8

❖ Wednesday after Epiphany

> First Reading: First John 4: 11-18
> Responsorial Psalm: Psalms 72: 1-2, 10, 12-13
> Alleluia: First Timothy 3: 16
> Gospel: Mark 6: 45-52
> Lectionary: 214

On this day after the feast of the Epiphany, the liturgy invites us to continue reflecting on the themes of love and faith. Today's readings deepen our understanding of how God's love perfects us and how faith in Jesus helps us navigate the challenges of life. As we meditate on these passages, we are encouraged to trust in God's presence and to live out His love in our daily lives.

➢ First Reading: 1 John 4: 11-18

In this passage, St. John speaks about the perfect love of God and how it casts out fear. He emphasizes that because God has loved us so much, we ought to love one another. John explains that love is made perfect among us when we live in God and He lives in us. Perfect love, rooted in God's presence, drives out fear and assures us of our relationship with Him.

Reflection:
St. John's teaching on perfect love highlights the transformative power of God's love in our lives. It is through God's love that we find freedom from fear and assurance of our place in His family. As we reflect on this passage, let us examine how God's love is evident in our lives and how it influences our interactions with others. Are we allowing God's love to perfect us and drive out fear? Let us strive to embody this love in our daily lives, fostering a deeper connection with God and with those around us.

Prayer:
Loving Father, Your perfect love casts out all fear. Help us to live in Your love and to let it transform our hearts and relationships. May we reflect Your love to others and find assurance in our relationship with You. Strengthen us to live boldly in Your grace and to overcome fear with the power of Your love. Amen.

➢ Gospel: Mark 6: 45-52

In this Gospel passage, Jesus compels His disciples to get into a boat and go ahead of Him to the other side of the Sea of Galilee while He dismisses the crowd. Later, He comes to them walking on the water. The disciples are terrified, but Jesus reassures them with the words, "Take heart; it is I. Do not be afraid." The wind ceases, and they are utterly astounded. Their lack of understanding about the loaves and fish is highlighted, showing their struggle to grasp Jesus' true identity.

Reflection:
Jesus walking on the water reveals His divine power and authority over nature, and His words, "It is I," remind us of His presence and reassurance in times of fear and uncertainty. The disciples' astonishment underscores the challenge of fully understanding and trusting in Jesus' true nature. As we reflect on this passage, we are invited to deepen our faith in Jesus' presence and power in our lives. In moments of fear or doubt, how can we remind ourselves of His reassurance and sovereignty? Let us place our trust in Jesus, knowing that He is with us even in the stormy seas of life.

Prayer:
Lord Jesus, we thank You for Your presence and reassurance in our lives. Help us to trust in Your power and to overcome our fears with the certainty of Your love and presence. As we face the challenges of life, remind us of Your words, "Do not be afraid," and strengthen our faith in Your divine authority. May we always find peace in Your presence and guidance. Amen.

Thursday, January 9

❖ Thursday after Epiphany

- ➢ First Reading: First John 4: 19 – 5: 4
- ➢ Responsorial Psalm: Psalms 72: 1-2, 14 and 15bc, 17
- ➢ Alleluia: Luke 4: 18
- ➢ Gospel: Luke 4: 14-22
- ➢ Lectionary: 215

As we continue reflecting on the mysteries of the Epiphany, today's readings focus on the nature of faith and the manifestation of Jesus' mission. The passages highlight the essence of love and the fulfillment of prophecy, inviting us to deepen our understanding of Christ's role in our lives and to embrace His message with faith and devotion.

➢ First Reading: 1 John 4: 19 – 5: 4

In this reading, St. John elaborates on the nature of love, emphasizing that our love for others is a response to God's love for us. He explains that those who love God must also love their brothers and sisters. John further highlights that faith in Jesus as the Son of God overcomes the world, and this faith is what allows us to live victoriously. The love of God and our faith in Jesus are intertwined, guiding us in our journey of faith.

Reflection:
St. John's message underscores the inseparable link between love and faith. God's love is the source from which our love for others flows, and faith in Jesus empowers us to overcome the challenges of the world. As we reflect on this passage, let us examine how our love and faith are manifesting in our lives. Are we responding to God's love by loving others, and are we trusting in Jesus to help us navigate life's difficulties? Let us commit to living out our faith through acts of love, trusting that God's love empowers us to live victoriously.

Prayer:
Heavenly Father, we thank You for Your immense love that guides and sustains us. Help us to respond to Your love by loving others and to live out our faith in Jesus with courage and conviction. Strengthen us to overcome the challenges of the world and to reflect Your love in all that we do. Amen.

> Gospel: Luke 4: 14-22

In this Gospel passage, Jesus returns to Galilee in the power of the Spirit and begins teaching in the synagogues. He reads from the prophet Isaiah, proclaiming the fulfillment of the prophecy: "The Spirit of the Lord is upon me, because he has anointed me to bring good news to the poor... to proclaim the year of the Lord's favor." Jesus declares that this scripture is fulfilled in their hearing. The people are amazed at His gracious words, yet their initial awe is mixed with skepticism.

Reflection:
Jesus' declaration of the fulfillment of Isaiah's prophecy marks the beginning of His public ministry and the manifestation of His mission to bring salvation and liberation. His words emphasize the arrival of a new era marked by the fulfillment of God's promises. As we reflect on this passage, let us consider how Jesus' mission impacts our understanding of His role in our lives. Are we open to the transformative message of Christ and willing to embrace the newness He brings? Let us invite Jesus to fulfill His promises in our lives and respond to His call with faith and openness.

Prayer:
Lord Jesus, we praise You for fulfilling the promises of God and bringing good news to the poor and oppressed. Help us to recognize Your mission in our lives and to respond with faith and openness. May we embrace the newness You offer and live in the light of Your grace. Guide us to share Your message of salvation with others and to reflect Your love and truth in our world. Amen.

Friday, January 10

❖ Friday after Epiphany

> First Reading: First John 5: 5-13
> Responsorial Psalm: Psalms 147: 12-13, 14-15, 19-20
> Alleluia: Matthew 4: 23
> Gospel: Luke 5: 12-16
> Lectionary: 216

As we continue the journey through the Epiphany season, today's readings focus on the assurance of faith and the healing power of Jesus. The readings invite us to reflect on the significance of believing in Jesus and experiencing His transformative presence in our lives.

> First Reading: 1 John 5: 5-13

In this passage, St. John emphasizes the assurance of eternal life through faith in Jesus Christ. He asserts that Jesus is the Son of God, and through believing in Him, we have the testimony of eternal life. John speaks about the confidence we can have in approaching God and the certainty of our salvation through Christ. This testimony is a foundation of Christian faith, offering hope and assurance to believers.

Reflection:
St. John's message provides a powerful affirmation of the assurance and confidence that come from faith in Jesus. The promise of eternal life and the certainty of God's testimony are central to Christian belief. As we reflect on this passage, let us consider the depth of our faith and the assurance it brings. Do we fully embrace the promise of eternal life and the confidence that comes from our relationship with Jesus? Let us strengthen our faith and live with the assurance that we are secure in God's love and promises.

Prayer:
Heavenly Father, we thank You for the assurance of eternal life through Your Son, Jesus Christ. Help us to deepen our faith and to live with confidence in Your promises. May we fully embrace the gift of salvation and reflect Your love and truth in our lives. Strengthen us to trust in Your testimony and to live with the hope and assurance You provide. Amen.

➢ Gospel: Luke 5: 12-16

In this Gospel passage, Jesus encounters a man suffering from leprosy who begs to be healed. Moved with compassion, Jesus touches him and heals him, commanding him to show himself to the priests and offer the sacrifices prescribed by Moses. Despite Jesus' instructions to keep the healing private, news of the miracle spreads widely, and crowds gather to hear Him and be healed of their diseases. Jesus, recognizing the need for solitude and prayer, withdraws to deserted places to pray.

Reflection:
Jesus' healing of the leper demonstrates His compassion and power, as well as His commitment to restoring individuals to wholeness. His instructions to show himself to the priests underscore the importance of following the law and giving testimony to God's work. Despite the growing fame and demands on His ministry, Jesus prioritizes time for prayer and solitude. As we reflect on this passage, let us consider how we respond to Jesus' healing and presence in our own lives. Are we attentive to His call for solitude and prayer amidst the demands of our daily lives? Let us seek to follow His example of compassion, obedience, and devotion.

Prayer:
Lord Jesus, we thank You for Your healing touch and for the compassion You show to all who come to You. Help us to respond to Your presence in our lives with gratitude and faith. Teach us to seek time for prayer and solitude, as You did, and to follow Your example of compassion and obedience. May we live in the light of Your healing and share Your love with those around us. Amen.

Saturday, January 11

❖ Saturday after Epiphany

> ➢ First Reading: First John 5: 14-21
> ➢ Responsorial Psalm: Psalms 149: 1-2, 3-4, 5 and 6a and 9b
> ➢ Alleluia: Matthew 4: 16
> ➢ Gospel: John 3: 22-30
> ➢ Lectionary: 217

As we conclude our week following the Epiphany, today's readings offer a reflection on the power of prayer and the role of Jesus in fulfilling God's plan. We are invited to consider our relationship with God through prayer and to recognize the central role of Christ in our faith.

> ➢ First Reading: 1 John 5: 14-21

In this passage, St. John reassures believers of the confidence they can have when approaching God in prayer. He emphasizes that if we ask anything according to God's will, He hears us and will grant our requests. John also warns against sin, particularly the sin leading to death, while encouraging the faithful to pray for one another and to keep themselves from idols. The passage concludes with the assurance that Jesus is the true God and eternal life.

Reflection:
St. John's teaching on prayer and the nature of sin offers deep insights into the Christian life. The confidence we have in approaching God is rooted in our relationship with Him and our alignment with His will. As we reflect on this passage, let us examine how we approach God in prayer and whether our requests align with His will. Are there areas in our lives where we need to seek His guidance and protection from sin? Let us also consider how we can support one another in faith and remain vigilant against anything that distracts us from God.

Prayer:
Loving Father, we thank You for the confidence we have in approaching You with our prayers. Help us to seek Your will in all things and to trust in Your guidance. Strengthen our faith and protect us from sin, and help us to support one another in our spiritual journeys. Keep us close to You and guard us from anything that might lead us away from Your truth. Amen.

> Gospel: John 3: 22-30

In this Gospel passage, Jesus and His disciples are baptizing in Judea, and John the Baptist's disciples raise a concern that Jesus is gaining more followers. John the Baptist responds by affirming that his role was to prepare the way for Jesus and that Jesus must increase while he himself must decrease. John acknowledges Jesus' divine role and authority, emphasizing that Jesus is the Bridegroom and he is merely the friend of the Bridegroom who rejoices at His presence.

Reflection:

John the Baptist's humble acknowledgment of Jesus' superior role highlights the essence of Christian humility and the recognition of Christ's central place in our faith. John's willingness to decrease so that Jesus might increase serves as a model for our own spiritual lives. As we reflect on this passage, let us consider how we can place Christ at the center of our lives and embrace humility in our service. Are we allowing Jesus to increase in our hearts and actions? Let us strive to follow John's example by joyfully supporting the work of Christ and recognizing His importance in our lives.

Prayer:

Lord Jesus, we thank You for the gift of Your presence and for the example of humility shown by John the Baptist. Help us to center our lives on You and to rejoice in Your role as our Savior. May we decrease so that You may increase in our hearts and actions. Guide us in serving You with humility and joy, and let our lives reflect Your grace and truth. Amen.

Sunday, January 12

❖ Baptism of the Lord - Feast

> First Reading: Isaiah 42: 1-4, 6-7 or Isaiah 40: 1-5, 9-11
> Responsorial Psalm: Psalms 104: 1b-2, 3-4, 24-25, 27-28, 29-30
> Second Reading: Titus 2: 11-14; 3: 4-7
> Alleluia: Luke 3: 16
> Gospel: Luke 3: 15-16, 21-22
> Lectionary: 21

Today we celebrate the Feast of the Baptism of the Lord, marking the event when Jesus was baptized by John in the Jordan River. This feast highlights the beginning of Jesus' public ministry and His identification with humanity. It also underscores the significance of baptism in our own lives and invites us to reflect on our own call to follow Christ.

> First Reading: Isaiah 42: 1-4, 6-7
>
> *or* Isaiah 40: 1-5, 9-11

Isaiah 42: 1-4, 6-7

This passage presents the "Servant Song," describing the chosen servant of the Lord who will bring justice and light to the nations. The servant is characterized by gentleness and a commitment to justice, and his mission includes opening the eyes of the blind and freeing those imprisoned.

Isaiah 40: 1-5, 9-11

This passage offers a message of comfort and hope, proclaiming the coming of the Lord and the preparation of a way in the wilderness. It describes the grandeur of God's coming, the leveling of mountains, and the promise of God's tender care for His people.

Reflection:
Both readings reflect the themes of preparation and revelation of God's mission. The passage from Isaiah 42 particularly aligns with the baptism of Jesus, as it speaks of the servant who will bring justice and light. Isaiah 40 emphasizes the preparation for God's coming and the transformative impact of His presence. As we reflect on these readings, let us consider how the baptism of Jesus fulfills these prophecies and how we are called to prepare the way for Christ in our own lives. How can we live out the message of justice, comfort, and transformation that these passages convey?

Prayer:
Lord God, we thank You for the prophecy and fulfillment of Your Servant who brings justice and light to the world. Help us to prepare our hearts for Your coming and to embrace the transformation You offer. May we reflect Your justice and comfort in our lives and be instruments of Your love and grace. Amen.

> Second Reading: Titus 2: 11-14; 3: 4-7

In this passage, St. Paul describes the grace of God that has appeared, bringing salvation to all people and teaching us to live godly lives. He speaks of Christ's sacrificial love and the renewal through the Holy Spirit. The reading highlights the transformative power of God's grace and the new life it brings through baptism.

Reflection:
St. Paul's message emphasizes the grace of God that appears through Jesus and the transformation it brings. The baptism of Jesus is a manifestation of this grace, marking the beginning of His public ministry and the revelation of His identity. As we reflect on this passage, let us consider how God's grace has appeared in our own lives and how it calls us to live transformed lives. How can we embody the grace and renewal that baptism represents? Let us commit to living in a way that reflects the new life we have received through Christ.

Prayer:
Gracious God, we thank You for the grace that has appeared through Jesus Christ, bringing us salvation and renewal. Help us to live transformed lives that reflect Your love and grace. Strengthen us to follow

the example of Christ and to embrace the new life You offer through baptism. May we be faithful witnesses of Your grace and live in a way that honors You. Amen.

> Gospel: Luke 3: 15-16, 21-22

In this Gospel passage, John the Baptist is questioned about whether he is the Messiah. He responds by pointing to Jesus, saying that He will baptize with the Holy Spirit and fire. The passage then describes Jesus' baptism, during which the heavens open, the Holy Spirit descends in bodily form like a dove, and a voice from heaven declares, "You are my Son, the Beloved; with you I am well pleased."

Reflection:
The account of Jesus' baptism highlights the divine confirmation of His identity as the Son of God and marks the beginning of His public ministry. The descending of the Holy Spirit and the voice from heaven affirm Jesus' divine sonship and mission. As we reflect on this passage, let us recognize the significance of Jesus' baptism in affirming His role and identity. How does this event shape our understanding of our own baptism and our relationship with God? Let us embrace the call to live as beloved children of God, empowered by the Holy Spirit.

Prayer:
Heavenly Father, we thank You for revealing Your Son at His baptism and for affirming His identity and mission. Help us to understand the significance of our own baptism and to live as Your beloved children. May the Holy Spirit guide and empower us to follow Christ faithfully and to fulfill the mission You have entrusted to us. Amen.

Monday, January 13

- ❖ Monday of the First week in Ordinary Time
- ❖ Saint Hilary, bishop and doctor - Optional Memorial

> First Reading: Hebrews 1: 1-6
> Responsorial Psalm: Psalms 97: 1 and 2b, 6 and 7c, 9
> Alleluia: Mark 1: 15
> Gospel: Mark 1: 14-20
> Lectionary: 305

Today, we enter the First Week of Ordinary Time and also commemorate Saint Hilary of Poitiers, a bishop and doctor of the Church renowned for his theological contributions and defense of the faith. The readings for today focus on the revelation of God through His Son and the call to follow Christ, exemplified in the early calling of the disciples.

➢ First Reading: Hebrews 1: 1-6

This passage from Hebrews speaks of how God has revealed Himself through His Son, Jesus Christ. The author contrasts the previous revelations through prophets with the final and complete revelation through Jesus, who is the exact imprint of God's nature. Jesus is described as the heir of all things and the one through whom God made the universe. The passage also highlights Jesus' superior status to angels, affirming His divine sonship and authority.

Reflection:
The opening verses of Hebrews underscore the significance of Jesus as the ultimate revelation of God. Unlike the partial revelations through the prophets, Jesus represents the fullness of God's self-disclosure. As we reflect on this passage, let us consider how Jesus, as the Son of God, fulfills the promises and prophecies of the Old Testament. How does this understanding deepen our relationship with Christ and our appreciation for His role in our faith? Let us seek to recognize Jesus as the central figure of our spiritual lives and to respond to His revelation with trust and devotion.

Prayer:
Heavenly Father, we thank You for revealing Yourself fully through Your Son, Jesus Christ. Help us to understand and embrace the significance of Jesus as the exact imprint of Your nature. Strengthen our faith in Him and guide us to respond to Your revelation with love and commitment. May we live in the light of Your truth and follow the example of Your Son. Amen.

➢ Gospel: Mark 1: 14-20

In this passage, Jesus begins His public ministry in Galilee, proclaiming the good news of God and calling people to repentance. He announces that "the kingdom of God has come near," and calls Simon Peter and his brother Andrew to become "fishers of men." He then calls James and John, the sons of Zebedee, to follow Him. The immediate response of these first disciples to Jesus' call is a powerful example of discipleship.

Reflection:
Jesus' call to the first disciples marks the beginning of His public ministry and highlights the transformative power of His invitation. The disciples' immediate response to leave their nets and follow Jesus demonstrates a profound trust and commitment. As we reflect on this passage, let us consider our own response to Jesus' call in our lives. Are we willing to leave behind our own "nets" and follow Him with the same readiness and dedication? Let us seek to embrace the call to discipleship and to respond to Jesus' invitation with faith and action.

Prayer:
Lord Jesus, we thank You for calling us to follow You and for inviting us to be part of Your mission. Help us to respond to Your call with the same readiness and commitment as Simon Peter, Andrew, James, and

John. Guide us in our journey of discipleship and empower us to live out Your message in our daily lives. May we be faithful in following You and sharing the good news of Your kingdom with others. Amen.

Tuesday, January 14

❖ Tuesday of the First week in Ordinary Time

- First Reading: Hebrews 2: 5-12
- Responsorial Psalm: Psalms 8: 2ab and 5, 6-7, 8-9
- Alleluia: First Thessalonians 2: 13
- Gospel: Mark 1: 21-28
- Lectionary: 306

In today's readings, we delve into the themes of Jesus' authority and His role in God's plan for salvation. The first reading from Hebrews emphasizes Jesus' humanity and His solidarity with us, while the Gospel passage highlights His authoritative teaching and power over evil spirits. These themes underscore the foundational aspects of Jesus' mission and His impact on our lives.

➤ First Reading: Hebrews 2: 5-12

This passage from Hebrews reflects on the role of Jesus as the one who fulfills God's plan for humanity. The author discusses how Jesus, though divine, became fully human to share in our experiences and to bring salvation. He refers to Jesus as the one who leads many children to glory and is not ashamed to call them brothers and sisters. By sharing in our humanity, Jesus is able to offer a perfect salvation and become a source of strength and help.

Reflection:
Hebrews highlights the profound mystery of the Incarnation—Jesus becoming human to bring salvation to humanity. This passage reassures us that Jesus, while being divine, fully understands our struggles and experiences because He shares in our humanity. As we reflect on this reading, let us ponder how Jesus' solidarity with us enhances our understanding of His role as Savior and Brother. How does knowing that Jesus is not ashamed to call us His brothers and sisters affect our relationship with Him? Let us embrace the comfort and strength that comes from Jesus' deep identification with our human condition.

Prayer:
Gracious God, we thank You for sending Your Son to share in our humanity and to bring us salvation. Help us to appreciate the depth of Jesus' love and solidarity with us. Strengthen our faith and trust in Him as our Savior and Brother. May we find comfort in His understanding and support as we journey through life. Amen.

> Gospel: Mark 1: 21-28

In this Gospel passage, Jesus teaches in the synagogue in Capernaum, and His teaching astonishes the people because He teaches with authority, unlike the scribes. During this time, a man with an unclean spirit interrupts the teaching, and Jesus commands the spirit to come out of him. The unclean spirit obeys, and the people are amazed at Jesus' authority over evil spirits, spreading the news about Him throughout the region.

Reflection:
Jesus' teaching with authority and His power over unclean spirits demonstrate His divine authority and mission. The astonishment of the people highlights the difference between Jesus' authority and that of the religious leaders of the time. His ability to command the unclean spirit illustrates His power over evil and His role in bringing about God's kingdom. As we reflect on this passage, let us consider how Jesus' authority impacts our lives. How can we recognize and respond to His authority in our daily decisions and actions? Let us invite Jesus' transformative power into our lives and seek to live under His authority.

Prayer:
Lord Jesus, we marvel at Your authority and power over evil. Thank You for teaching us with such authority and for your victory over unclean spirits. Help us to recognize Your authority in our lives and to live according to Your teachings. Empower us to resist evil and to seek Your guidance in all things. May Your authority bring transformation and peace to our hearts and lives. Amen.

Wednesday, January 15

❖ Wednesday of the First week in Ordinary Time

> First Reading: Hebrews 2: 14-18
> Responsorial Psalm: Psalms 105: 1-2, 3-4, 6-7, 8-9
> Alleluia: John 10: 27
> Gospel: Mark 1: 29-39
> Lectionary: 307

Today's readings continue to explore the profound impact of Jesus' ministry and His role as our compassionate Savior. The first reading from Hebrews speaks about Jesus' solidarity with humanity and His role as a merciful High Priest. The Gospel passage highlights Jesus' healing ministry and His commitment to preaching the Good News. These readings invite us to reflect on Jesus' deep compassion and His mission to bring healing and salvation.

➢ First Reading: Hebrews 2: 14-18

In this passage, the author of Hebrews explains how Jesus shared in our humanity to break the power of death and the devil. By becoming fully human, Jesus was able to offer a perfect sacrifice for our sins and to help those who are tempted. His humanity allows Him to be a merciful and faithful High Priest, able to sympathize with our weaknesses and offer aid in our struggles.

Reflection:
Hebrews underscores the significance of Jesus' Incarnation—His sharing in our human nature allows Him to be our compassionate High Priest. By experiencing our vulnerabilities and temptations, Jesus is able to offer us genuine help and understanding. As we reflect on this passage, let us appreciate the depth of Jesus' empathy and the strength He offers in our moments of weakness. How does this understanding of Jesus as our merciful High Priest influence our relationship with Him and our trust in His aid? Let us draw near to Him with confidence, knowing that He fully understands and supports us.

Prayer:
Merciful Lord, we thank You for sharing in our humanity and becoming our faithful High Priest. Help us to trust in Your understanding and to seek Your aid in our struggles. Strengthen us in our temptations and guide us with Your compassion. May we always turn to You for comfort and support, knowing that You fully understand our needs. Amen.

➢ Gospel: Mark 1: 29-39

In this Gospel passage, Jesus heals Simon Peter's mother-in-law, who is suffering from a fever. After healing her, she begins to serve them, and that evening, many who were sick or possessed by demons come to Jesus for healing. Jesus heals many and drives out demons, but He also retreats to a deserted place to pray. When Simon and the others find Him, Jesus says that He must continue His mission to preach in other towns.

Reflection:
This passage highlights Jesus' compassion and His dedication to His mission. His healing of Simon Peter's mother-in-law and many others demonstrates His care for those who are suffering. Despite the demands of His ministry, Jesus takes time for prayer and seeks to continue His mission of preaching the Good News. As we reflect on this passage, let us consider how Jesus' example of service, prayer, and mission can inspire our own lives. How can we balance our commitments with time for prayer and reflection? Let us follow Jesus' example by serving others, maintaining a strong prayer life, and staying committed to our own mission.

Prayer:
Lord Jesus, we thank You for Your healing touch and Your dedication to serving others. Help us to follow Your example of compassion and service. Guide us to balance our responsibilities with time for prayer and reflection. Empower us to continue Your mission in our own lives, sharing Your love and truth with those around us. May we serve with the same dedication and care that You have shown. Amen.

Thursday, January 16

❖ **Thursday of the First week in Ordinary Time**

> ➢ First Reading: Hebrews 3: 7-14
> ➢ Responsorial Psalm: Psalms 95: 6-7c, 8-9, 10-11
> ➢ Alleluia: Matthew 4: 23
> ➢ Gospel: Mark 1: 40-45
> ➢ Lectionary: 308

Today's readings highlight themes of faith, obedience, and healing. The first reading from Hebrews calls for perseverance and faithfulness, warning against hardening our hearts. The Gospel passage features a dramatic healing of a leper by Jesus, demonstrating His compassion and the power of faith. These readings invite us to reflect on our own faithfulness and the transformative power of encountering Christ.

> ➢ First Reading: Hebrews 3: 7-14

In this passage, the author of Hebrews recalls the Israelites' history of disobedience and warns against hardening one's heart as they did in the wilderness. He urges believers to remain steadfast in their faith and to encourage one another daily, so that none may be hardened by sin's deceitfulness. The reading emphasizes the importance of holding firm to our confidence in Christ and remaining faithful until the end.

Reflection:
Hebrews challenges us to reflect on our own faithfulness and openness to God. The warning against hardening our hearts serves as a reminder to stay vigilant and engaged in our relationship with God. As we consider this passage, let us ask ourselves how we can remain faithful and avoid the pitfalls of unbelief and disobedience. How can we support and encourage one another in our faith journey? Let us strive to keep our hearts open to God's guidance and to remain steadfast in our commitment to Him.

Prayer:
Lord God, we thank You for the call to remain faithful and to encourage one another in our journey of faith. Help us to avoid hardening our hearts and to stay open to Your guidance. Strengthen our confidence in Christ and keep us steadfast in our commitment to You. May we support one another with love and encouragement, and remain faithful until the end. Amen.

> Gospel: Mark 1: 40-45

In this Gospel passage, a leper approaches Jesus, begging to be healed. Jesus, moved with compassion, touches the leper and heals him, instructing him to show himself to the priest and offer the sacrifices required by Moses. Despite Jesus' instructions to keep the healing private, the man spreads the news widely, causing crowds to gather around Jesus, making it difficult for Him to enter towns openly.

Reflection:
Jesus' healing of the leper demonstrates His profound compassion and willingness to touch and heal those who are marginalized and suffering. His instructions to the leper emphasize the importance of following the law and giving testimony to God's work. Despite the man's disobedience, which leads to increased crowds and challenges for Jesus, the healing act reveals the power of faith and the transformative impact of Jesus' ministry. As we reflect on this passage, let us consider our own faith and openness to Jesus' healing touch. How can we embody His compassion in our interactions with others? Let us seek to follow Jesus' example in reaching out to those in need and in sharing the Good News with humility and grace.

Prayer:
Compassionate Lord Jesus, we thank You for Your healing touch and for Your willingness to reach out to those who are suffering. Help us to embody Your compassion and to follow Your example of love and service. Guide us to share the Good News with humility and to support those in need with kindness and grace. May Your healing presence transform our lives and empower us to be instruments of Your love. Amen.

Friday, January 17

❖ Saint Anthony, abbot - Memorial

> First Reading: Hebrews 4: 1-5, 11
> Responsorial Psalm: Psalms 78: 3 and 4bc, 6c-7, 8
> Alleluia: Luke 7: 16
> Gospel: Mark 2: 1-12
> Lectionary: 309

Today we celebrate Saint Anthony the Abbot, a key figure in the early monastic tradition. His life of asceticism and devotion paved the way for monasticism as we know it. The readings for today underscore themes of faith, rest, and healing, inviting us to reflect on our own journey towards spiritual rest and wholeness.

➢ First Reading: Hebrews 4: 1-5, 11

In this passage, the author of Hebrews discusses the promise of entering God's rest and the importance of faith in achieving it. He reflects on the failure of the Israelites to enter the promised rest due to their disobedience and unbelief. The reading emphasizes that the rest God offers is a place of spiritual peace and fulfillment that remains available to those who are faithful and diligent in their walk with God.

Reflection:

The promise of entering God's rest speaks to the ultimate fulfillment and peace that comes from a faithful relationship with Him. The Israelites' failure to enter the rest due to unbelief serves as a warning to us to remain faithful and diligent. As we reflect on this passage, let us examine our own faith and commitment. Are there areas in our lives where we are struggling with unbelief or disobedience? How can we strive to enter into God's rest by living faithfully and obediently? Let us seek to align our lives with God's promises and to find true peace in Him.

Prayer:

Lord God, we thank You for the promise of Your rest and the peace that comes from a faithful relationship with You. Help us to remain diligent and obedient in our walk with You. Guide us to enter into Your rest and to find fulfillment in Your presence. Strengthen our faith and help us to overcome any obstacles that keep us from experiencing Your peace. Amen.

➢ Gospel: Mark 2: 1-12

In this Gospel passage, Jesus heals a paralyzed man who is brought to Him by his friends. Seeing their faith, Jesus first forgives the man's sins, which provokes skepticism from the scribes present. To demonstrate His authority to forgive sins, Jesus then heals the man, telling him to pick up his mat and walk. The crowd is amazed and praises God for the miracles they witness.

Reflection:

Jesus' healing of the paralyzed man illustrates His divine authority and the importance of faith. By first addressing the man's spiritual needs through forgiveness and then his physical needs through healing, Jesus reveals the connection between sin, healing, and restoration. The faith of the man's friends plays a crucial role in the miracle, showing the power of communal faith and support. As we reflect on this passage, let us consider the role of faith in our own lives and how we can support one another spiritually and physically. How can we bring others to Christ and seek His healing and forgiveness in our own lives?

Prayer:

Lord Jesus, we thank You for the healing and forgiveness You offer to us. Strengthen our faith and help us to support one another in our spiritual journey. Guide us to experience Your healing in our lives and to share Your love and forgiveness with those around us. May we be instruments of Your grace and witness Your miracles in our daily lives. Amen.

Saturday, January 18

- ❖ Saturday of the First week in Ordinary Time
- ❖ Blessed Virgin Mary - Optional Memorial

> First Reading: Hebrews 4: 12-16
> Responsorial Psalm: Psalms 19: 8, 9, 10, 15
> Alleluia: Luke 4: 18
> Gospel: Mark 2: 13-17
> Lectionary: 310

Today, we honor the Blessed Virgin Mary, the mother of Jesus, whose faith and obedience exemplify the ideal response to God's call. The readings for today highlight the power of God's Word and the inclusive nature of Jesus' mission. As we reflect on Mary's role and the teachings in the readings, we are invited to deepen our understanding of God's Word and His call to bring all people to His table.

> First Reading: Hebrews 4: 12-16

This passage from Hebrews emphasizes the living and active nature of God's Word, which is sharper than a double-edged sword, penetrating to the depths of our being. The reading underscores that Jesus, as our High Priest, is able to empathize with our weaknesses because He has been tempted in every way yet remained without sin. We are encouraged to approach the throne of grace with confidence to receive mercy and find grace in our time of need.

Reflection:
The power of God's Word is central to this passage, highlighting its ability to discern our innermost thoughts and intentions. Jesus' empathy as our High Priest assures us that He understands our struggles and is ready to offer mercy and grace. As we reflect on this reading, let us consider how we respond to the Word of God in our lives. Are we open to its transformative power? How do we approach God's throne of grace, and how does Jesus' empathy influence our relationship with Him? Let us strive to approach God with confidence and trust, knowing that His Word and His grace are always available to us.

Prayer:
Lord God, we thank You for the living and active power of Your Word. Help us to be receptive to its guidance and to approach Your throne of grace with confidence. Strengthen our faith and trust in Jesus as our compassionate High Priest. May we find mercy and grace in our time of need and live according to the transformative power of Your Word. Amen.

> Gospel: Mark 2: 13-17

In this Gospel passage, Jesus calls Levi (Matthew) to follow Him while he is at his tax booth. Levi immediately leaves his work and follows Jesus. Later, Jesus dines with Levi and other tax collectors and sinners, prompting criticism from the Pharisees. Jesus responds by saying that He has come not to call the righteous, but sinners, to repentance.

Reflection:
Jesus' call to Levi and His association with tax collectors and sinners reveal the inclusive nature of His mission. By dining with those considered outcasts, Jesus demonstrates that His ministry is for everyone, especially those in need of repentance. His response to the Pharisees underscores the essence of His mission: to seek and save those who are lost. As we reflect on this passage, let us consider our own openness to Jesus' call and His mission to reach out to all people. How can we embrace this inclusive vision in our own lives and communities? Let us be inspired by Jesus' example to reach out with compassion and to welcome those who are in need of grace and repentance.

Prayer:
Lord Jesus, we thank You for Your inclusive call to all people and for Your compassion toward sinners. Help us to follow Your example by reaching out to those in need and welcoming them with love and grace. Guide us to embrace Your mission of bringing all people to repentance and to live with openness and compassion. May we be instruments of Your mercy and grace in our communities. Amen.

Sunday, January 19

❖ Second Sunday in Ordinary Time

> First Reading: Isaiah 62: 1-5
> Responsorial Psalm: Psalms 96: 1-2a, 2b-3, 7-8, 9-10
> Second Reading: First Corinthians 12: 4-11
> Alleluia: Second Thessalonians 2: 14
> Gospel: John 2: 1-11
> Lectionary: 66

Today's readings celebrate the revelation of God's glory and the manifestations of His gifts among us. The first reading from Isaiah anticipates the joy and transformation that God will bring to His people. The second reading from 1 Corinthians discusses the diverse spiritual gifts given by the Holy Spirit for the common good. The Gospel recounts the miracle at the wedding in Cana, where Jesus performs His first miracle, revealing His divine glory. These readings invite us to reflect on the joy of God's presence, the diversity of His gifts, and the transformative power of Jesus.

➢ First Reading: Isaiah 62: 1-5

In this passage, the prophet Isaiah speaks of a future time when Jerusalem will be restored and honored, reflecting the joy and transformation that God will bring. God promises that His people will no longer be forsaken or desolate but will be called "My Delight" and "Married" because of His love and blessing. The imagery of marriage symbolizes the deep and intimate relationship between God and His people, highlighting His commitment and joy in their union.

Reflection:
Isaiah's prophecy paints a picture of restoration and joy for Jerusalem, symbolizing the transformative power of God's love. The imagery of marriage reflects the profound relationship God desires with His people. As we reflect on this passage, let us consider how God's love and commitment to us bring transformation and joy into our lives. How does the promise of restoration and intimacy with God influence our faith and our relationship with Him? Let us embrace the joy and hope that come from being united with God and experiencing His transformative love.

Prayer:
Lord God, we thank You for Your promise of restoration and joy. Help us to recognize and embrace the depth of Your love and commitment to us. Transform our lives with Your presence and guide us in our relationship with You. May we find joy in our union with You and reflect Your love in our interactions with others. Amen.

➢ Second Reading: 1 Corinthians 12: 4-11

In this reading, Saint Paul discusses the variety of spiritual gifts bestowed upon believers by the Holy Spirit. He emphasizes that while there are many different gifts, they all come from the same Spirit and are given for the common good. Paul highlights that these gifts are meant to build up the Church and to serve others, demonstrating the diverse ways in which God works through individuals to achieve His purposes.

Reflection:
The diversity of spiritual gifts within the Church underscores the richness and unity of the Body of Christ. Each gift, while unique, contributes to the common good and the mission of the Church. As we reflect on this passage, let us consider our own spiritual gifts and how we can use them to serve others and build up the Church. How can we better recognize and appreciate the gifts of others? Let us seek to use our gifts for the glory of God and the benefit of the community, fostering unity and mutual support.

Prayer:
Holy Spirit, we thank You for the diverse gifts You bestow upon us. Help us to recognize and appreciate the gifts of others and to use our own gifts for the common good. Guide us in our service to others and in building up the Church. May Your gifts inspire us to work together in unity and love, reflecting Your grace in all that we do. Amen.

> Gospel: John 2: 1-11

The Gospel recounts the story of the wedding at Cana, where Jesus performs His first miracle by turning water into wine. This miracle, done at the request of His mother, reveals Jesus' divine power and the abundance of His grace. The transformation of water into wine symbolizes the new and abundant life that Jesus brings. The miracle also demonstrates Jesus' attention to the needs of individuals and His desire to bless and provide for them.

Reflection:

The wedding at Cana reveals the abundance and generosity of Jesus' miracles. By transforming water into wine, Jesus not only meets the immediate needs of the wedding guests but also symbolizes the new covenant and abundant life He offers. As we reflect on this miracle, let us consider how Jesus' presence in our lives brings transformation and abundance. How can we recognize and appreciate the ways Jesus blesses and provides for us? Let us seek to experience and share the joy and abundance that come from a relationship with Christ.

Prayer:

Lord Jesus, we thank You for the miracle at Cana and for the abundance of grace and blessings You bring into our lives. Help us to recognize Your presence and provision in our daily lives. May we experience the joy and transformation that come from knowing You and sharing Your love with others. Guide us to reflect Your generosity and grace in all that we do. Amen.

Monday, January 20

- ❖ Monday of the Second week in Ordinary Time
- ❖ Saint Fabian, pope and martyr - Optional Memorial
- ❖ Saint Sebastian, martyr - Optional Memorial

> First Reading: Hebrews 5: 1-10
> Responsorial Psalm: Psalms 110: 1, 2, 3, 4
> Alleluia: Hebrews 4: 12
> Gospel: Mark 2: 18-22
> Lectionary: 311

Today, we remember Saints Fabian and Sebastian, both martyrs whose lives exemplified courage and unwavering faith. The readings focus on the nature of Jesus' mission and the transformation He brings. The first reading from Hebrews explores the role of Jesus as our High Priest, while the Gospel contrasts the new ways brought by Jesus with old traditions. These readings invite us to reflect on the transformative power of Christ and how we live out His call in our lives.

➢ First Reading: Hebrews 5: 1-10

In this passage, the author of Hebrews discusses the role of the High Priest, who is appointed to offer gifts and sacrifices for sins. Jesus is presented as the ultimate High Priest, chosen by God and designated to mediate between God and humanity. Unlike the Levitical priests, Jesus' priesthood is eternal and perfect, established by His obedience and sacrifice. His suffering and obedience qualify Him to be the source of eternal salvation for all who obey Him.

Reflection:

The reading highlights the unique and eternal nature of Jesus' priesthood compared to the Old Testament priests. Jesus' role as High Priest is characterized by His deep empathy, suffering, and perfect obedience, which enable Him to offer an eternal and complete salvation. As we reflect on this passage, let us consider the significance of Jesus' priesthood in our lives. How does His role as our High Priest impact our relationship with God? How can we live in obedience to His call and find strength in His eternal salvation? Let us appreciate the depth of Jesus' sacrifice and embrace His role as our mediator and Savior.

Prayer:

Lord Jesus, we thank You for Your role as our eternal High Priest. Help us to appreciate the depth of Your sacrifice and to live in obedience to Your call. Strengthen our faith in Your eternal salvation and guide us in our relationship with You. May we trust in Your perfect mediation and find peace and hope in Your grace. Amen.

➢ Gospel: Mark 2: 18-22

In this passage, Jesus is questioned about why His disciples do not fast, unlike the disciples of John the Baptist and the Pharisees. Jesus responds by explaining that fasting is not appropriate while the bridegroom is with them, symbolizing His presence and the joy it brings. He then uses the metaphors of new wine and new wineskins to illustrate that His teachings and ministry bring a new order that cannot be contained within old structures.

Reflection:

Jesus' response to the question about fasting highlights the transformative nature of His ministry. His presence brings joy and a new way of relating to God that surpasses old traditions. The metaphors of new wine and new wineskins emphasize that the new covenant Jesus brings cannot be confined by old practices. As we reflect on this passage, let us consider how Jesus' teachings and presence in our lives bring renewal and transformation. How can we embrace the newness that Jesus offers and avoid clinging to outdated traditions? Let us seek to experience and share the joy of the new covenant and the transformative power of Christ in our daily lives.

Prayer:

Lord Jesus, we thank You for the newness and joy You bring into our lives. Help us to embrace the transformation of Your teachings and to live in the light of Your new covenant. Guide us to move beyond old practices and to experience the fullness of life in You. May we share the joy and renewal that comes from Your presence and reflect Your love and grace in all that we do. Amen.

Tuesday, January 21

❖ Saint Agnes, virgin and martyr - Memorial

- First Reading: Hebrews 6: 10-20
- Responsorial Psalm: Psalms 111: 1-2, 4-5, 9 and 10c
- Alleluia: Ephesians 1: 17-18
- Gospel: Mark 2: 23-28
- Lectionary: 312

Today we honor Saint Agnes, a young martyr whose steadfast faith and commitment to Christ made her a powerful example of courage and purity. The readings highlight themes of hope, perseverance, and the authority of Jesus over religious traditions. As we reflect on Saint Agnes's life and the teachings of today's readings, we are invited to deepen our faith and commitment to Christ.

First Reading: Hebrews 6: 10-20

In this passage, the author of Hebrews encourages believers to remain steadfast and diligent in their faith, assuring them that God will not forget their labor of love. The reading emphasizes the promise of God's faithfulness and the hope we have in His promises. The passage also speaks of Jesus as the anchor of our hope, offering a firm and secure foundation for our faith, much like the promises made to Abraham were fulfilled by God.

Reflection:
The assurance of God's faithfulness and the hope we find in Christ are central to this passage. Just as God fulfilled His promises to Abraham, we are reminded that He remains faithful to His promises to us. Jesus is described as the anchor of our hope, providing stability and security in our journey of faith. As we reflect on this passage, let us consider how we can remain steadfast and diligent in our faith, trusting in God's promises. How does the hope we have in Christ anchor our lives? Let us seek to strengthen our commitment to God and to trust in His unwavering faithfulness.

Prayer:
Lord God, we thank You for Your faithfulness and the hope we find in Your promises. Help us to remain steadfast in our faith and to trust in the security and stability that Jesus provides as the anchor of our hope. Guide us to live with confidence in Your promises and to reflect Your love and faithfulness in our daily lives. Amen.

> Gospel: Mark 2: 23-28

In this Gospel passage, Jesus is questioned by the Pharisees about His disciples picking grain on the Sabbath. Jesus responds by reminding them of David's actions when he ate the consecrated bread, which was reserved for priests. He then declares that "the Sabbath was made for man, not man for the Sabbath," and asserts His authority as Lord of the Sabbath. Jesus' response highlights the purpose and flexibility of the Sabbath as a gift for human well-being rather than a strict legal obligation.

Reflection:
Jesus' teaching on the Sabbath reveals His authority and His understanding of its true purpose. By referencing David's actions and emphasizing that the Sabbath is for human benefit, Jesus challenges the rigid interpretations of religious laws. His statement that He is the Lord of the Sabbath redefines its role as a source of rest and blessing rather than mere ritual compliance. As we reflect on this passage, let us consider how we honor the Sabbath in our own lives. How can we ensure that our observance of religious practices aligns with their intended purpose of fostering our well-being and relationship with God? Let us seek to live in a way that honors the spirit of the law and reflects Jesus' understanding of grace and mercy.

Prayer:
Lord Jesus, we thank You for Your teaching on the Sabbath and for revealing its true purpose as a gift for our well-being. Help us to understand and embrace the spirit of Your laws, focusing on their role in fostering our relationship with You. Guide us to live with grace and mercy, reflecting Your authority and love in our observance of religious practices. May we find rest and renewal in You, Lord of the Sabbath. Amen.

Wednesday, January 22

- ❖ Wednesday of the Second week in Ordinary Time
- ❖ Saint Vincent, deacon and martyr - Optional Memorial
- ❖ In the United States-Day of Prayer for the Legal Protection of Unborn Children

> First Reading: Hebrews 7: 1-3, 15-17
> Responsorial Psalm: Psalms 110: 1, 2, 3, 4
> Alleluia: Matthew 4: 23
> Gospel: Mark 3: 1-6
> Lectionary: 313

Today we remember Saint Vincent, a deacon and martyr whose unwavering faith and commitment to the Church exemplify the power of steadfast witness. The readings emphasize the nature of Jesus' priesthood and His authority to bring healing and challenge the status quo. As we also observe the Day of Prayer for the Legal Protection of Unborn Children, we are called to reflect on the sanctity of life and the protection of the most vulnerable among us.

➢ First Reading: Hebrews 7: 1-3, 15-17

This passage from Hebrews highlights the unique and eternal priesthood of Jesus, comparing it to the priesthood of Melchizedek. Melchizedek, who blessed Abraham and received tithes from him, is presented as a type of Christ, whose priesthood is both eternal and superior to the Levitical priesthood. Jesus' priesthood is established not by ancestral lineage but by His divine authority and eternal nature, making Him the perfect mediator between God and humanity.

Reflection:
The comparison between Melchizedek and Jesus underscores the exceptional nature of Jesus' priesthood. While Melchizedek's priesthood was a precursor to the true and eternal priesthood of Christ, Jesus' role as High Priest is perfect and everlasting. This passage invites us to reflect on the significance of Jesus' eternal priesthood in our lives. How does understanding Jesus as our eternal High Priest impact our relationship with God? Let us appreciate the depth of Christ's mediation and His role in our spiritual lives, recognizing the profound significance of His eternal and unchanging priesthood.

Prayer:
Lord Jesus, we thank You for Your eternal priesthood and Your role as our perfect mediator. Help us to understand and appreciate the depth of Your sacrifice and the significance of Your divine authority. Strengthen our faith in Your role as our High Priest and guide us to live in accordance with Your teachings. May we find peace and assurance in Your eternal mediation. Amen.

➢ Gospel: Mark 3: 1-6

In this Gospel passage, Jesus heals a man with a withered hand on the Sabbath, which prompts controversy among the Pharisees. They are more concerned with the legality of Jesus' actions than the healing itself. Jesus challenges their rigid interpretation of the law, asking whether it is lawful to do good or evil on the Sabbath. He then heals the man, demonstrating that doing good and showing mercy is always in accordance with God's will. This act intensifies the Pharisees' resolve to destroy Him.

Reflection:
Jesus' healing on the Sabbath reveals His commitment to compassion and mercy over rigid legalism. His challenge to the Pharisees highlights the true purpose of the law: to do good and to serve others, not merely to follow rules. As we reflect on this passage, let us consider how we live out our faith. Are we focused on the letter of the law, or are we guided by principles of love and mercy? Let us strive to embody Jesus' example by prioritizing compassion and kindness in our daily lives and in our interactions with others.

Prayer:
Lord Jesus, we thank You for Your example of compassion and mercy. Help us to follow Your lead by prioritizing love and goodness over rigid adherence to rules. Guide us to act with kindness and to do good

in all circumstances. May we reflect Your mercy in our lives and seek to serve others with the same compassion that You have shown us. Amen.

> ➤ Day of Prayer for the Legal Protection of Unborn Children

Today, as we also observe the Day of Prayer for the Legal Protection of Unborn Children, we are called to pray for the protection of the most vulnerable and to advocate for the sanctity of life. This observance highlights the importance of upholding the dignity and rights of every human being from conception to natural death.

Prayer for the Day of Prayer for the Legal Protection of Unborn Children:

Heavenly Father, we pray for the protection of unborn children and for the upholding of their right to life. Strengthen our resolve to advocate for the sanctity of life and to support those in need of compassion and care. Guide us to be instruments of Your love and to work towards a culture that values and protects every human life. May our prayers and actions reflect Your commitment to the most vulnerable and bring about positive change in our world. Amen.

Thursday, January 23

- ❖ Thursday of the Second week in Ordinary Time
- ❖ In the United States- Thursday of the Second week in Ordinary Time
- ❖ Saint Vincent, deacon and martyr - Optional Memorial
- ❖ Saint Marianne Cope, Virgin - Optional Memorial

> ➤ First Reading: Hebrews 7: 25 – 8: 6
> ➤ Responsorial Psalm: Psalms 40: 7-8a, 8b-9, 10, 17
> ➤ Alleluia: Second Timothy 1: 10
> ➤ Gospel: Mark 3: 7-12
> ➤ Lectionary: 314

Today we honor both Saint Vincent and Saint Marianne Cope, whose lives and ministries exemplify devotion and service. The readings focus on Jesus' role as our eternal High Priest and the power of His presence. As we reflect on these readings and the witness of the saints, we are called to deepen our understanding of Christ's role in our lives and to respond with faith and service.

➢ First Reading: Hebrews 7: 25 – 8: 6

This passage from Hebrews highlights the unique and eternal nature of Jesus' priesthood. Jesus is described as a High Priest who is able to save completely those who come to God through Him because He always lives to intercede for them. The reading contrasts Jesus' perfect and eternal priesthood with the temporary and imperfect Levitical priesthood. The passage also speaks of the new covenant established by Jesus, which is superior to the old covenant, bringing a more profound relationship with God and greater promises.

Reflection:

Jesus' eternal priesthood and the new covenant He establishes highlight the depth of His commitment to humanity. Unlike the Levitical priests, who offered sacrifices repeatedly, Jesus' sacrifice is once and for all, providing complete and eternal salvation. The new covenant represents a deeper and more intimate relationship with God, built on grace rather than law. As we reflect on this passage, let us consider how the eternal nature of Jesus' priesthood influences our faith and relationship with God. How does understanding Jesus as our eternal High Priest impact our daily lives and our approach to the new covenant? Let us embrace the fullness of this relationship and live in the grace and promises of the new covenant.

Prayer:

Lord Jesus, we thank You for Your eternal priesthood and the new covenant You have established. Help us to understand and appreciate the depth of Your sacrifice and the relationship we have with You through this covenant. Strengthen our faith and guide us to live in accordance with Your grace and promises. May we find peace and hope in Your eternal mediation. Amen.

➢ Gospel: Mark 3: 7-12

In this passage, Jesus retreats to the sea with His disciples due to the large crowds that are following Him. The people come from various regions, bringing those who are afflicted, and Jesus heals many. Even unclean spirits recognize Him as the Son of God and acknowledge His authority. Jesus commands them not to reveal His identity, emphasizing His desire to avoid premature or false declarations about His mission.

Reflection:

The Gospel reveals the power and authority of Jesus, as evidenced by His healing miracles and the recognition of His divine identity by unclean spirits. Jesus' command to the spirits not to reveal His identity reflects His intention to guide His mission according to divine timing and purpose. As we reflect on this passage, let us consider how we respond to Jesus' authority in our own lives. How do we recognize and respond to His presence and power? Let us seek to understand Jesus' mission more deeply and to align our lives with His divine purpose, embracing the healing and transformation He offers.

Prayer:

Lord Jesus, we thank You for Your healing power and Your authority over all things. Help us to recognize Your presence and to respond to Your call in our lives. Guide us to understand Your mission and to live in alignment with Your divine purpose. May we experience Your healing and transformation and reflect Your love and authority in all that we do. Amen.

Friday, January 24

❖ Saint Francis de Sales, bishop and doctor - Memorial

> ➢ First Reading: Hebrews 8: 6-13
> ➢ Responsorial Psalm: Psalms 85: 8 and 10, 11-12, 13-14
> ➢ Gospel: Mark 3: 13-19
> ➢ Lectionary: 315

Today, we celebrate Saint Francis de Sales, renowned for his gentle and pastoral approach to spirituality and his deep commitment to the teachings of the Church. The readings focus on the new covenant established by Jesus and His selection of the twelve apostles. As we honor Saint Francis de Sales, we are invited to reflect on the transformative power of the new covenant and the role of the apostles in spreading the Gospel.

> ➢ First Reading: Hebrews 8: 6-13

This passage from Hebrews contrasts the new covenant with the old one, emphasizing the superiority of the new covenant established by Jesus. The author highlights that Jesus is the mediator of a better covenant, which is based on better promises. The new covenant involves a more intimate relationship with God, where His laws are written on the hearts of His people rather than on tablets of stone. The old covenant is described as outdated and obsolete, making way for the new covenant which fulfills God's promises in a deeper and more personal way.

Reflection:
The new covenant represents a profound transformation in our relationship with God. Unlike the old covenant, which was based on external laws, the new covenant brings a deeper, internal transformation where God's laws are written on our hearts. This shift highlights the intimacy and personal connection that Jesus' covenant offers. As we reflect on this passage, let us consider how the new covenant affects our relationship with God and our approach to living out His commands. How can we better embrace and live according to the promises of the new covenant? Let us open our hearts to the transformative power of God's grace and seek to live in accordance with His will.

Prayer:
Lord Jesus, we thank You for the new covenant You have established and for the transformation it brings to our relationship with You. Help us to embrace the promises of this covenant and to live in accordance with Your will. Write Your laws on our hearts and guide us in our daily lives. May we experience the fullness of Your grace and reflect Your love in all that we do. Amen.

> Gospel: Mark 3: 13-19

In this Gospel passage, Jesus selects the twelve apostles from among His disciples. He appoints them to be with Him, to preach, and to have authority to drive out demons. The twelve apostles, including Simon (Peter), James, John, and others, are chosen to carry out Jesus' mission and to establish the foundations of the Church. Their selection signifies a new phase in Jesus' ministry, where He formalizes the leadership and mission of His followers.

Reflection:

The appointment of the twelve apostles marks a significant moment in Jesus' ministry, as He formalizes their role in His mission and entrusts them with authority. Each apostle is chosen to participate in the work of spreading the Gospel and building the Church. As we reflect on this passage, let us consider our own call to follow Jesus and to participate in His mission. How can we respond to Jesus' call in our own lives? Let us seek to fulfill our roles in the Church with dedication and commitment, inspired by the example of the apostles.

Prayer:

Lord Jesus, we thank You for calling the twelve apostles to be Your closest followers and to carry out Your mission. Help us to respond to Your call in our own lives and to fulfill our roles in the Church with dedication and faithfulness. Guide us in our participation in Your mission and empower us to spread Your message of love and grace. May we follow the example of the apostles and be steadfast in our commitment to You. Amen.

Saturday, January 25

❖ **Conversion of Saint Paul, apostle - Feast**

> First Reading: Acts 22: 3-16 or Acts 9: 1-22
> Responsorial Psalm: Psalms 117: 1bc, 2
> Alleluia: John 15: 16
> Gospel: Mark 16: 15-18
> Lectionary: 519

Today, we celebrate the Conversion of Saint Paul, a pivotal event in the history of the early Church. Paul's dramatic transformation from a persecutor of Christians to a passionate apostle of Christ exemplifies the power of God's grace and the call to conversion. The readings reflect the significance of Paul's conversion and the universal mission of spreading the Gospel. As we honor this feast, we are invited to reflect on our own call to conversion and mission.

> ### First Reading: Acts 22: 3-16 or Acts 9: 1-22

Acts 22: 3-16

In this account, Paul recounts his dramatic conversion experience to a Jewish audience in Jerusalem. He describes his past as a persecutor of Christians and his encounter with Jesus on the road to Damascus. Jesus' words to him, "Saul, Saul, why are you persecuting me?" highlight the personal nature of the call. Ananias, a disciple, is sent by God to restore Paul's sight and baptize him, marking the beginning of his mission to spread the Gospel.

Acts 9: 1-22

This passage provides a detailed narrative of Paul's conversion on the road to Damascus. Saul, blinded by a heavenly light, hears Jesus asking why he is persecuting Him. After three days of blindness, Ananias lays hands on Saul, restoring his sight and filling him with the Holy Spirit. Saul is baptized and begins to preach that Jesus is the Son of God, astonishing those who knew him as a persecutor.

Reflection:
Paul's conversion is a profound example of God's transformative power. His radical change from persecutor to preacher illustrates how an encounter with Christ can fundamentally alter one's life and mission. As we reflect on this event, let us consider our own experiences of conversion and transformation. How has God worked in our lives to bring about change? How can we respond to His call to spread the Gospel? Let us be inspired by Paul's example to embrace our own calls to conversion and to be bold in sharing our faith.

Prayer:
Lord Jesus, we thank You for the dramatic conversion of Saint Paul and for the example of Your transforming grace. Help us to open our hearts to Your call and to embrace the changes You wish to bring about in our lives. Empower us to boldly share the Gospel and to follow in the footsteps of Saint Paul. May Your grace continue to work in us, transforming our hearts and guiding us in Your mission. Amen.

> ### Gospel: Mark 16: 15-18

In this passage, Jesus commissions His disciples to go into the whole world and proclaim the Gospel to all creation. He promises signs that will accompany those who believe, including the casting out of demons, speaking in new tongues, and healing the sick. This commissioning underscores the universal mission of the Church and the power of faith to effect change and miracles.

Reflection:
Jesus' commission to His disciples highlights the expansive and inclusive nature of the Gospel message. The signs that accompany belief serve as affirmations of the power and truth of the message being proclaimed. As we reflect on this passage, let us consider how we can actively participate in the mission of spreading the Gospel in our own contexts. How can we embody the signs of faith in our lives and communities? Let us be motivated by Jesus' commissioning to engage in the mission of the Church with faith and courage.

Prayer:
Lord Jesus, we thank You for commissioning Your disciples to spread the Gospel to all creation. Help us to respond to this call in our own lives and to be active participants in Your mission. Empower us with faith and courage to share Your message and to live out the signs of Your presence in the world. May we be faithful to Your commission and dedicated to bringing Your love and grace to others. Amen.

Sunday, January 26

❖ Third Sunday in Ordinary Time

- First Reading: Nehemiah 8: 2-4a, 5-6, 8-10
- Responsorial Psalm: Psalms 19: 8, 9, 10, 15
- Second Reading: First Corinthians 12: 12-30 or First Corinthians 12: 12-14, 27
- Alleluia: Luke 4: 18
- Gospel: Luke 1: 1-4; 4: 14-21
- Lectionary: 69

On this Third Sunday in Ordinary Time, the readings focus on the themes of the Word of God, the unity of the Church, and the fulfillment of prophecy. As we reflect on these passages, we are invited to embrace the transformative power of God's Word and recognize our role within the Body of Christ. The readings underscore the importance of both hearing and living out the message of salvation.

- First Reading: Nehemiah 8: 2-4a, 5-6, 8-10

In this passage from Nehemiah, Ezra the scribe reads the Law to the people of Israel, who have gathered in Jerusalem. The reading occurs during the Feast of Tabernacles and marks a moment of renewal and dedication. The people listen attentively, and Ezra's reading of the Law is accompanied by explanations to help the people understand its meaning. The passage highlights the reverence for the Word of God and its role in guiding and reforming the community.

Reflection:
The reading from Nehemiah illustrates the profound impact of hearing and understanding God's Word. Ezra's reading and explanation of the Law serve as a reminder of the importance of engaging with Scripture and allowing it to shape our lives. As we reflect on this passage, let us consider how we approach the Word of God in our own lives. How can we better listen to and understand the Scriptures? How does God's Word guide and transform us? Let us seek to deepen our engagement with the Bible and to apply its teachings in our daily lives.

Prayer:
Lord God, we thank You for the gift of Your Word and for the guidance it provides. Help us to listen attentively to Your Scriptures and to understand their meaning for our lives. May Your Word inspire and transform us, leading us to live according to Your will. Grant us the grace to seek Your guidance and to be faithful to Your teachings. Amen.

> ### Second Reading: 1 Corinthians 12: 12-30 or 1 Corinthians 12: 12-14, 27

1 Corinthians 12: 12-30

In this passage, Paul uses the analogy of the body to describe the unity and diversity within the Church. Just as the body has many parts, each with a distinct role, so too does the Church consist of many members, each contributing to the whole. Paul emphasizes that all members are essential and that the Church functions best when each person fulfills their role. The reading underscores the importance of mutual respect and collaboration within the community of believers.

1 Corinthians 12: 12-14, 27

This shorter selection from the same chapter also uses the analogy of the body to describe the Church. It highlights that while there are many parts, there is one body, and each member plays a crucial role. Paul concludes with the affirmation that "you are the body of Christ and individually members of it," emphasizing the unity and interdependence of the Christian community.

Reflection:
Paul's analogy of the body illustrates the unity and diversity within the Church. Each member has a unique role and contributes to the functioning of the whole body. This passage invites us to reflect on our own place within the Church and our contributions to the community. How can we better understand and fulfill our roles within the Body of Christ? Let us recognize and appreciate the diverse gifts within the Church and strive to work together harmoniously for the common good.

Prayer:
Lord Jesus, we thank You for the gift of Your Church and for the diversity of gifts and roles within it. Help us to understand our place within the Body of Christ and to use our gifts for the good of the community. May we work together in unity and respect, building up the Church and reflecting Your love in all that we do. Guide us to fulfill our roles faithfully and to contribute to the growth and mission of Your Church. Amen.

> ### Gospel: Luke 1: 1-4; 4: 14-21

Luke 1: 1-4

This introduction to the Gospel of Luke establishes the author's intention to write an orderly and accurate account of the events concerning Jesus, based on the testimonies of those who were eyewitnesses and servants of the Word. Luke's careful approach aims to provide a clear and trustworthy narrative of the life and teachings of Jesus.

Luke 4: 14-21

In this passage, Jesus returns to Galilee in the power of the Spirit and teaches in the synagogues. He reads from the scroll of the prophet Isaiah in the synagogue at Nazareth, proclaiming that the prophecy has been fulfilled in Him. Jesus announces that He is the fulfillment of the Messianic prophecy, bringing good news to the poor, freedom for prisoners, sight for the blind, and liberation for the oppressed.

Reflection:
The readings from Luke highlight the fulfillment of prophecy and the mission of Jesus. By declaring that He fulfills the prophecy from Isaiah, Jesus reveals His role as the anointed one who brings salvation and liberation. As we reflect on this passage, let us consider how we respond to Jesus' mission in our own lives. How does Jesus' fulfillment of prophecy shape our understanding of His role and His message? Let us open our hearts to the transformative power of Jesus' ministry and seek to live in accordance with His mission.

Prayer:
Lord Jesus, we thank You for the fulfillment of the prophecy and for Your mission to bring salvation and liberation. Help us to recognize and embrace Your role as the anointed one who brings good news and transformation. Guide us to live in accordance with Your message and to share Your love and grace with others. May we be inspired by Your mission and committed to living out Your teachings in our daily lives. Amen.

Monday, January 27

- ❖ Monday of the Third week in Ordinary Time
- ❖ Saint Angela Merici, virgin - Optional Memorial

> First Reading: Hebrews 9: 15, 24-28
> Responsorial Psalm: Psalms 98: 1, 2-3ab, 3cd-4, 5-6
> Alleluia: Second Timothy 1: 10
> Gospel: Mark 3: 22-30
> Lectionary: 317

Today, we remember Saint Angela Merici, founder of the Ursuline Order, known for her commitment to education and spiritual development. The readings for today focus on Christ's role as the mediator of the new covenant and the opposition He faced from religious authorities. As we honor Saint Angela, we are invited to reflect on the power of Christ's sacrifice and the importance of discerning true wisdom from false teachings.

➢ First Reading: Hebrews 9: 15, 24-28

This passage from Hebrews emphasizes Jesus as the mediator of a new covenant, contrasting His role with that of the old covenant priests. It describes how Christ's sacrifice, once for all, redeems humanity from sin. Unlike the Levitical priests who entered the earthly sanctuary, Jesus entered the heavenly sanctuary to offer His own blood for our salvation. His sacrifice provides eternal redemption and cleanses our consciences from dead works.

Reflection:

The reading highlights the profound nature of Christ's sacrifice and His role as the mediator of the new covenant. While the old covenant required repeated sacrifices, Jesus' single offering is sufficient for the redemption of humanity. This passage invites us to reflect on the significance of Christ's sacrifice in our lives. How does understanding Jesus as the mediator of the new covenant shape our relationship with God? Let us embrace the grace and redemption offered through Christ and live in the freedom it brings.

Prayer:

Lord Jesus, we thank You for Your sacrifice and for mediating the new covenant. Help us to fully understand and appreciate the depth of Your offering and to live in the freedom and grace it provides. Cleanse our hearts and guide us to live according to Your will. May Your sacrifice inspire us to follow Your example and to share Your love with others. Amen.

➢ Gospel: Mark 3: 22-30

In this Gospel passage, the scribes accuse Jesus of being possessed by Beelzebul, claiming He drives out demons by the power of the prince of demons. Jesus responds by explaining the absurdity of such accusations and using parables to illustrate His authority over demons. He warns against blaspheming the Holy Spirit, which He describes as an unforgivable sin. The passage underscores the conflict between Jesus and the religious authorities and highlights the importance of recognizing the true nature of His mission.

Reflection:

Jesus' response to the accusations from the scribes reveals the importance of discerning true from false teachings. His authority over demons demonstrates His divine power and the presence of God's kingdom. The warning against blaspheming the Holy Spirit emphasizes the gravity of rejecting the work of God's Spirit. As we reflect on this passage, let us consider how we discern and respond to God's work in our lives. How do we recognize and embrace the true nature of Jesus' mission? Let us be open to the Holy Spirit and guard against the rejection of divine truth.

Prayer:

Lord Jesus, we thank You for Your authority and for revealing the truth of Your mission. Help us to discern Your work in our lives and to recognize the presence of Your Spirit. Guard us from rejecting Your truth and guide us to follow Your example with humility and faith. May we always seek to understand and embrace the true nature of Your mission and share Your message with others. Amen.

Tuesday, January 28

❖ Saint Thomas Aquinas, priest and doctor - Memorial

> First Reading: Hebrews 10: 1-10
> Responsorial Psalm: Psalms 40: 2 and 4ab, 7-8a, 10, 11
> Alleluia: Matthew 11: 25
> Gospel: Mark 3: 31-35
> Lectionary: 318

Today, we honor Saint Thomas Aquinas, a profound theologian and philosopher whose works have significantly shaped Catholic thought. Known for his synthesis of faith and reason, Aquinas made immense contributions to theological and philosophical inquiry. The readings for today highlight the nature of Christ's sacrifice and the true family of Jesus, which is based on doing God's will.

> First Reading: Hebrews 10: 1-10

In this passage from Hebrews, the author reflects on the inadequacy of the old covenant's sacrifices, which had to be repeated annually and could never fully remove sin. Jesus' sacrifice, however, is presented as a once-for-all offering that perfects those who are being sanctified. The reading underscores the fulfillment of God's will through Christ's offering, which establishes a new and perfect covenant.

Reflection:
The reading emphasizes the transition from the old covenant, characterized by repeated sacrifices, to the new covenant established by Christ's single, perfect sacrifice. Jesus' offering is portrayed as both fulfilling and surpassing the old system. This passage invites us to reflect on the profound impact of Christ's sacrifice and its role in our spiritual lives. How do we understand and appreciate the significance of Christ's once-for-all offering? Let us embrace the grace of this new covenant and allow it to transform our relationship with God.

Prayer:
Lord Jesus, we thank You for Your perfect sacrifice and for establishing a new covenant through Your offering. Help us to understand the depth of this grace and to live in accordance with Your will. May Your sacrifice inspire us to deepen our relationship with You and to reflect Your love in our daily lives. Guide us to live fully in the freedom and redemption You have provided. Amen.

> Gospel: Mark 3: 31-35

In this Gospel passage, Jesus is told that His mother and brothers are seeking Him. He responds by redefining the concept of family, stating that those who do the will of God are His true family. Jesus emphasizes that His spiritual family is made up of those who follow God's commandments and live in alignment with His will.

Reflection:
Jesus' redefinition of family highlights the importance of spiritual relationships over biological ones. The true family of Jesus is characterized by doing God's will, which transcends traditional familial bonds. This passage invites us to reflect on our own relationship with Jesus and our place in His spiritual family. How do we align our lives with God's will? Let us strive to be part of Jesus' true family by living out His commandments and reflecting His love in our actions.

Prayer:
Lord Jesus, we thank You for redefining what it means to be part of Your family. Help us to live according to Your will and to embrace our role in Your spiritual family. May we seek to align our lives with Your teachings and to reflect Your love in our daily actions. Guide us in our journey to be faithful members of Your true family and to share Your message with others. Amen.

Wednesday, January 29

❖ **Wednesday of the Third week in Ordinary Time**

> First Reading: Hebrews 10: 11-18
> Responsorial Psalm: Psalms 110: 1, 2, 3, 4
> Gospel: Mark 4: 1-20
> Lectionary: 319

Today's readings explore the transformative power of Christ's sacrifice and the impact of His teachings on our lives. The First Reading reflects on the finality of Christ's offering, while the Gospel presents the Parable of the Sower, illustrating how the reception of God's Word can vary among individuals. As we reflect on these readings, we are invited to examine our response to Christ's message and its effect on our spiritual growth.

> First Reading: Hebrews 10: 11-18

In this passage, the author of Hebrews contrasts the repetitive sacrifices of the old covenant with Christ's single, perfect offering. While the old priests had to continually offer sacrifices for sins, Jesus' sacrifice was once and for all, and it accomplished the forgiveness of sins. The reading emphasizes that Jesus' offering has made the old sacrificial system obsolete and established a new, perfect covenant.

Reflection:

The reading underscores the significance of Christ's sacrifice in the context of salvation history. Unlike the old covenant sacrifices that were temporary and needed repetition, Jesus' sacrifice is complete and final. This passage invites us to reflect on the permanence and efficacy of Christ's offering. How does this understanding shape our faith and our relationship with God? Let us embrace the new covenant established by Jesus and live in the light of His ultimate sacrifice.

Prayer:

Lord Jesus, we thank You for Your perfect and final sacrifice, which has brought us forgiveness and established a new covenant. Help us to fully appreciate the significance of Your offering and to live in accordance with the grace You have provided. May Your sacrifice inspire us to deepen our faith and to live in the freedom and redemption You have given us. Amen.

➢ Gospel: Mark 4: 1-20

In this passage, Jesus tells the Parable of the Sower, describing how different types of soil represent various responses to the Word of God. The seed sown on different soils—path, rocky ground, thorns, and good soil—symbolizes how people receive and act upon the message of the Kingdom. The parable highlights the importance of cultivating a receptive heart and understanding to bear fruit from the Word.

Reflection:

The Parable of the Sower serves as a powerful metaphor for how we receive and respond to God's Word. The different types of soil represent the various ways people can respond to spiritual teachings—some with openness and growth, others with resistance or distraction. This passage challenges us to reflect on the condition of our own hearts. How do we receive and act upon the Word of God in our lives? Let us strive to cultivate a heart that is fertile soil for God's message, allowing it to take root and bear fruit in our lives.

Prayer:

Lord Jesus, we thank You for teaching us through the Parable of the Sower. Help us to cultivate our hearts to be receptive to Your Word and to live out Your teachings with faithfulness and dedication. Guide us to remove any obstacles that prevent Your Word from taking root in our lives and to bear fruit that reflects Your love and grace. May we always seek to grow in our understanding and response to Your message. Amen.

Thursday, January 30

❖ Thursday of the Third week in Ordinary Time

> First Reading: Hebrews 10: 19-25
> Responsorial Psalm: Psalms 24: 1-2, 3-4ab, 5-6
> Alleluia: Psalms 119: 105
> Gospel: Mark 4: 21-25
> Lectionary: 320

Today's readings call us to deepen our relationship with God through faith and action. The First Reading from Hebrews encourages us to approach God with confidence and mutual support within the Christian community. The Gospel from Mark presents teachings about the light of Christ and the importance of how we receive and respond to it. As we reflect on these passages, we are invited to examine our faithfulness and our role in sharing the light of Christ.

> First Reading: Hebrews 10: 19-25

In this passage, the author of Hebrews exhorts the believers to draw near to God with a sincere heart, full of faith, and to hold fast to their hope without wavering. The passage emphasizes the importance of communal support in the faith journey, encouraging believers to stimulate one another to love and good works and to not neglect gathering together. It highlights the new access to God through Christ's sacrifice and the communal aspect of Christian life.

Reflection:
The reading emphasizes the transformative power of Christ's sacrifice, which grants us bold access to God. It also highlights the importance of community and mutual encouragement in the faith. This passage invites us to reflect on our approach to God and our role within the Christian community. How can we better support and encourage one another in our spiritual lives? Let us embrace the new way of approaching God with confidence and foster a sense of unity and mutual support within our faith community.

Prayer:
Lord Jesus, we thank You for granting us bold access to God through Your sacrifice. Help us to draw near to You with sincere hearts and to support and encourage one another in our faith. May we live out Your teachings with commitment and love, and build a strong, supportive Christian community. Guide us to faithfully hold on to our hope and to inspire one another to live according to Your will. Amen.

> Gospel: Mark 4: 21-25

In this Gospel passage, Jesus teaches about the purpose of light. He compares His teachings to a lamp that should not be hidden but placed where it can give light to all. Jesus emphasizes that the measure we use will be the measure we receive, and to those who have, more will be given. The passage underscores the importance of how we respond to and share the light of Christ.

Reflection:
The Gospel passage highlights the role of Jesus' teachings as a source of light meant to illuminate and guide. The teaching about not hiding the lamp signifies the need for openness and the sharing of the light of Christ with others. It also emphasizes that our response to the light we have been given will determine how much more we receive. As we reflect on this passage, let us consider how we can better share the light of Christ in our own lives. How can we ensure that our actions and responses to Christ's teachings reflect His light and love?

Prayer:
Lord Jesus, we thank You for being the light that guides us. Help us to let Your light shine brightly in our lives and to share it with others. May we be faithful stewards of the grace You have given us and reflect Your love and truth in all we do. Guide us to live openly and generously, allowing Your light to shine through us and to illuminate the path for others. Amen.

Friday, January 31

❖ Saint John Bosco, priest - Memorial

> First Reading: Hebrews 10: 32-39
> Responsorial Psalm: Psalms 37: 3-4, 5-6, 23-24, 39-40
> Alleluia: Matthew 11: 25
> Gospel: Mark 4: 26-34
> Lectionary: 321

Today, we honor Saint John Bosco, known for his dedication to the education and formation of young people through his innovative approach and loving care. His life and work inspire us to live out our faith with zeal and compassion. The readings today highlight the theme of perseverance in faith and the growth of God's kingdom, using the imagery of seeds and mustard plants to illustrate the expansive and transformative power of the Gospel.

➢ First Reading: Hebrews 10: 32-39

In this passage, the author of Hebrews encourages believers to recall their past endurance and faithfulness in the face of suffering and persecution. He calls them to persevere in their faith, confident in the promise of salvation. The passage emphasizes that those who have faith and do not shrink back will receive what God has promised. It is a call to hold fast to faith and remain steadfast even in adversity.

Reflection:
The reading reminds us of the importance of perseverance and steadfastness in our faith journey. The early Christians faced significant challenges, but their faith and endurance were pivotal in their spiritual growth. This passage invites us to reflect on our own experiences of suffering or difficulty and to consider how we can maintain our faith and trust in God's promises. How can we cultivate a spirit of perseverance in our own lives? Let us draw strength from the example of the faithful and remain committed to our spiritual journey.

Prayer:
Lord Jesus, we thank You for the examples of faithfulness and perseverance set by Your followers. Help us to remain steadfast in our faith, especially during times of challenge and difficulty. Strengthen our trust in Your promises and guide us to live with unwavering hope and commitment. May we follow the example of saints like John Bosco and be a source of encouragement and inspiration to others. Amen.

➢ Gospel: Mark 4: 26-34

In this Gospel passage, Jesus uses parables to describe the growth of God's kingdom. He compares the kingdom of God to a seed sown in the ground, which grows mysteriously and gradually into a large plant. He also likens the kingdom to a mustard seed, which, though small, grows into a large tree. These parables illustrate the seemingly small beginnings and the eventual expansive growth of God's kingdom.

Reflection:
The parables of the growing seed and the mustard seed convey the idea that God's kingdom starts from humble beginnings but grows beyond our expectations. The gradual and often hidden growth of the seed mirrors the way the Gospel spreads and transforms lives over time. This passage encourages us to be patient and faithful, recognizing that even small acts of faith can lead to significant spiritual growth. How can we contribute to the growth of God's kingdom in our daily lives? Let us trust in the process and be patient, knowing that our efforts, no matter how small, are part of a larger, divine plan.

Prayer:
Lord Jesus, we thank You for the parables that reveal the nature of Your kingdom. Help us to understand that even small acts of faith and love contribute to the growth of Your kingdom. May we trust in Your timing and remain patient as we work to spread Your message and live out Your teachings. Guide us to be active participants in the growth of Your kingdom and to witness the transformative power of Your love in our lives and in the world. Amen.

February 2025

Saturday, February 1

- ❖ First Saturday
- ❖ Saturday of the Third week in Ordinary Time
- ❖ Blessed Virgin Mary - Optional Memorial

> First Reading: Hebrews 11: 1-2, 8-19
> Responsorial Psalm: Luke 1: 69, 70-72, 73-75
> Alleluia: John 3: 16
> Gospel: Mark 4: 35-41
> Lectionary: 322

On this First Saturday, traditionally devoted to the Blessed Virgin Mary, we reflect on the virtues of faith and trust in God's promises. The First Reading from Hebrews recounts the faith of the patriarchs, emphasizing the profound trust they placed in God. The Gospel from Mark describes the calming of the storm, reminding us of Jesus' power and our call to trust in Him, even in life's turbulent moments.

> First Reading: Hebrews 11: 1-2, 8-19

This passage from Hebrews is often referred to as the "Faith Hall of Fame," highlighting the extraordinary faith of key figures in salvation history. The reading begins by defining faith as "the assurance of things hoped for, the conviction of things not seen." It recounts how Abraham, by faith, obeyed God's call to leave his homeland, trusted in God's promise of descendants, and was willing to sacrifice his son Isaac, believing that God could raise him from the dead.

Reflection:
The reading from Hebrews underscores the importance of faith as the foundation of our relationship with God. The examples of Abraham and other patriarchs remind us that faith often requires stepping into the unknown, trusting in God's promises even when they seem impossible. This passage invites us to examine the strength of our own faith. How can we deepen our trust in God's plans, especially when faced with uncertainty? Let us draw inspiration from the patriarchs and strive to cultivate a faith that is unwavering and rooted in God's promises.

Prayer:
Lord God, we thank You for the examples of faith set by the patriarchs. Help us to deepen our trust in You, even when Your plans seem unclear or difficult to understand. May we, like Abraham, respond to Your call with obedience and confidence in Your promises. Strengthen our faith so that we may always walk in the assurance of Your love and guidance. Amen.

> Gospel: Mark 4: 35-41

In this passage, Jesus and His disciples are crossing the Sea of Galilee when a fierce storm arises, threatening to capsize their boat. While the disciples panic, Jesus is asleep. When they wake Him, He rebukes the wind and calms the sea with the words, "Peace! Be still!" The disciples are amazed and fearful, questioning who Jesus is that even the wind and sea obey Him. Jesus, in turn, challenges them, asking, "Why are you afraid? Have you still no faith?"

Reflection:

The calming of the storm is a powerful reminder of Jesus' authority over creation and His ability to bring peace in the midst of chaos. The disciples' fear contrasts with Jesus' calm, highlighting their need for greater faith. This passage invites us to reflect on how we respond to the storms in our own lives. Do we trust in Jesus' power to calm our fears and anxieties? How can we cultivate a deeper faith that remains steadfast even in times of turmoil? Let us turn to Jesus with confidence, knowing that He is always with us, ready to bring peace to our troubled hearts.

Prayer:

Lord Jesus, we thank You for Your power and presence in our lives, especially during times of fear and uncertainty. Help us to trust in Your ability to calm the storms we face and to bring peace to our hearts. Strengthen our faith so that we may always turn to You with confidence, knowing that You are in control. May we find comfort in Your words, "Peace! Be still!" and live with the assurance of Your constant care and protection. Amen.

Sunday, February 2

❖ Presentation of the Lord - Feast

> First Reading: Malachi 3: 1-4
> Responsorial Psalm: Psalms 24: 7, 8, 9, 10
> Second Reading: Hebrews 2: 14-18
> Alleluia: Luke 2: 32
> Gospel: Luke 2: 22-40 or Luke 2: 22-32
> Lectionary: 524

The Feast of the Presentation of the Lord, also known as Candlemas, commemorates the moment when Mary and Joseph brought the infant Jesus to the Temple in Jerusalem to present Him to the Lord, as prescribed by Jewish law. This event is filled with symbolism, as Jesus, the Light of the World, is recognized by Simeon and Anna as the promised Savior. The readings today emphasize the fulfillment of God's promises and the revelation of Christ as a light to the nations.

➢ First Reading: Malachi 3: 1-4

In this prophetic passage, Malachi speaks of the coming of the Lord's messenger, who will prepare the way before Him. The Lord is described as a refiner and purifier, who will cleanse and purify the sons of Levi so that they may offer pleasing sacrifices to God. This passage foreshadows the coming of Christ, who purifies us through His sacrifice and prepares us to live in holiness.

Reflection:

Malachi's prophecy speaks to the transformative power of God's presence, which purifies and refines us as gold and silver are refined. The coming of the Lord is not merely a moment of joy but also a call to purification and holiness. This reading invites us to reflect on how we can open our hearts to God's refining work. Are we willing to be purified and transformed by His grace? Let us seek to offer our lives as pleasing sacrifices, purified by the love and mercy of God.

Prayer:

Lord God, we thank You for the promise of Your coming and the purification that You bring. Help us to be open to Your refining work in our lives, so that we may be made pure and holy in Your sight. May we offer ourselves to You as living sacrifices, pleasing and acceptable in Your sight. Purify our hearts and guide us in the way of righteousness. Amen.

➢ Second Reading: Hebrews 2: 14-18

In this passage, the author of Hebrews reflects on the humanity of Christ, who became like us in every way except sin. By taking on flesh and blood, Jesus was able to destroy the power of death and the devil, freeing those who were held in slavery by fear of death. As a merciful and faithful high priest, He made atonement for the sins of the people, and through His own suffering, He is able to help those who are being tested.

Reflection:

This reading emphasizes the profound mystery of the Incarnation—Christ becoming fully human so that He could redeem humanity. It reminds us of the depth of God's love, as Jesus shared in our sufferings and weaknesses to bring us salvation. This passage invites us to reflect on the significance of Jesus' humanity in our own lives. How does His shared experience of our struggles and sufferings bring us comfort and strength? Let us turn to Him in our times of need, knowing that He understands and cares for us deeply.

Prayer:

Lord Jesus, we thank You for becoming one of us, sharing in our humanity so that You might bring us salvation. Help us to draw near to You in our times of suffering and trial, confident that You understand our struggles and are always ready to help us. May we find comfort and strength in Your presence, and may Your love guide us through every challenge we face. Amen.

> Gospel: Luke 2: 22-40 or Luke 2: 22-32

In this Gospel passage, Mary and Joseph bring the infant Jesus to the Temple to present Him to the Lord, as was the custom according to the Law of Moses. In the Temple, they encounter Simeon, a righteous and devout man who had been promised by the Holy Spirit that he would not die before seeing the Messiah. Simeon takes Jesus in his arms and praises God, declaring that Jesus is the light for revelation to the Gentiles and the glory of Israel. The prophetess Anna also recognizes Jesus as the Redeemer and speaks about Him to all who were waiting for the redemption of Jerusalem.

Reflection:

The Presentation of the Lord is a moment of revelation and recognition. Simeon and Anna, guided by the Holy Spirit, recognize Jesus as the long-awaited Messiah, the light to the nations. This passage invites us to reflect on how we recognize and respond to Christ in our own lives. Do we see Him as the light that guides our path? How do we share the light of Christ with others? Let us follow the example of Simeon and Anna, who, with patience and faith, awaited the fulfillment of God's promises and rejoiced in their fulfillment.

Prayer:

Lord Jesus, we thank You for being the light that shines in our darkness. Help us to recognize You in our daily lives and to welcome You into our hearts with joy. May we, like Simeon and Anna, live in hope and faith, always trusting in Your promises. Guide us to be bearers of Your light in the world, sharing Your love and truth with all those we encounter. Amen.

Monday, February 3

- ❖ Monday of the Fourth week in Ordinary Time
- ❖ Saint Blase, bishop and martyr - Optional Memorial
- ❖ Saint Ansgar, bishop - Optional Memorial

> First Reading: Hebrews 11: 32-40
> Responsorial Psalm: Psalms 31: 20, 21, 22, 23, 24
> Alleluia: Luke 7: 16
> Gospel: Mark 5: 1-20
> Lectionary: 323

On this day, we celebrate the optional memorials of Saint Blase, known for the blessing of throats, and Saint Ansgar, a missionary bishop who brought the Gospel to Scandinavia. The readings focus on the power of faith, as we see in the first reading from Hebrews, and the transformative power of Jesus, as depicted in the Gospel of Mark.

➤ First Reading: Hebrews 11: 32-40

This passage from Hebrews continues the theme of faith, recounting the extraordinary deeds accomplished by those who trusted in God. The author mentions figures such as Gideon, Barak, Samson, and David, who through faith conquered kingdoms, administered justice, and gained what was promised. The reading also acknowledges the suffering endured by others, who remained faithful despite torture, imprisonment, and death, looking forward to something better.

Reflection:

This reading serves as a powerful reminder of the strength and resilience that come from faith. The examples of the heroes of faith encourage us to remain steadfast in our own faith, regardless of the challenges we face. The passage also highlights that faith is not only about triumphs but also about enduring trials with the hope of God's promises. It invites us to consider how we can deepen our faith and trust in God, even when the path is difficult.

Prayer:

Lord God, we thank You for the examples of faith given to us by the saints and heroes of Scripture. Help us to grow in faith and to trust in Your promises, even in the face of trials and hardships. Strengthen our resolve to follow You with courage and perseverance, knowing that our faith in You will be rewarded. Amen.

➤ Gospel: Mark 5: 1-20

In this Gospel passage, Jesus encounters a man possessed by a legion of demons in the region of the Gerasenes. The man lives among the tombs, uncontrollable and isolated. When Jesus arrives, the demons recognize Him and beg not to be sent out of the area. Jesus grants their request to enter a herd of pigs, which then rush into the sea and drown. The healed man begs to stay with Jesus, but Jesus sends him home, telling him to share what God has done for him.

Reflection:

This dramatic encounter demonstrates Jesus' authority over evil and His compassion for those who are suffering. The man's transformation from a tormented outcast to a proclaimer of God's mercy highlights the power of Jesus to bring healing and restoration. This passage invites us to reflect on the ways Jesus has brought healing and transformation into our own lives. How can we share the story of what God has done for us? It also challenges us to trust in Jesus' power to overcome the forces of darkness and to bring light and peace into our lives.

Prayer:

Lord Jesus, we thank You for Your power to heal and restore. Help us to trust in Your ability to bring light into the darkest areas of our lives. May we, like the man healed in today's Gospel, go forth and share the story of Your mercy and grace with others. Strengthen our faith and fill us with the peace that only You can give. Amen.

Tuesday, February 4

❖ Tuesday of the Fourth week in Ordinary Time

- ➢ First Reading: Hebrews 12: 1-4
- ➢ Responsorial Psalm: Psalms 22: 26b-27, 28 and 30, 31-32
- ➢ Alleluia: Matthew 8: 17
- ➢ Gospel: Mark 5: 21-43
- ➢ Lectionary: 324

As we journey through the Fourth Week in Ordinary Time, today's readings encourage us to persevere in our faith and trust in the healing power of Jesus. The first reading from Hebrews speaks of the endurance required in the Christian life, while the Gospel of Mark recounts two miraculous healings that demonstrate Jesus' compassion and power.

➢ First Reading: Hebrews 12: 1-4

In this passage, the author of Hebrews urges believers to persevere in their faith, drawing strength from the "great cloud of witnesses" that surrounds them. We are called to lay aside every weight and sin that hinders us, and to run with endurance the race set before us, keeping our eyes fixed on Jesus, the pioneer and perfecter of our faith. The reading also reminds us that, in our struggle against sin, we have not yet resisted to the point of shedding blood.

Reflection:
The image of running a race with endurance is a powerful metaphor for the Christian life. It reminds us that faith requires perseverance, especially when we face challenges and obstacles. The "great cloud of witnesses" refers to the saints and faithful who have gone before us, offering us inspiration and encouragement. This reading invites us to reflect on the ways we can shed the sins and distractions that weigh us down, so that we can follow Jesus more closely. It also challenges us to keep our eyes on Jesus, who not only shows us the way but also gives us the strength to endure.

Prayer:
Lord Jesus, we thank You for the example of the saints who have run the race of faith before us. Help us to persevere in our own journey, laying aside the sins and distractions that hinder us. May we keep our eyes fixed on You, drawing strength from Your love and grace. Grant us the endurance to follow You faithfully, even in the face of trials. Amen.

> Gospel: Mark 5: 21-43

In this Gospel passage, Jesus performs two miraculous healings: the raising of Jairus' daughter and the healing of a woman who had been suffering from a hemorrhage for twelve years. Jairus, a synagogue leader, pleads with Jesus to heal his dying daughter. As Jesus is on His way to Jairus' house, a woman in the crowd touches His cloak, believing that it will heal her. Jesus feels power go out from Him and, turning to the crowd, He acknowledges the woman's faith, telling her that her faith has made her well. When Jesus arrives at Jairus' house, He finds the child has died, but He takes her by the hand and tells her to rise, and she comes back to life.

Reflection:
This Gospel passage reveals the transformative power of faith and the deep compassion of Jesus. The woman's faith in reaching out to touch Jesus, and Jairus' faith in seeking Jesus' help for his daughter, both result in miraculous healings. These stories invite us to reflect on our own faith—how do we reach out to Jesus in our time of need? Do we trust in His power to heal and restore us? This passage also challenges us to have faith even in seemingly hopeless situations, trusting that Jesus has the power to bring new life where there is death and despair.

Prayer:
Lord Jesus, we thank You for Your compassion and healing power. Help us to reach out to You in faith, trusting in Your ability to heal and restore us. Strengthen our faith, especially in times of difficulty, and help us to trust in Your presence and power in our lives. May we, like the woman and Jairus, experience the transformative power of Your love and grace. Amen.

Wednesday, February 5

❖ Saint Agatha, virgin and martyr - Memorial

> First Reading: Hebrews 12: 4-7, 11-15
> Responsorial Psalm: Psalms 103: 1-2, 13-14, 17-18a
> Alleluia: John 10: 27
> Gospel: Mark 6: 1-6
> Lectionary: 325

Today, we celebrate the memorial of Saint Agatha, a virgin and martyr who gave her life for her faith in Christ. Her courage and unwavering devotion are a powerful testimony to the strength that comes from faith. The readings for today remind us of the importance of discipline in our spiritual lives and the challenge of believing in Jesus, even when others around us do not.

➢ First Reading: Hebrews 12: 4-7, 11-15

In this passage, the author of Hebrews speaks about the discipline that comes from the Lord, comparing it to the discipline a father gives to his children. The reading reminds us that God's discipline, though difficult at the time, ultimately produces righteousness and peace for those who are trained by it. The author urges us to strengthen our resolve, to make "straight paths" for our feet, and to strive for peace and holiness. We are also warned to be vigilant, ensuring that no one falls short of God's grace and that no root of bitterness takes hold among us.

Reflection:

Discipline is often seen as something unpleasant, but in the context of our spiritual lives, it is a sign of God's love and care for us. Just as a parent disciplines a child to guide them toward growth and maturity, God's discipline is meant to help us grow in holiness. This reading invites us to embrace the challenges and corrections that come our way, knowing that they are opportunities for spiritual growth. It also encourages us to support one another in our faith journey, ensuring that we all experience the fullness of God's grace.

Prayer:

Heavenly Father, we thank You for Your loving discipline that shapes us into the people You call us to be. Help us to accept Your guidance with humility and trust, knowing that it leads to righteousness and peace. Strengthen our resolve to walk in Your ways and to encourage one another in our journey of faith. May we always seek peace and holiness, reflecting Your grace in all that we do. Amen.

➢ Gospel: Mark 6: 1-6

In this Gospel passage, Jesus returns to His hometown of Nazareth, where He teaches in the synagogue. Despite His wisdom and the mighty works He has performed, the people of Nazareth take offense at Him, questioning how someone they know so well could possess such authority. Their lack of faith astonishes Jesus, and as a result, He is unable to perform many miracles there, except for a few healings.

Reflection:

This passage highlights the difficulty of faith when familiarity breeds contempt. The people of Nazareth, who knew Jesus as the carpenter, struggled to believe in His divine authority and mission. Their skepticism and lack of faith limited the miracles Jesus could perform among them. This story challenges us to examine our own faith—do we sometimes take Jesus for granted because of our familiarity with Him? Are there areas in our lives where we struggle to believe in His power? It reminds us that faith is essential for experiencing the fullness of God's grace and blessings.

Prayer:

Lord Jesus, we thank You for Your presence in our lives, even when we sometimes take it for granted. Help us to approach You with faith and trust, recognizing Your power and authority in every aspect of our lives. Strengthen our belief in Your ability to work miracles in us and through us. May we never let familiarity or doubt hinder the fullness of Your grace in our lives. Amen.

Thursday, February 6

❖ Saint Paul Miki and companions, martyrs - Memorial

- First Reading: Hebrews 12: 18-19, 21-24
- Responsorial Psalm: Psalms 48: 2-3ab, 3cd-4, 9, 10-11
- Alleluia: Mark 1: 15
- Gospel: Mark 6: 7-13
- Lectionary: 326

Today, we honor the memory of Saint Paul Miki and his companions, who were martyred for their faith in Japan. Their sacrifice is a powerful testament to the strength of faith in the face of persecution. The readings for today remind us of the profound relationship we have with God through Christ and the mission we are called to as His disciples.

- First Reading: Hebrews 12: 18-19, 21-24

In this passage, the author of Hebrews contrasts the experience of the Israelites at Mount Sinai with that of Christians under the new covenant. The Israelites approached a terrifying and unapproachable mountain, filled with fire, darkness, and a fearful voice. In contrast, Christians are invited to approach Mount Zion, the city of the living God, the heavenly Jerusalem. This passage speaks of the joy and communion with countless angels and the spirits of the righteous, with Jesus, the mediator of the new covenant, whose blood speaks more graciously than Abel's.

Reflection:
This reading highlights the transformative nature of our relationship with God through Jesus Christ. The fearful distance of the old covenant has been replaced by the intimate and joyful communion of the new covenant. Through Christ, we are invited into the very presence of God, where grace, mercy, and love abound. This passage invites us to reflect on the privilege and responsibility of being part of this new covenant community. It also challenges us to live in a way that reflects our heavenly citizenship, embracing the grace that Jesus offers.

Prayer:
Heavenly Father, we thank You for the new covenant made possible through Jesus Christ. Help us to live in the joy and freedom of this relationship, always mindful of the grace that has been given to us. May we approach You with reverence and gratitude, knowing that through Jesus, we are welcomed into Your presence. Strengthen our faith and help us to live as true citizens of Your heavenly kingdom. Amen.

> Gospel: Mark 6: 7-13

In this Gospel passage, Jesus sends out the twelve apostles in pairs, giving them authority over unclean spirits. He instructs them to take nothing for their journey except a staff—no bread, no bag, no money in their belts—but to wear sandals and not put on two tunics. They are to stay in whatever house they enter until they leave that place, and if any place does not welcome them, they are to shake off the dust from their feet as a testimony against them. The apostles go out and preach repentance, cast out demons, and heal many who are sick.

Reflection:

This passage illustrates the mission of the disciples and the simplicity with which they are to carry it out. Jesus' instructions emphasize reliance on God's provision and the urgency of the mission. The apostles' success in preaching, exorcism, and healing shows the power of God at work through those who are faithful to His call. This Gospel challenges us to reflect on our own mission as disciples of Christ. Are we willing to trust in God's provision and step out in faith to share the Good News? It also reminds us of the power and authority we have been given through Christ to bring healing and hope to others.

Prayer:

Lord Jesus, we thank You for the mission You have entrusted to us as Your disciples. Help us to trust in Your provision and to step out in faith, sharing the Good News with those around us. May we always rely on Your power and authority as we seek to bring healing, hope, and repentance to the world. Strengthen us to be faithful witnesses of Your love and grace. Amen.

Friday, February 7

❖ First Friday
❖ Friday of the Fourth week in Ordinary Time

> First Reading: Hebrews 13: 1-8
> Responsorial Psalm: Psalms 27: 1, 3, 5, 8b-9abc
> Alleluia: Luke 8: 15
> Gospel: Mark 6: 14-29
> Lectionary: 327

On this First Friday, a day traditionally dedicated to the Sacred Heart of Jesus, we reflect on the steadfast love and presence of Christ in our lives. The readings today call us to a life of love, integrity, and trust in God's unchanging nature. As we meditate on these passages, we are reminded of the importance of living out our faith with sincerity and courage.

➢ First Reading: Hebrews 13: 1-8

In this passage, the author of Hebrews provides practical instructions for Christian living, emphasizing love, hospitality, compassion for those in prison, purity in marriage, and contentment with what one has. The reading encourages believers to remember and imitate the faith of their leaders, holding fast to the truth that "Jesus Christ is the same yesterday, today, and forever."

Reflection:
This reading offers a beautiful blueprint for a life that honors God. It reminds us of the importance of love in our interactions with others, the need for integrity in our relationships, and the call to be content with God's provision. The reassurance that Jesus is unchanging provides a foundation of stability and trust in a world that is often uncertain. As we reflect on these words, we are encouraged to live out our faith in practical ways, knowing that Christ's presence and guidance are constant in our lives.

Prayer:
Lord Jesus, we thank You for Your unchanging love and faithfulness. Help us to live lives that reflect Your love, showing kindness and compassion to those around us. May we be content with what we have, trusting in Your provision and guidance. Strengthen our faith so that we may stand firm in the truth of Your unchanging nature, and inspire us to live with integrity and love in all that we do. Amen.

➢ Gospel: Mark 6: 14-29

This Gospel passage recounts the story of the beheading of John the Baptist. King Herod, though fascinated by John's message, ultimately orders his execution because of a rash vow made during a banquet. Herodias, Herod's wife, seizes the opportunity to silence John, who had openly criticized her marriage to Herod. Despite Herod's reluctance, he fulfills his promise to Herodias' daughter, leading to John's martyrdom.

Reflection:
The story of John the Baptist's martyrdom is a powerful reminder of the cost of speaking the truth and standing up for righteousness. John's unwavering commitment to God's message, even in the face of danger, challenges us to examine our own courage in witnessing to our faith. Herod's weakness and susceptibility to pressure contrast sharply with John's steadfastness. This passage calls us to be firm in our convictions, to speak the truth with love, and to trust in God's justice, even when it comes at a great personal cost.

Prayer:
Heavenly Father, we thank You for the example of John the Baptist, who courageously proclaimed the truth and remained faithful to You even unto death. Grant us the courage to stand up for what is right and to speak the truth in love, no matter the consequences. Help us to rely on Your strength when we face challenges and opposition in our lives. May we, like John, remain steadfast in our faith, trusting in Your ultimate justice and mercy. Amen.

Saturday, February 8

- ❖ Saturday of the Fourth week in Ordinary Time
- ❖ Saint Jerome Emiliani - Optional Memorial
- ❖ Saint Josephine Bakhita - Optional Memorial
- ❖ Blessed Virgin Mary - Optional Memorial

- ➢ First Reading: Hebrews 13: 15-17, 20-21
- ➢ Responsorial Psalm: Psalms 23: 1-3a, 3b-4, 5, 6
- ➢ Alleluia: John 10: 27
- ➢ Gospel: Mark 6: 30-34
- ➢ Lectionary: 328

On this Saturday, we are invited to reflect on the example of Saint Jerome Emiliani, the patron of orphans and abandoned children, and Saint Josephine Bakhita, a symbol of resilience and forgiveness. These saints inspire us to live lives of charity, trust in God, and perseverance. The readings today guide us in offering praise to God and in following Christ's compassionate example.

- ➢ First Reading: Hebrews 13: 15-17, 20-21

In this passage, the author of Hebrews encourages believers to continually offer a sacrifice of praise to God, the fruit of lips that openly profess His name. The reading also calls for obedience to spiritual leaders, as they keep watch over souls, and for prayers that God may equip the faithful with everything good to do His will. The passage concludes with a blessing, asking that the God of peace, who brought back Jesus from the dead, may equip believers with all that is needed to do His will, working in them what is pleasing to Him through Jesus Christ.

Reflection:
This reading emphasizes the importance of living a life of praise, obedience, and service to God. The "sacrifice of praise" is a continual offering that flows from a heart that acknowledges God's goodness and sovereignty. The call to obey spiritual leaders reminds us of the need for humility and unity within the Christian community. The blessing at the end is a powerful reminder that it is God who equips and enables us to do His will. As we reflect on these words, we are encouraged to live in a way that is pleasing to God, trusting that He will provide us with the grace and strength needed to fulfill His purposes in our lives.

Prayer:
Gracious God, we offer You our sacrifice of praise, acknowledging Your goodness and mercy in our lives.

Help us to live in obedience to Your will, guided by the leaders You have placed in our lives. Equip us with all that we need to do what pleases You, and may our lives be a testimony of Your love and grace. We ask this through Jesus Christ, who lives and reigns with You forever and ever. Amen.

> Gospel: Mark 6: 30-34

In this Gospel passage, the apostles return to Jesus after their missionary journey, reporting all they had done and taught. Jesus, seeing that they were tired and had not even had time to eat, invites them to come away to a deserted place to rest. However, the crowds see them leaving and follow them. When Jesus sees the large crowd, He is moved with compassion, for they are like sheep without a shepherd. He begins to teach them many things.

Reflection:
This passage reveals the compassionate heart of Jesus, who cares for both the physical and spiritual needs of His followers. Despite His desire to give the apostles rest, Jesus is moved by the needs of the crowd and takes the time to teach them. This scene invites us to reflect on the balance between rest and service in our own lives. It also challenges us to cultivate a heart of compassion, being attentive to the needs of others even when we ourselves are weary. Jesus' example teaches us that true leadership and discipleship involve a willingness to serve, even at personal cost.

Prayer:
Lord Jesus, we thank You for Your compassion and care for us. Help us to follow Your example by being attentive to the needs of others, even when we are tired or in need of rest. Give us the strength and grace to serve with love and humility, and to find our rest in You. May we always be shepherds to those who are lost, guiding them to Your truth and love. Amen.

Sunday, February 9

❖ Fifth Sunday in Ordinary Time

> First Reading: Isaiah 6: 1-2a, 3-8
> Responsorial Psalm: Psalms 138: 1-2ab, 2cd-3, 4-5, 7c-8
> Second Reading: First Corinthians 15: 1-11 or First Corinthians 15: 3-8, 11
> Alleluia: Matthew 4: 19
> Gospel: Luke 5: 1-11
> Lectionary: 75

On this Fifth Sunday in Ordinary Time, the liturgy invites us to encounter God's holiness and respond to His call with humility and faith. The readings focus on moments of divine revelation, human unworthiness, and the transformative power of God's grace. As we reflect on these passages, we are encouraged to recognize our own limitations, embrace God's mercy, and commit ourselves to His service.

➢ First Reading: Isaiah 6: 1-2a, 3-8

This reading from Isaiah describes the prophet's vision of the Lord seated on a high and lofty throne, surrounded by seraphim who proclaim God's holiness. In the presence of such holiness, Isaiah becomes acutely aware of his own sinfulness, crying out, "Woe is me, I am doomed!" A seraph then touches Isaiah's lips with a burning coal, cleansing him of his sin. When the Lord asks, "Whom shall I send?", Isaiah responds, "Here I am, send me!"

Reflection:

Isaiah's vision is a powerful reminder of the majesty and holiness of God. It highlights the contrast between God's purity and human sinfulness, but also reveals God's desire to cleanse and use us for His purposes. Isaiah's immediate response to God's call—despite his initial feelings of unworthiness—challenges us to be open and willing to serve the Lord, trusting in His ability to purify and equip us for the mission He has for us. This passage invites us to encounter God's holiness, acknowledge our need for His mercy, and respond to His call with a willing heart.

Prayer:

Holy God, we stand in awe of Your majesty and holiness. Like Isaiah, we recognize our own unworthiness in Your presence, but we thank You for Your mercy that cleanses and renews us. Grant us the courage to respond to Your call with a willing heart, saying, "Here I am, send me." Equip us to serve You faithfully and to proclaim Your holiness to the world. Amen.

➢ Second Reading: First Corinthians 15: 1-11 or First Corinthians 15: 3-8, 11

In this passage, Paul reminds the Corinthians of the Gospel message he preached to them, which they received and in which they stand firm. He recounts the key events of the Gospel: Christ's death for our sins, His burial, and His resurrection on the third day, all according to the Scriptures. Paul also emphasizes the appearances of the risen Christ to various individuals and groups, including himself. He humbly acknowledges that he is the least of the apostles, unworthy to be called an apostle because of his past persecution of the Church, but he attributes his ministry to God's grace.

Reflection:

Paul's words remind us of the foundational truth of the Gospel: Christ's death and resurrection. This message is the cornerstone of our faith and the source of our hope. Paul's humility and recognition of God's grace in his life challenge us to reflect on our own journeys of faith. No matter our past, God's grace is sufficient to transform us and use us for His glory. This passage calls us to stand firm in the Gospel, to recognize the power of grace at work in our lives, and to share this message with others.

Prayer:

Gracious God, we thank You for the Gospel, the good news of Christ's death and resurrection that brings us hope and salvation. Help us to stand firm in this truth and to live out its implications in our daily lives. We acknowledge that it is only by Your grace that we are who we are, and we ask for the strength to faithfully share this message with others. May we always give glory to You for the work You do in and through us. Amen.

➤ Gospel: Luke 5: 1-11

In this Gospel passage, Jesus calls His first disciples. After teaching the crowds from Simon Peter's boat, Jesus instructs Peter to put out into deep water and lower the nets for a catch. Despite having caught nothing all night, Peter obeys Jesus' command, and they catch such a large number of fish that their nets begin to tear. Astonished by the miracle, Peter falls at Jesus' knees, saying, "Depart from me, Lord, for I am a sinful man." Jesus reassures him, saying, "Do not be afraid; from now on you will be catching men." Peter and the other fishermen leave everything and follow Jesus.

Reflection:

This passage illustrates the power of obedience to Christ, even when it goes against our human understanding or experience. Peter's willingness to trust Jesus' command leads to a miraculous catch, revealing Jesus' authority and divinity. Peter's recognition of his own sinfulness in the presence of Jesus echoes Isaiah's experience in the first reading, yet Jesus does not reject him. Instead, He calls Peter to a new mission—becoming a fisher of men. This encounter reminds us that Jesus sees beyond our weaknesses and calls us to participate in His mission. Our response, like Peter's, should be one of trust and total surrender to His will.

Prayer:

Lord Jesus, we thank You for Your call to follow You, despite our weaknesses and imperfections. Help us to trust in Your word and to obey Your commands, even when we do not fully understand. Give us the courage to leave behind anything that hinders our discipleship and to embrace the mission You have for us. May we, like Peter, respond to Your call with faith and surrender, and may our lives be a testament to Your power and grace. Amen.

Monday, February 10

❖ Saint Scholastica, virgin - Memorial

- ➤ First Reading: Genesis 1: 1-19
- ➤ Responsorial Psalm: Psalms 104: 1-2a, 5-6, 10 and 12, 24 and 35c
- ➤ Alleluia: Matthew 4: 23
- ➤ Gospel: Mark 6: 53-56
- ➤ Lectionary: 329

Today we honor Saint Scholastica, the twin sister of Saint Benedict and a dedicated virgin who devoted her life to prayer and monastic life. Her life is a testament to the power of prayer and the importance of community in the spiritual life. The readings reflect on the beginnings of creation and the healing power of Jesus, themes that resonate with Saint Scholastica's life of devotion and faith.

➢ First Reading: Genesis 1: 1-19

This passage from Genesis describes the first four days of creation. It recounts how God created the heavens and the earth, separated light from darkness, and established the heavens and the earth with distinct purposes. On the first day, God said, "Let there be light," and there was light. He then separated the light from the darkness, calling the light "day" and the darkness "night." On the second day, God created the sky, and on the third day, He gathered the waters to reveal dry land and created vegetation. The fourth day saw the creation of the sun, moon, and stars to separate day from night and to mark seasons, days, and years.

Reflection:
The creation narrative emphasizes the order and intentionality of God's work. Each act of creation is a deliberate and purposeful step in establishing the world. This passage reminds us of the fundamental truth that God is the Creator of all things, and His creation is good. As we reflect on the beauty and order of creation, we are invited to recognize God's hand in our own lives and to honor His work in the world. Saint Scholastica's life mirrored this sense of order and purpose, as she dedicated herself to the monastic life with intention and devotion.

Prayer:
Creator God, we praise You for the wonder and order of Your creation. Help us to recognize Your hand in all things and to live our lives in harmony with Your will. We thank You for the example of Saint Scholastica, who dedicated her life to Your service. May we, too, find purpose and meaning in our daily lives as we seek to honor You in all that we do. Amen.

➢ Gospel: Mark 6: 53-56

In this Gospel passage, Jesus and His disciples arrive at Gennesaret, where people recognize Him and bring all the sick to Him. The people beg to touch even the fringe of His cloak, and all who touch it are healed. Jesus' healing power is evident as He responds to the faith and desperation of the people, demonstrating His compassion and divine authority.

Reflection:
This passage highlights Jesus' healing power and His willingness to respond to the faith of those who seek Him. The people's belief that even touching the fringe of His cloak could bring healing underscores their trust in His power. This story encourages us to approach Jesus with faith and confidence in His ability to heal and transform our lives. It also reminds us of the importance of reaching out to those in need, following Jesus' example of compassion and service. Saint Scholastica, through her dedicated prayer and life of service, exemplifies this spirit of reaching out to God and others with trust and devotion.

Prayer:
Lord Jesus, we are in awe of Your healing power and Your compassion for those who are suffering. We ask for the grace to approach You with faith, trusting in Your ability to heal and transform our lives. Help us to follow Your example of love and service, reaching out to those in need with compassion. We thank You for the life of Saint Scholastica, who devoted herself to prayer and service. May we be inspired by her example to live lives of faith and dedication. Amen.

Tuesday, February 11

- Tuesday of the Fifth week in Ordinary Time
- Our Lady of Lourdes - Optional Memorial

- First Reading: Genesis 1: 20 – 2: 4a
- Responsorial Psalm: Psalms 8: 4-5, 6-7, 8-9
- Alleluia: Psalms 119: 36, 29b
- Gospel: Mark 7: 1-13
- Lectionary: 330

Today, we commemorate Our Lady of Lourdes, a special day that reminds us of the apparitions of the Blessed Virgin Mary to Saint Bernadette Soubirous in Lourdes, France, in 1858. This day is also recognized as the World Day of the Sick, inviting us to reflect on the healing grace of God and the intercession of the Blessed Mother. The readings today focus on the ongoing creation and the importance of inner purity over external observance, inviting us to trust in God's creative power and seek purity of heart.

- First Reading: Genesis 1: 20 – 2: 4a

This continuation of the creation story describes the fifth and sixth days, where God creates the creatures of the sea and air, followed by the animals on the land and humankind. On the sixth day, God creates man and woman in His image, giving them dominion over all the earth. After completing His creation, God rests on the seventh day, blessing it as a day of rest.

Reflection:
The creation narrative reaches its climax with the creation of humanity, made in the image and likeness of God. This passage highlights the unique dignity and responsibility given to human beings to care for creation. It also introduces the concept of the Sabbath, a day of rest and reflection on God's goodness. As we reflect on the grandeur of creation, we are reminded of our call to be stewards of the earth and to live in harmony with all of God's creation. The commemoration of Our Lady of Lourdes today also draws our

attention to the beauty and sanctity of life, as we honor the Blessed Mother, who always points us toward her Son, the source of all life and healing.

Prayer:
Gracious God, we thank You for the gift of creation and for making us in Your image. Help us to be good stewards of the earth and to recognize the sanctity of all life. We ask for the intercession of Our Lady of Lourdes, that we may experience Your healing grace and be filled with a deeper love for You. Guide us to live each day in a way that honors You and reflects Your love to the world. Amen.

> ➢ Gospel: Mark 7: 1-13

In this passage, the Pharisees and some scribes criticize Jesus' disciples for eating with unwashed hands, a violation of traditional rituals. Jesus responds by calling out their hypocrisy, emphasizing that what defiles a person is not what enters from the outside but what comes from within, from the heart. He rebukes them for prioritizing human traditions over the commandments of God.

Reflection:
Jesus' words in this passage challenge us to examine our own hearts and motivations. It is easy to become focused on external observances and miss the deeper call to inner purity and righteousness. True holiness comes from a heart aligned with God's will, not merely from following rituals. The optional memorial of Our Lady of Lourdes reminds us of the importance of seeking spiritual healing and renewal, just as Mary always leads us to her Son, who alone can purify and transform our hearts.

Prayer:
Lord Jesus, You call us to true holiness, which begins in the heart. Help us to seek purity of heart and to live in accordance with Your will. We ask for the intercession of Our Lady of Lourdes, that we may receive the grace of inner healing and grow in our love for You. May our lives reflect Your goodness and bring glory to Your name. Amen.

Wednesday, February 12

❖ **Wednesday of the Fifth week in Ordinary Time**

> ➢ First Reading: Genesis 2: 4b-9, 15-17
> ➢ Responsorial Psalm: Psalms 104: 1-2a, 27-28, 29bc-30
> ➢ Alleluia: John 17: 17b, 17a
> ➢ Gospel: Mark 7: 14-23
> ➢ Lectionary: 331

As we continue our journey through Ordinary Time, today's readings invite us to reflect on the origin of humanity and the importance of inner purity. The Genesis account takes us back to the creation of man and the Garden of Eden, while the Gospel challenges us to consider the condition of our hearts. Together, these readings remind us of our dependence on God as our Creator and the need to cultivate a pure and righteous heart.

➤ First Reading: Genesis 2: 4b-9, 15-17

This passage recounts the creation of the first human being, formed by God from the dust of the ground and given the breath of life. God places the man in the Garden of Eden, a place of beauty and abundance, with the command to till and keep it. In the center of the garden stand the tree of life and the tree of the knowledge of good and evil. God commands the man not to eat from the tree of the knowledge of good and evil, warning that doing so would lead to death.

Reflection:
The creation of man and the Garden of Eden symbolize the intimate relationship between God and humanity. God forms man with His own hands and breathes life into him, highlighting our dependence on God for life and purpose. The Garden of Eden represents the ideal state of harmony between God, humanity, and creation. The command not to eat from the tree of the knowledge of good and evil serves as a reminder of the importance of obedience and trust in God's wisdom. This reading invites us to reflect on our own relationship with God and our call to live in accordance with His will, recognizing that true freedom is found in obedience to His commands.

Prayer:
Creator God, You formed us from the dust of the earth and breathed life into us. Help us to live in harmony with Your creation and to follow Your commandments with trust and obedience. May we always seek Your wisdom and live in a way that honors You. Amen.

➤ Gospel: Mark 7: 14-23

In this passage, Jesus calls the crowd to Him and teaches that it is not what goes into a person that defiles them, but what comes out from their heart. He explains that evil thoughts, words, and actions—such as theft, murder, adultery, greed, malice, deceit, envy, and pride—are what truly defile a person. These sins originate from within and reveal the true condition of a person's heart.

Reflection:
Jesus' teaching challenges us to look beyond external actions and appearances to the deeper issues of the heart. It is easy to focus on outward observances and neglect the inner transformation that God desires. True holiness and purity come from a heart that is aligned with God's will and filled with His love. This passage invites us to examine our own hearts and to seek God's grace in purifying our thoughts, words, and actions. By allowing God to transform our hearts, we can live in a way that reflects His holiness and love to the world.

Prayer:
Lord Jesus, cleanse our hearts from all that defiles and leads us away from You. Help us to recognize the

importance of inner purity and to seek Your grace in transforming our lives. May our thoughts, words, and actions be pleasing to You, and may we reflect Your love and holiness in all that we do. Amen.

Thursday, February 13

❖ Thursday of the Fifth week in Ordinary Time

- ➢ First Reading: Genesis 2: 18-25
- ➢ Responsorial Psalm: Psalms 128: 1-2, 3, 4-5
- ➢ Alleluia: James 1: 21bc
- ➢ Gospel: Mark 7: 24-30
- ➢ Lectionary: 332

Today's readings bring us deeper into the creation narrative and reveal a touching moment in Jesus' ministry. In Genesis, we witness the creation of woman, emphasizing the beauty and complementarity of man and woman in God's design. In the Gospel, Jesus' encounter with the Syrophoenician woman demonstrates His compassion and the breaking of barriers to extend God's mercy to all people. These passages invite us to reflect on relationships—both human and divine—and the universality of God's love.

➢ First Reading: Genesis 2: 18-25

In this passage, God observes that it is not good for the man to be alone, and He decides to make a suitable partner for him. God forms every creature and brings them to the man, who names them, but none of them are a suitable partner. God then causes the man to fall into a deep sleep, takes one of his ribs, and forms a woman from it. When the man awakes, he recognizes her as "bone of my bones and flesh of my flesh," and she is named "woman" because she was taken out of man. This passage concludes with the institution of marriage, where a man leaves his father and mother and is united with his wife, and they become one flesh.

Reflection:

This passage beautifully illustrates the profound connection between man and woman, highlighting the divine origin of human relationships. The creation of woman from the man's side signifies equality, partnership, and mutual support in God's plan for humanity. The institution of marriage as a union of one flesh underscores the sacredness and depth of the marital bond. In our relationships, whether in marriage or community, we are called to reflect the love, unity, and mutual respect that God intended from the beginning. This reading invites us to cherish and nurture our relationships, seeing them as a reflection of God's love and a gift to be honored.

Prayer:
Loving Creator, You formed us for one another and established the sacred bond of marriage. Help us to honor and cherish the relationships You have given us. May our love for one another reflect Your divine love, and may we live in harmony and mutual respect. Guide us in building strong, loving, and supportive relationships that glorify Your name. Amen.

> ➤ **Gospel: Mark 7: 24-30**

In this passage, Jesus travels to the region of Tyre and enters a house, hoping to remain unnoticed. However, a Syrophoenician woman, a Gentile, hears of His presence and comes to Him, begging Him to cast a demon out of her daughter. Jesus initially responds with a remark about the children (the Jews) being fed first and not giving the children's bread to dogs (a term used for Gentiles at the time). The woman, undeterred, humbly replies that even the dogs under the table eat the children's crumbs. Impressed by her faith, Jesus tells her that the demon has left her daughter, and when she returns home, she finds her daughter healed.

Reflection:
The encounter between Jesus and the Syrophoenician woman is a powerful reminder of the boundless nature of God's mercy and the importance of persistent faith. Despite cultural and religious barriers, the woman's faith in Jesus' power to heal her daughter led to her request being granted. Jesus' response to her persistence and humility shows that God's love and grace extend beyond human boundaries and are available to all who seek Him with genuine faith. This passage challenges us to approach God with humility, persistence, and trust, knowing that His love and mercy are without limit.

Prayer:
Merciful Lord, You respond to all who seek You with faith, regardless of who they are or where they come from. Help us to approach You with the same humility and trust as the Syrophoenician woman. May we recognize that Your love and mercy know no bounds, and may we be instruments of that love to all people, breaking down barriers and extending Your grace to those in need. Amen.

Friday, February 14

❖ Saint Cyril, monk, and Methodius, bishop - Memorial

> ➤ First Reading: Genesis 3: 1-8
> ➤ Responsorial Psalm: Psalms 32: 1-2, 5, 6, 7
> ➤ Alleluia: Acts 16: 14b
> ➤ Gospel: Mark 7: 31-37
> ➤ Lectionary: 333

On this day, we celebrate the memorial of Saints Cyril and Methodius, brothers who were missionaries to the Slavic peoples and are known as the "Apostles to the Slavs." Their work in spreading the Gospel and creating the Glagolitic alphabet to translate the Scriptures into the Slavic language had a lasting impact on the Christian faith in Eastern Europe. The readings today reflect on the consequences of sin and the power of Jesus' healing touch, calling us to consider our own need for repentance and the healing that Christ offers.

➢ First Reading: Genesis 3: 1-8

This passage describes the fall of humanity through the disobedience of Adam and Eve. The serpent, the most cunning of all the wild animals, deceives Eve by questioning God's command not to eat from the tree of the knowledge of good and evil. Eve, seeing that the fruit was desirable, eats it and gives some to Adam, who also eats. Their eyes are opened, and they realize they are naked, leading them to sew fig leaves together to cover themselves. When they hear the sound of the Lord God walking in the garden, they hide among the trees.

Reflection:

The fall of Adam and Eve represents the introduction of sin into the world, a moment that altered the course of human history. Their disobedience stemmed from doubt and a desire for wisdom apart from God. The consequences of their actions—shame, fear, and separation from God—highlight the destructive power of sin. This reading invites us to reflect on our own lives, recognizing the ways in which we may be tempted to stray from God's commandments. It calls us to acknowledge our sins, seek God's forgiveness, and restore our relationship with Him. The story of the fall is not just about the past; it is a reminder of the ongoing battle between good and evil in our own hearts.

Prayer:

Merciful God, in our weakness, we often fall into sin and stray from Your path. Help us to recognize the subtle temptations that lead us away from You and give us the strength to resist them. Grant us the grace to seek Your forgiveness and to walk in the light of Your truth. May we always turn to You, trusting in Your mercy and love. Amen.

➢ Gospel: Mark 7: 31-37

In this passage, Jesus travels through the region of the Decapolis and encounters a man who is deaf and has a speech impediment. The people bring the man to Jesus, begging Him to lay His hand on him. Jesus takes the man aside, away from the crowd, and performs a healing by putting His fingers into the man's ears, spitting, and touching the man's tongue. Jesus then looks up to heaven, sighs, and says, "Ephphatha," meaning "Be opened." Immediately, the man's ears are opened, his tongue is loosened, and he begins to speak plainly. The people are astonished and proclaim, "He has done all things well. He makes the deaf hear and the mute speak."

Reflection:

This miracle demonstrates Jesus' compassion and power to heal both physically and spiritually. By healing the deaf man, Jesus not only restores his hearing and speech but also brings him back into full communion with the community. The act of taking the man aside and performing the healing in a personal and intimate way shows the depth of Jesus' care for each individual. This passage invites us to consider how Jesus desires to heal us, especially in areas where we feel isolated or silenced. His command "Be opened" is not only for the man in the story but also for us—calling us to open our hearts to His love and healing power.

Prayer:

Lord Jesus, You open the ears of the deaf and loosen the tongues of the mute. Open our hearts to hear Your word and to speak Your truth with courage and clarity. Heal us from all that separates us from You and from one another. May we, like the people in the Gospel, proclaim Your goodness and the wonders You have done in our lives. Amen.

Saturday, February 15

- ❖ Saturday of the Fifth week in Ordinary Time
- ❖ Blessed Virgin Mary - Optional Memorial

- ➢ First Reading: Genesis 3: 9-24
- ➢ Responsorial Psalm: Psalms 90: 2, 3-4abc, 5-6, 12-13
- ➢ Alleluia: Matthew 4: 4b
- ➢ Gospel: Mark 8: 1-10
- ➢ Lectionary: 334

As we continue our journey through Ordinary Time, the readings for today present us with a deep reflection on the consequences of sin and the mercy of God. The story of Adam and Eve's expulsion from the Garden of Eden reminds us of the gravity of sin and its impact on humanity. The Gospel passage then contrasts this with the compassion of Jesus, who feeds the multitude, showing us the abundance of God's providence and love. When celebrated as a memorial, the Blessed Virgin Mary's role as a mother who intercedes for us is also honored today.

- ➢ First Reading: Genesis 3: 9-24

In this reading, we witness the aftermath of Adam and Eve's disobedience. God calls out to Adam, asking, "Where are you?" Adam responds, confessing that he hid because he was naked. God questions them, leading to the revelation that they have eaten from the forbidden tree. As a result, God pronounces the consequences of their actions: the serpent is cursed to crawl on its belly, Eve is told she will experience pain in childbirth, and Adam is told that he will toil for his food from the cursed ground. The reading concludes with God driving them out of the Garden of Eden, placing cherubim and a flaming sword to guard the way to the tree of life.

Reflection:

This passage marks a turning point in the biblical narrative, illustrating the profound effects of sin on human life. The loss of innocence and the beginning of suffering and death are direct results of Adam and Eve's choice to disobey God. Yet, even in this moment of judgment, there is a glimmer of hope—the protoevangelium, the first announcement of the Gospel, where God hints at future redemption. This reading invites us to reflect on our own lives, acknowledging the ways sin separates us from God and each other. It also reminds us of the hope we have in Christ, who has overcome sin and death.

Prayer:

Loving Father, we acknowledge our sins and the ways in which we have fallen short of Your glory. We are sorry for the times we have disobeyed You and sought our own will instead of Yours. Help us to turn back to You with contrite hearts, trusting in Your mercy and the promise of redemption through Jesus Christ, our Lord. Amen.

➢ Gospel: Mark 8: 1-10

In this Gospel passage, Jesus is surrounded by a large crowd that has been with Him for three days without anything to eat. Moved with compassion, He expresses concern for the crowd, not wanting to send them away hungry, lest they faint on the way. The disciples are doubtful, asking where they could get enough bread in such a remote place. Jesus asks them how many loaves they have, and they reply, "Seven." Jesus then gives thanks, breaks the bread, and distributes it to the people. They also have a few small fish, which He blesses and shares. The crowd, numbering about four thousand, eats and is satisfied, and seven baskets of leftovers are collected. Afterward, Jesus dismisses the crowd and travels to the region of Dalmanutha.

Reflection:

This miracle of the feeding of the four thousand reveals Jesus' deep compassion and His ability to provide abundantly for the needs of His people. The disciples' initial doubt is met with Jesus' miraculous provision, reminding us that with God, nothing is impossible. This passage encourages us to trust in God's providence, even when resources seem scarce and situations appear hopeless. Jesus' ability to satisfy the physical hunger of the crowd also points to His power to satisfy our spiritual hunger. In Him, we find the fullness of life.

Prayer:

Lord Jesus, we thank You for Your boundless compassion and generosity. Just as You fed the multitude in the wilderness, we ask that You feed us with Your grace and love. Help us to trust in Your providence, especially in times of need, and to share what we have with others, knowing that in Your hands, our offerings can be multiplied to bless many. Amen.

Sunday, February 16

❖ Sixth Sunday in Ordinary Time

- First Reading: Jeremiah 17: 5-8
- Responsorial Psalm: Psalms 1: 1-2, 3, 4 and 6
- Second Reading: First Corinthians 15: 12, 16-20
- Alleluia: Luke 6: 23ab
- Gospel: Luke 6: 17, 20-26
- Lectionary: 78

On this Sixth Sunday in Ordinary Time, the Scriptures present us with a profound contrast between the blessings of those who trust in the Lord and the woes of those who place their trust in worldly things. The readings invite us to reflect on where we place our confidence and to recognize that true happiness and eternal life come from God alone. Jesus' teachings in the Gospel challenge us to examine our priorities and align our lives with the values of the Kingdom of God.

➢ First Reading: Jeremiah 17: 5-8

The prophet Jeremiah speaks of the contrast between those who trust in human strength and those who trust in the Lord. He begins with a curse: "Cursed is the one who trusts in man, who draws strength from mere flesh and whose heart turns away from the Lord." Such a person is like a shrub in the desert, parched and unfruitful. In contrast, "Blessed is the one who trusts in the Lord, whose confidence is in Him." This person is like a tree planted by water, sending out its roots by the stream. It does not fear when heat comes; its leaves are always green. In the year of drought, it is not anxious and never fails to bear fruit.

Reflection:
Jeremiah's imagery vividly portrays the consequences of where we place our trust. Trusting in human strength leads to a barren, unfulfilling life, while trusting in God brings nourishment, growth, and stability, even in difficult times. This reading challenges us to examine our own lives: Are we like the shrub in the desert, relying on our own abilities and resources? Or are we like the tree by the water, rooted in God's love and sustained by His grace? The choice we make will determine the fruitfulness and peace of our lives.

Prayer:
Heavenly Father, help us to place our trust entirely in You. May we be like the tree planted by water, drawing our strength and sustenance from Your endless grace. When challenges arise, keep us grounded in faith, so that we may continue to flourish and bear fruit for Your Kingdom. Amen.

➢ Second Reading: First Corinthians 15: 12, 16-20

In this passage, Paul addresses the Corinthians' doubts about the resurrection of the dead. He asserts that if there is no resurrection of the dead, then not even Christ has been raised, and if Christ has not been raised, our preaching and faith are in vain. But Christ has indeed been raised from the dead, the firstfruits of those who have fallen asleep. Paul emphasizes that the resurrection is central to the Christian faith, affirming that if Christ has not been raised, our hope is futile, and we are still in our sins.

Reflection:
Paul's teaching underscores the importance of the resurrection in the Christian faith. The resurrection of Jesus is the cornerstone of our hope, ensuring that death is not the end and that eternal life awaits those who believe in Him. This reading challenges us to renew our faith in the resurrection and to live in the hope that Christ's victory over death has secured our own future resurrection. It also encourages us to share this hope with others, reminding them that our faith is not in vain.

Prayer:
Lord Jesus, we praise You for Your victory over sin and death. Strengthen our faith in Your resurrection, and fill our hearts with the hope of eternal life. May this hope guide our lives and inspire us to live with courage and joy, knowing that our future is secure in You. Amen.

➢ Gospel: Luke 6: 17, 20-26

In this Gospel passage, Jesus delivers the Beatitudes and Woes during His Sermon on the Plain. He begins by declaring blessings on the poor, the hungry, those who weep, and those who are hated because of the Son of Man. These blessings promise that they will inherit the Kingdom of God, be satisfied, laugh, and receive a great reward in heaven. Conversely, Jesus pronounces woes on the rich, those who are full, those who laugh now, and those who are praised by everyone, warning that they have already received their comfort and will face sorrow.

Reflection:
The Beatitudes and Woes are a radical inversion of worldly values. Jesus blesses those who are often seen as unfortunate and challenges those who seem to have everything. This teaching invites us to reflect on what we truly value and seek in life. Are we striving for earthly success and comfort, or are we pursuing the things of God, even if it means sacrifice and suffering? Jesus' words remind us that true blessedness is found in dependence on God and living according to His will, not in the temporary pleasures and accolades of this world.

Prayer:
Gracious God, we thank You for the Beatitudes that reveal the values of Your Kingdom. Help us to embrace the blessings You offer, even when they challenge us to live differently from the world around us. Teach us to seek Your approval above all and to trust in Your promise of eternal reward. May our lives reflect the values of Your Kingdom in all that we do. Amen.

Monday, February 17

- ❖ Monday of the Sixth week in Ordinary Time
- ❖ Seven Founders of the Order of Servites - Optional Memorial

> First Reading: Genesis 4: 1-15, 25

> Responsorial Psalm: Psalms 50: 1 and 8, 16bc-17, 20-21

> Alleluia: John 14: 6

> Gospel: Mark 8: 11-13

> Lectionary: 335

Today's readings offer a stark reminder of the consequences of sin and the importance of faithfulness. In Genesis, we see the tragic outcome of jealousy and anger, while in the Gospel, Jesus faces opposition from those who demand signs. On this day, we also remember the Seven Founders of the Servite Order, who dedicated their lives to prayer and service. Their example calls us to live in harmony with others and to seek God's will above our own desires.

> First Reading: Genesis 4: 1-15, 25

This passage recounts the story of Cain and Abel, the first sons of Adam and Eve. Cain, driven by jealousy and anger, kills his brother Abel after God shows favor to Abel's offering over his own. When God asks Cain about Abel's whereabouts, Cain responds with the infamous line, "Am I my brother's keeper?" God then punishes Cain, making him a restless wanderer on the earth, but also marks him to protect him from being killed.

Reflection:
The story of Cain and Abel is a powerful reflection on the destructive nature of envy and anger. Cain's inability to master his emotions leads him to commit the first murder, severing his relationship with God and his brother. This passage challenges us to consider how we handle our own feelings of jealousy and resentment. Do we allow them to fester and lead us to harm others, or do we seek God's help in overcoming them? The narrative also reminds us of the importance of being our "brother's keeper," taking responsibility for the well-being of others.

Prayer:
Lord, help us to overcome the destructive emotions of jealousy and anger that can lead us away from You and harm our relationships with others. Teach us to be true caretakers of our brothers and sisters, showing love and compassion in all we do. May Your grace guide us to live in harmony and peace. Amen.

> Gospel: Mark 8: 11-13

In this brief Gospel passage, the Pharisees confront Jesus, demanding a sign from heaven to test Him. Jesus, deeply grieved by their lack of faith, refuses to give them a sign and departs from them. He recognizes that their demand for signs is not rooted in genuine faith but in a desire to challenge and discredit Him.

Reflection:
The Pharisees' demand for a sign highlights a fundamental misunderstanding of faith. True faith does not require constant proof or miraculous signs; it trusts in God even without tangible evidence. Jesus' refusal to perform a sign for the Pharisees serves as a reminder that faith is not about testing God but about trusting in His presence and guidance, even when we do not see immediate results. This passage challenges us to examine our own faith: Do we seek God with a sincere heart, or do we demand signs to bolster our belief?

Prayer:
Heavenly Father, grant us a faith that trusts in You without demanding signs or proof. Help us to recognize Your presence in our lives, even in the ordinary and unseen moments. Strengthen our belief in Your goodness and guide us to live by faith and not by sight. Amen.

Tuesday, February 18

❖ Tuesday of the Sixth week in Ordinary Time

> First Reading: Genesis 6: 5-8; 7: 1-5, 10
> Responsorial Psalm: Psalms 29: 1a and 2, 3ac-4, 3b and 9c-10
> Alleluia: John 14: 23
> Gospel: Mark 8: 14-21
> Lectionary: 336

Today's readings invite us to reflect on the consequences of humanity's sinfulness and the importance of spiritual awareness. In Genesis, we witness the deep sorrow of God over the wickedness of the world, leading to the decision to cleanse the earth through the flood. In the Gospel, Jesus warns His disciples to be wary of the "leaven" of the Pharisees, urging them to open their hearts to true understanding and faith.

➢ First Reading: Genesis 6: 5-8; 7: 1-5, 10

This passage details God's grief over the pervasive wickedness in humanity and His decision to send a great flood to cleanse the earth. However, Noah finds favor with God because of his righteousness. God instructs Noah to build an ark and take his family, along with pairs of every living creature, into it. Noah obeys God's commands, and the floodwaters come as He foretold.

Reflection:
The story of Noah and the flood is a sobering reminder of the devastating effects of sin on the world. It highlights God's deep sorrow over the corruption that had spread among humanity, but also His mercy in sparing Noah, a righteous man. This passage encourages us to examine our own lives and the world around us. Are we contributing to the spread of righteousness, or are we allowing sin to fester? Noah's obedience and trust in God remind us that even in the face of overwhelming challenges, we are called to remain faithful to God's commands.

Prayer:
Lord, grant us the grace to walk in righteousness as Noah did, trusting in Your guidance even when the world around us turns away from You. Help us to be instruments of Your mercy and love, spreading goodness in a world that often chooses otherwise. May we always seek to align our lives with Your will. Amen.

➢ Gospel: Mark 8: 14-21

In this passage, Jesus cautions His disciples to beware of the "leaven" of the Pharisees and Herod, which represents their corrupting influence and lack of true faith. The disciples, concerned about their lack of bread, miss the deeper spiritual warning. Jesus reminds them of the miracles He has performed—feeding thousands with just a few loaves—urging them to understand that He provides for their needs and to trust in Him.

Reflection:
Jesus' warning about the "leaven" of the Pharisees and Herod speaks to the subtle and pervasive nature of negative influences. Just as a small amount of leaven can affect an entire loaf, so too can doubt, hypocrisy, and cynicism infiltrate our hearts and minds. The disciples' focus on their immediate concerns blinded them to the greater spiritual lesson Jesus was teaching. This passage challenges us to remain spiritually alert, trusting in God's provision and not allowing worldly concerns or negative influences to cloud our faith.

Prayer:
Heavenly Father, help us to remain vigilant against the negative influences that can take root in our hearts. Open our eyes to Your truth and deepen our trust in Your providence. May we always seek to understand Your teachings and live by them, confident in Your care for us. Amen.

Wednesday, February 19

❖ Wednesday of the Sixth week in Ordinary Time

- ➢ First Reading: Genesis 8: 6-13, 20-22
- ➢ Responsorial Psalm: Psalms 116: 12-13, 14-15, 18-19
- ➢ Alleluia: Ephesians 1: 17-18
- ➢ Gospel: Mark 8: 22-26
- ➢ Lectionary: 337

Today's readings present powerful images of renewal and healing. In Genesis, we witness the end of the great flood and God's promise to sustain life on earth, while in the Gospel, Jesus heals a blind man, restoring his sight gradually. These passages invite us to trust in God's ongoing work of restoration and healing in our lives and in the world.

➢ First Reading: Genesis 8: 6-13, 20-22

This passage describes the conclusion of the great flood. After forty days, Noah sends out a dove to see if the waters had receded from the earth. When the dove returns with an olive leaf, Noah knows that the floodwaters have diminished. Eventually, Noah, his family, and all the animals leave the ark. Noah then builds an altar to the Lord and offers sacrifices. God is pleased and makes a covenant, promising never to curse the ground again or destroy all living creatures as He had done.

Reflection:
The story of Noah's release from the ark symbolizes new beginnings and the enduring faithfulness of God. After a time of immense trial and judgment, God's promise to sustain life brings hope and assurance. Noah's immediate response is to offer thanksgiving, recognizing God's mercy and protection. This passage encourages us to trust in God's covenant with us and to respond with gratitude, even after enduring our own periods of trial. It reminds us that after every storm, God brings renewal and new opportunities to live according to His will.

Prayer:
Loving God, we thank You for Your unending faithfulness and the promise of renewal after times of trial. Help us to trust in Your covenant with us and to respond with hearts full of gratitude. May we always recognize Your presence and guidance in our lives, especially when we emerge from difficult circumstances. Amen.

> **Gospel: Mark 8: 22-26**

In this passage, Jesus heals a blind man in Bethsaida. The healing occurs in two stages: initially, the man's sight is partially restored, and he sees people who look like "walking trees." After Jesus lays His hands on the man's eyes a second time, his sight is fully restored, and he sees everything clearly.

Reflection:

This two-step healing is unique in the Gospels and highlights the gradual process of spiritual enlightenment. Sometimes, our understanding of God's work in our lives unfolds slowly, and we need time to fully grasp His will. Jesus' methodical approach in this miracle encourages us to be patient with our own spiritual growth and that of others. The passage also serves as a reminder that true sight—both physical and spiritual—comes through Jesus, who is always willing to guide us to clearer understanding if we remain open to His touch.

Prayer:

Lord Jesus, open our eyes to see clearly the path You have set before us. Help us to trust in Your healing power, even when our progress seems slow. Grant us patience and faith as You work within us, restoring our vision and guiding us toward greater spiritual clarity. Amen.

Thursday, February 20

❖ Thursday of the Sixth week in Ordinary Time

> First Reading: Genesis 9: 1-13
> Responsorial Psalm: Psalms 102: 16-18, 19-21, 29 and 22-23
> Alleluia: John 6: 63c, 68c
> Gospel: Mark 8: 27-33
> Lectionary: 338

Today's readings highlight the themes of covenant and understanding the true nature of Jesus. In Genesis, God establishes His covenant with Noah and all living creatures, symbolized by the rainbow. In the Gospel, Peter confesses Jesus as the Christ, but struggles to grasp the full meaning of His mission. These passages invite us to reflect on our own understanding of God's promises and the mission of Christ.

> **First Reading: Genesis 9: 1-13**

In this passage, God blesses Noah and his sons, giving them dominion over all living creatures and instructing them to be fruitful and multiply. God then establishes a covenant with Noah and all living beings, promising never again to destroy the earth with a flood. The rainbow is given as the sign of this covenant, a reminder of God's mercy and faithfulness.

Reflection:

The covenant with Noah marks a new beginning for humanity, a divine promise of preservation and hope. The rainbow, a beautiful and natural sign, serves as a reminder of God's enduring faithfulness. This passage reassures us that despite the sins and failures of humanity, God's commitment to life and creation remains steadfast. It calls us to live in a way that honors this covenant, respecting the life and beauty of the world God has entrusted to us.

Prayer:

Faithful God, we thank You for the covenant You made with Noah and all creation. May the rainbow always remind us of Your mercy and the promise of new beginnings. Help us to live in harmony with Your creation, respecting the life You have given us and trusting in Your everlasting faithfulness. Amen.

➢ Gospel: Mark 8: 27-33

In this passage, Jesus asks His disciples who people say He is, and then who they believe He is. Peter confesses, "You are the Christ." However, when Jesus begins to teach them that the Son of Man must suffer, be rejected, and killed, Peter rebukes Him. Jesus responds by rebuking Peter, saying, "Get behind me, Satan! For you are not thinking as God does, but as human beings do."

Reflection:

Peter's confession of Jesus as the Christ is a pivotal moment, yet his misunderstanding of what that means reveals the difficulty in fully grasping God's plan. Peter, like many of us, wants to avoid suffering and struggles to accept that the path to salvation involves sacrifice. Jesus' rebuke is a call to all of us to align our understanding with God's ways, even when it challenges our human desires. This passage encourages us to embrace the full message of the Gospel, including the call to carry our own crosses in following Christ.

Prayer:

Lord Jesus, we confess that You are the Christ, the Son of the living God. Help us to understand and accept the full truth of Your mission, even when it involves the cross. Strengthen our faith so that we may follow You with hearts and minds aligned with God's will, trusting in Your promise of resurrection and life. Amen.

Friday, February 21

- ❖ Friday of the Sixth week in Ordinary Time
- ❖ Saint Peter Damian, bishop and doctor - Optional Memorial

> First Reading: Genesis 11: 1-9
> Responsorial Psalm: Psalms 33: 10-11, 12-13, 14-15
> Alleluia: John 15: 15b
> Gospel: Mark 8: 34 – 9:1
> Lectionary: 339

Today's readings confront us with the consequences of human pride and the cost of discipleship. In Genesis, the story of the Tower of Babel illustrates how humanity's ambition to reach the heavens led to division and confusion. In the Gospel, Jesus speaks of the need to take up our crosses and follow Him. These passages challenge us to reflect on our ambitions and the sacrifices we are willing to make in our journey of faith.

> First Reading: Genesis 11: 1-9

This passage recounts the story of the Tower of Babel. The people of the earth, speaking a single language, come together to build a city and a tower that reaches the heavens, intending to make a name for themselves. In response, God confuses their language, causing them to stop their building and scatter across the earth. The place is called Babel, symbolizing the confusion that arose from their prideful attempt to reach the heavens.

Reflection:
The story of Babel serves as a powerful reminder of the dangers of pride and the desire for self-exaltation. The people's ambition to build a tower to the heavens reflects humanity's tendency to rely on their own strength and wisdom, rather than seeking God's guidance. The resulting confusion and scattering are consequences of their prideful disobedience. This passage invites us to consider where we may be building our own "towers" in life, relying on our abilities rather than humbly seeking God's will. It calls us to trust in God and to build our lives on the foundation of His wisdom and grace, not on our ambition or pride.

Prayer:
Lord God, keep us from the pride that leads to separation from You and others. Teach us to rely not on our strength but on Your wisdom and grace. May we build our lives on the solid foundation of Your love, seeking always to honor Your name rather than making a name for ourselves. Amen.

> Gospel: Mark 8: 34 – 9:1

In this passage, Jesus calls the crowd and His disciples to Him and says, "If anyone would come after me, let him deny himself and take up his cross and follow me." He explains that those who want to save their lives will lose them, but those who lose their lives for His sake and for the Gospel will save them. Jesus concludes by saying that some standing there will not taste death before they see the kingdom of God come with power.

Reflection:

Jesus' call to take up our crosses and follow Him is a profound challenge to all who seek to be His disciples. It requires a radical reorientation of our lives, where self-denial and sacrifice take precedence over personal gain. The paradox that losing our lives for Christ's sake leads to true life invites us to embrace the Gospel fully, even when it demands suffering or sacrifice. This passage reminds us that true discipleship is not about seeking comfort or glory but about following Christ's example of love, humility, and obedience to the Father's will.

Prayer:

Lord Jesus, give us the courage to take up our crosses and follow You, even when the path is difficult. Help us to understand that true life is found not in preserving our own comfort but in giving ourselves fully to You and Your mission. May we trust in Your promise that those who lose their lives for Your sake will find them in abundance. Amen.

Saturday, February 22

❖ Chair of Saint Peter, apostle - Feast

> First Reading: First Peter 5: 1-4
> Responsorial Psalm: Psalms 23: 1-3a, 4, 5, 6
> Alleluia: Matthew 16: 18
> Gospel: Matthew 16: 13-19
> Lectionary: 535

Today, we celebrate the Feast of the Chair of Saint Peter, a day that honors the role of Saint Peter and his successors in leading and shepherding the Church. This feast reminds us of the unity and authority entrusted to Peter and his successors, ensuring that the Church remains guided by the truth of Christ. The readings today highlight the pastoral responsibility and the foundational role of Peter in the life of the Church.

➢ First Reading: 1 Peter 5: 1-4

In this passage, Saint Peter exhorts the elders of the Church to shepherd the flock of God among them, not out of compulsion but willingly, as God would have them. They are to serve as examples to the flock, not lording their authority over others. Peter assures them that when the Chief Shepherd appears, they will receive the unfading crown of glory.

Reflection:
Peter's message to the leaders of the Church is one of humility, service, and responsibility. He emphasizes that leadership in the Church is not about power or control but about serving others with a willing and loving heart. The true leader, according to Peter, is one who leads by example, guiding the flock with the same love and care that Christ, the Chief Shepherd, shows to His people. This reading invites us to reflect on how we exercise leadership in our own lives—whether as parents, teachers, or community members—and encourages us to lead with humility and a spirit of service.

Prayer:
Lord, help us to lead with humility and love, following the example of Saint Peter. May we always seek to serve others, guided by Your example of selfless love and sacrifice. Strengthen our leaders in the Church to be faithful shepherds, caring for the flock entrusted to them with wisdom and compassion. Amen.

➢ Gospel: Matthew 16: 13-19

In this Gospel passage, Jesus asks His disciples who people say He is. After hearing various answers, He asks them directly, "But who do you say that I am?" Peter responds, "You are the Christ, the Son of the living God." Jesus blesses Peter for this confession and declares, "You are Peter, and on this rock I will build my church, and the gates of Hades will not prevail against it." Jesus also gives Peter the keys to the kingdom of heaven, with the authority to bind and loose on earth and in heaven.

Reflection:
This moment is pivotal in the life of the Church. Peter's recognition of Jesus as the Christ is a revelation from God, and Jesus' response establishes Peter's unique role as the rock upon which the Church will be built. The authority given to Peter signifies the trust and responsibility placed on him to guide the Church in truth and faithfulness. As we celebrate this feast, we are reminded of the importance of unity and fidelity to the teachings of Christ, as entrusted to Peter and his successors. This passage challenges us to reaffirm our own faith in Jesus and our commitment to the Church He established.

Prayer:
Lord Jesus, we thank You for the gift of the Church, built on the solid foundation of Peter's faith. Strengthen us in our faith and help us to remain united with the Church in truth and love. Grant wisdom and courage to the successors of Peter as they guide us on the path of salvation. May we always proclaim You as the Christ, the Son of the living God. Amen.

Sunday, February 23

❖ Seventh Sunday in Ordinary Time

- First Reading: First Samuel 26: 2, 7-9, 12-13, 22-23
- Responsorial Psalm: Psalms 103: 1-2, 3-4, 8, 10, 12-13
- Second Reading: First Corinthians 15: 45-49
- Alleluia: John 13: 34
- Gospel: Luke 6: 27-38
- Lectionary: 81

On this Seventh Sunday in Ordinary Time, the readings challenge us to embrace the radical love and mercy that Christ calls us to live out in our daily lives. We are invited to go beyond what is expected, loving even our enemies and offering forgiveness in a world that often seeks revenge. This Sunday is an opportunity to reflect on the depth of God's mercy and how we can mirror that mercy in our interactions with others.

➢ First Reading: 1 Samuel 26: 2, 7-9, 12-13, 22-23

In this passage, we find David being pursued by King Saul, who seeks to kill him out of jealousy. Despite having the opportunity to kill Saul in his sleep, David chooses to spare his life, taking only Saul's spear and water jug as proof of his presence. David's refusal to harm Saul, despite being persecuted by him, demonstrates his deep respect for the Lord's anointed and his commitment to God's justice rather than seeking revenge.

Reflection:
David's mercy towards Saul is a powerful example of what it means to trust in God's justice rather than taking matters into our own hands. In a situation where revenge would have seemed justified, David chooses the path of mercy, demonstrating that true strength lies in restraint and forgiveness. This reading encourages us to consider how we handle conflicts and wrongs done to us. Are we quick to seek revenge, or do we trust in God's timing and justice, choosing instead to forgive and show mercy?

Prayer:
Merciful God, give us the strength to forgive those who have wronged us, just as David forgave Saul. Help us to choose mercy over revenge, trusting in Your perfect justice and timing. May our actions reflect Your love and grace in all that we do. Amen.

➢ Second Reading: 1 Corinthians 15: 45-49

Paul contrasts Adam, the first man, who was made a living being, with Christ, the last Adam, who became a life-giving spirit. Just as we have borne the image of the earthly man, Adam, we are also called to bear the image of the heavenly man, Christ. This passage reminds us of the transformation that takes place in us through Christ, calling us to live according to the Spirit and not merely the flesh.

Reflection:
This passage highlights the contrast between our earthly nature and the new life we have in Christ. While we are all born in the image of Adam, subject to sin and death, through Christ, we are given the opportunity to be reborn in the image of the heavenly man. This transformation calls us to live in a way that reflects the life-giving spirit of Christ, embracing virtues such as love, mercy, and forgiveness. It challenges us to rise above our natural inclinations and live as citizens of heaven, embodying the character of Christ in our daily lives.

Prayer:
Lord Jesus, help us to shed our earthly inclinations and embrace the new life You offer. May we bear Your image in all that we do, living in the power of the Spirit and reflecting Your love and mercy to the world. Transform our hearts and minds to be more like Yours, guiding us on the path of righteousness. Amen.

➢ Gospel: Luke 6: 27-38

In this Gospel passage, Jesus delivers one of His most challenging teachings: love your enemies, do good to those who hate you, bless those who curse you, and pray for those who mistreat you. He goes on to say that if someone strikes you on one cheek, offer the other, and if someone takes your cloak, do not withhold your tunic. Jesus calls us to a radical way of living, one that defies the logic of the world and is rooted in the boundless mercy and love of God. He concludes with the Golden Rule: "Do to others as you would have them do to you."

Reflection:
Jesus' teachings in this passage are difficult to live out, but they are at the heart of what it means to follow Him. Loving our enemies and showing kindness to those who harm us goes against our natural instincts, yet it is this radical love that sets us apart as followers of Christ. By choosing to love and forgive, we reflect the mercy that God shows us every day. This passage challenges us to examine our hearts and ask ourselves if we are truly living out the Gospel message in our relationships, especially with those who are difficult to love.

Prayer:
Lord, give us the courage to love as You love, even when it is difficult. Help us to forgive those who hurt us and to show kindness to those who do not deserve it. May our lives be a reflection of Your radical love and mercy, bringing light to a world in need of Your grace. Amen.

Monday, February 24

❖ Monday of the Seventh week in Ordinary Time

- ➢ First Reading: Sirach 1: 1-10
- ➢ Responsorial Psalm: Psalms 93: 1ab, 1cd-2, 5
- ➢ Alleluia: Second Timothy 1: 10
- ➢ Gospel: Mark 9: 14-29
- ➢ Lectionary: 341

As we begin a new week, today's readings remind us of the infinite wisdom of God and the power of faith in overcoming the challenges we face. We are invited to reflect on how we seek God's wisdom in our daily lives and how our faith can move mountains when we rely on God's strength rather than our own.

➢ First Reading: Sirach 1: 1-10

The book of Sirach opens by extolling the wisdom of God, declaring that all wisdom comes from the Lord and remains with Him forever. Sirach emphasizes that wisdom was created before all things, and it is poured out upon all His works and given to those who love and fear Him. The passage highlights that wisdom is both a divine gift and an essential aspect of God's creation, intricately woven into the fabric of the universe.

Reflection:

In a world that often values knowledge over wisdom, this reading reminds us that true wisdom is a gift from God, rooted in reverence for the Creator. It calls us to seek God's wisdom in our decisions and actions, recognizing that human understanding is limited, but God's wisdom is boundless. By turning to God in prayer and humility, we open ourselves to receiving the wisdom that guides us on the path of righteousness.

Prayer:

O God of all wisdom, we seek Your divine insight in our lives. Grant us the humility to acknowledge our limitations and the grace to receive Your wisdom. Help us to live in a way that reflects Your eternal truth and to make decisions that align with Your will. Amen.

➢ Gospel: Mark 9: 14-29

In this Gospel passage, Jesus encounters a crowd gathered around a boy possessed by a spirit that causes seizures. The boy's father pleads with Jesus, expressing doubt after the disciples were unable to drive out the spirit. Jesus rebukes the unbelief of the generation, but when the father asks for help, saying, "I do believe; help my unbelief," Jesus responds with compassion. He heals the boy, driving out the unclean spirit, and later tells the disciples that this kind of spirit can only come out through prayer.

Reflection:

This passage underscores the power of faith and the necessity of prayer in overcoming spiritual challenges. The father's plea, "I do believe; help my unbelief," is a profound expression of the human struggle with doubt. It reminds us that even when our faith feels weak, we can turn to Jesus for strength and guidance. The disciples' failure to heal the boy reveals the importance of relying not on our own abilities but on God's power, accessed through prayer. This story encourages us to deepen our faith through constant prayer and trust in God's ability to work miracles in our lives.

Prayer:
Lord Jesus, strengthen our faith, especially when we struggle with doubt. Help us to trust in Your power and to rely on prayer as the foundation of our spiritual lives. May we always turn to You in times of need, believing that through You, all things are possible. Amen.

Tuesday, February 25

❖ Tuesday of the Seventh week in Ordinary Time

- ➤ First Reading: Sirach 2: 1-11
- ➤ Responsorial Psalm: Psalms 37: 3-4, 18-19, 27-28, 39-40
- ➤ Alleluia: Galatians 6: 14
- ➤ Gospel: Mark 9: 30-37
- ➤ Lectionary: 342

Today's readings invite us to reflect on the themes of trust in God amidst trials and humility in our relationships with others. We are called to remain steadfast in faith, even when faced with difficulties, and to embrace a spirit of service and humility as modeled by Christ.

➤ First Reading: Sirach 2: 1-11

The book of Sirach offers counsel to those who seek to serve the Lord, warning them to prepare for trials. The passage encourages perseverance, patience, and trust in God during times of hardship, promising that the Lord is compassionate and merciful to those who remain faithful. Sirach reassures believers that those who trust in the Lord will not be disappointed, for God will never abandon those who fear Him.

Reflection:

This reading provides a powerful reminder that following God is not always easy; it often involves challenges and tests of faith. However, these trials are opportunities for spiritual growth and deeper reliance on God. When we encounter difficulties, we are called to remain patient, to trust in God's plan, and to believe that He will provide for us. The reassurance that God is compassionate and merciful offers comfort and hope, reminding us that our perseverance in faith will be rewarded.

Prayer:

Merciful Father, grant us the strength to endure the trials we face in our journey of faith. Help us to trust in Your divine providence and to remain steadfast in our commitment to You. May we find comfort in Your compassion and be encouraged by the promise that You will never abandon those who seek You. Amen.

➤ Gospel: Mark 9: 30-37

In this Gospel passage, Jesus foretells His suffering, death, and resurrection to His disciples, but they do not understand and are afraid to ask Him about it. Later, as they travel, the disciples argue among themselves about who is the greatest. Jesus, knowing their thoughts, teaches them that true greatness lies in being the least and serving others. He then takes a child, places the child among them, and says, "Whoever receives one child such as this in my name, receives me; and whoever receives me, receives not me but the one who sent me."

Reflection:

This passage challenges our understanding of greatness, turning worldly values upside down. Jesus teaches that greatness in the Kingdom of God is not about power, status, or recognition, but about humility, service, and welcoming the lowly. The example of a child represents simplicity, dependence, and innocence—qualities that Jesus calls us to embrace. By serving others, especially those who are vulnerable, we embody the love and humility of Christ. This Gospel invites us to examine our ambitions and desires, encouraging us to seek greatness through service rather than self-promotion.

Prayer:

Lord Jesus, teach us to embrace humility and to serve others with love and compassion. Help us to set aside our pride and ambitions, seeking instead to follow Your example of selfless service. May we always be mindful of the needs of those around us, especially the vulnerable, and welcome them as we would welcome You. Amen.

Wednesday, February 26

❖ Wednesday of the Seventh week in Ordinary Time

- First Reading: Sirach 4: 11-19
- Responsorial Psalm: Psalms 119: 165, 168, 171, 172, 174, 175
- Alleluia: John 14: 6
- Gospel: Mark 9: 38-40
- Lectionary: 343

The readings for today focus on the wisdom and guidance that come from God and the openness required in our discipleship. We are invited to embrace divine wisdom in our lives and to recognize the unity in serving God, regardless of where that service comes from.

➤ First Reading: Sirach 4: 11-19

In this passage, Sirach personifies wisdom as a caring mother who nurtures and protects those who seek her. Wisdom leads, tests, and teaches, offering support in times of trouble. While the path of wisdom may involve trials and challenges, those who remain faithful will be blessed. Wisdom is portrayed as a guiding force that remains close to those who trust in her, ensuring their ultimate success and fulfillment.

Reflection:
The pursuit of wisdom requires patience, perseverance, and a willingness to learn through life's experiences. This passage reminds us that God's wisdom is not always easy to grasp; it requires us to face challenges and endure trials. However, these difficulties are part of our spiritual growth. By embracing wisdom, we allow God to guide us through life's complexities, leading us to a deeper understanding of His will and purpose for us.

Prayer:
Heavenly Father, grant us the wisdom to navigate the challenges of life with faith and courage. Help us to trust in Your guidance and to learn from the experiences that shape us. May we remain open to the lessons of wisdom, knowing that You are always with us, leading us toward fulfillment and peace. Amen.

➤ Gospel: Mark 9: 38-40

In this brief Gospel passage, the apostle John tells Jesus that they saw someone driving out demons in His name and tried to stop him because he was not part of their group. Jesus, however, responds by saying,

"Do not stop him, for whoever is not against us is for us." Jesus teaches that the work of God is not limited to a specific group or community; rather, it transcends human boundaries.

Reflection:
This passage calls us to recognize the broader scope of God's work in the world. It challenges the notion of exclusivity in discipleship and reminds us that God can work through anyone who acts in His name, regardless of their affiliation. Jesus invites us to see unity in the diversity of God's servants and to support rather than hinder those who do good in His name. This openness fosters a spirit of collaboration and inclusiveness in our mission as followers of Christ.

Prayer:
Lord Jesus, open our hearts to see Your work in all people, regardless of where they come from or who they are. Help us to embrace a spirit of unity and collaboration, recognizing that Your love knows no boundaries. May we support and encourage those who serve You, wherever they may be, and join together in spreading Your message of hope and love. Amen.

Thursday, February 27

❖ Thursday of the Seventh week in Ordinary Time

- First Reading: Sirach 5: 1-8
- Responsorial Psalm: Psalms 1: 1-2, 3, 4 and 6
- Alleluia: First Thessalonians 2: 13
- Gospel: Mark 9: 41-50
- Lectionary: 344

Today's readings emphasize the importance of humility, vigilance, and repentance. We are reminded to avoid complacency in our spiritual lives and to take seriously the call to holiness, recognizing the need for constant self-examination and a commitment to living in accordance with God's will.

- First Reading: Sirach 5: 1-8

In this passage, Sirach warns against complacency and the presumption of God's mercy as a license to sin. He cautions against delaying repentance and relying on wealth or worldly security, reminding us that God's judgment is certain and swift. The passage urges us to live with a sense of urgency, recognizing that our actions have consequences, and that true wisdom involves living in the fear of the Lord.

Reflection:
This reading challenges us to reflect on our spiritual priorities and to avoid the trap of complacency. It's

easy to fall into the mindset that there is always more time to turn away from sin and seek God's mercy. However, Sirach calls us to a more disciplined approach to our faith, one that recognizes the immediacy of God's call to holiness. True repentance and conversion cannot be delayed, for we do not know the hour of the Lord's coming.

Prayer:
Merciful God, help us to live each day with a renewed commitment to Your will. Keep us vigilant and aware of the need for repentance, and grant us the grace to turn away from sin without delay. May we seek Your wisdom and guidance in all that we do, knowing that our time is in Your hands. Amen.

> Gospel: Mark 9: 41-50

In this Gospel passage, Jesus speaks strongly about the seriousness of sin and the need for radical measures to avoid it. He warns against leading others into sin and emphasizes the importance of cutting off anything that causes us to sin, even if it is as essential as a hand, foot, or eye. Jesus uses hyperbole to stress the gravity of sin and the eternal consequences it can have. He concludes with a call to live in peace with one another, seasoning our lives with the fire of God's love and purification.

Reflection:
This passage is a sobering reminder of the seriousness with which we must approach our spiritual lives. Jesus' words may seem harsh, but they underscore the radical commitment required to follow Him. Sin is not something to be taken lightly, and we are called to be ruthless in removing anything from our lives that leads us away from God. At the same time, we are also reminded to live in peace and harmony with others, allowing the fire of God's love to purify and refine us.

Prayer:
Lord Jesus, give us the strength to remove from our lives anything that leads us away from You. Help us to be vigilant against sin and to strive for holiness in all that we do. May we live in peace with others, allowing Your love to purify our hearts and guide our actions. Teach us to be faithful and to walk in Your ways, trusting in Your mercy and grace. Amen.

Friday, February 28

❖ **Friday of the Seventh week in Ordinary Time**

> First Reading: Sirach 6: 5-17
> Responsorial Psalm: Psalms 119: 12, 16, 18, 27, 34, 35
> Alleluia: John 17: 17b, 17a
> Gospel: Mark 10: 1-12
> Lectionary: 345

Today's readings delve into the themes of friendship, loyalty, and the sanctity of marriage. We are invited to reflect on the importance of faithfulness in our relationships, whether with friends or within the bond of marriage. The readings challenge us to cultivate relationships that are rooted in love, honesty, and commitment, aligning with God's design for human connection.

➢ First Reading: Sirach 6: 5-17

In this passage, Sirach speaks about the value of true friendship, emphasizing that a faithful friend is a treasure beyond measure. He warns against being quick to trust just anyone and advises discernment in choosing friends. A true friend, according to Sirach, is someone who stands by you in times of adversity, offering steadfast loyalty and support. The reading highlights that cultivating such friendships requires time, patience, and mutual respect.

Reflection:

This reading invites us to consider the quality of our friendships and the importance of loyalty and faithfulness. True friendship is a gift from God and requires a foundation of trust, honesty, and mutual care. Sirach's wisdom reminds us that genuine friends are rare and should be cherished. In a world where relationships can often be superficial or self-serving, we are called to seek and nurture friendships that are grounded in love and guided by virtue.

Prayer:

Loving God, thank You for the gift of friendship. Help us to be faithful friends who support and uplift one another in all circumstances. Grant us the wisdom to choose our companions wisely and to build relationships that reflect Your love and goodness. May our friendships be a source of strength and encouragement, leading us closer to You. Amen.

➢ Gospel: Mark 10: 1-12

In this Gospel passage, Jesus addresses the issue of divorce, reaffirming the sanctity and permanence of marriage. When questioned by the Pharisees, He points back to God's original design for marriage, where a man and woman become one flesh, united in a bond that is not meant to be broken. Jesus emphasizes that marriage is a sacred covenant, and what God has joined together, no one should separate. His teaching underscores the seriousness of marriage and the commitment it requires.

Reflection:

Jesus' words in this passage challenge us to view marriage as a lifelong commitment that reflects God's unbreakable covenant with His people. In a society where the permanence of marriage is often questioned, Jesus calls us to honor the sacredness of this union. Marriage is not just a social contract but a divine vocation that demands fidelity, self-giving love, and perseverance through challenges. This teaching reminds us to approach marriage with reverence and to support those who are married in living out their vows.

Prayer:

Heavenly Father, we pray for all married couples, that they may be strengthened in their commitment to one another. Help them to live out their marriage vows with love, patience, and faithfulness. For those facing difficulties, grant them the grace to persevere and to seek Your guidance in all things. May their union be a reflection of Your eternal love for us, and may they find joy and peace in their shared life together. Amen.

March 2025

Saturday, March 1

- ❖ First Saturday
- ❖ Saturday of the Seventh week in Ordinary Time
- ❖ Blessed Virgin Mary - Optional Memorial

> First Reading: Sirach 17: 1-15

> Responsorial Psalm: Psalms 103: 13-14, 15-16, 17-18

> Alleluia: Matthew 11: 25

> Gospel: Mark 10: 13-16

> Lectionary: 346

Today's readings highlight the themes of divine care and the significance of welcoming others, especially the innocent and vulnerable. As we honor the Blessed Virgin Mary, we reflect on her role as a model of openness and trust in God, and we are reminded of the value of nurturing a childlike faith.

> First Reading: Sirach 17: 1-15

In this passage, Sirach describes how God has endowed humanity with wisdom, understanding, and the knowledge of good and evil. He reflects on God's generosity in guiding people and providing them with the means to understand and follow His will. Sirach speaks of the covenant relationship between God and humanity, emphasizing that God has made known to us the way of righteousness and the blessings that come from following His commands.

Reflection:

This reading underscores the profound care and guidance that God provides to His people. Sirach reminds us of the privileges and responsibilities that come with knowing God's ways. We are called to appreciate and respond to this divine guidance with gratitude and obedience. Reflecting on God's covenant helps us to recognize the importance of living according to His teachings and appreciating the wisdom He imparts to us.

Prayer:

Lord God, we thank You for the wisdom and understanding You provide. Help us to live in accordance with Your teachings and to follow the path You have set before us. May we respond to Your guidance with humility and gratitude, and may we grow in our knowledge of Your will. Amen.

> Gospel: Mark 10: 13-16

In this Gospel passage, Jesus expresses His displeasure with His disciples for preventing children from coming to Him. He welcomes the children, saying that the kingdom of God belongs to such as these. Jesus emphasizes that one must receive the kingdom of God with the trust and openness of a child. He then embraces the children, blessing them and demonstrating His love and acceptance for the most vulnerable members of society.

Reflection:
Jesus' actions in this passage highlight the importance of childlike faith and the openness required to enter the kingdom of God. By welcoming the children, Jesus challenges us to approach our relationship with God with simplicity and trust. This Gospel passage calls us to be open-hearted and receptive, recognizing that the kingdom of God is accessible to all who come with humility and faith. It also reminds us to value and nurture the innocence and faith of children.

Prayer:
Lord Jesus, teach us to approach You with the simplicity and trust of a child. Help us to embrace Your kingdom with a pure heart and to welcome others with the same love and acceptance You showed to the children. May we strive to live out our faith with openness and humility, reflecting Your grace in all that we do. Amen.

Sunday, March 2

❖ Eighth Sunday in Ordinary Time

> First Reading: Sirach 27: 4-7
> Responsorial Psalm: Psalms 92: 2-3, 13-14, 15-16
> Second Reading: First Corinthians 15: 54-58
> Alleluia: Philippians 2: 15d, 16a
> Gospel: Luke 6: 39-45
> Lectionary: 84

As we gather to celebrate the Eighth Sunday in Ordinary Time, today's readings invite us to reflect on the power of our words and actions. They remind us that what is in our hearts will inevitably show itself in how we live and speak. We are called to cultivate lives rooted in integrity, truth, and love, reflecting the goodness of God in all that we do.

➢ First Reading: Sirach 27: 4-7

This passage from Sirach emphasizes the idea that one's true nature is revealed through speech. Just as a sieve separates unwanted particles from grain, so too do a person's words reveal what is in their heart. The wise man cautions us to be mindful of our speech, for it is a reflection of our inner character.

Reflection:

Sirach challenges us to examine the integrity of our hearts, knowing that our words and actions are the fruit of our inner life. What we say and how we behave are clear indicators of our spiritual health. We are encouraged to cultivate virtue within, so that our words and deeds reflect God's truth and love.

Prayer:

Heavenly Father, help us to nurture hearts filled with Your love and truth. May our words and actions be reflections of a pure and faithful spirit, glorifying You in all that we do. Give us the wisdom to speak and act with integrity, guided always by Your Holy Spirit. Amen.

➢ Second Reading: First Corinthians 15: 54-58

In this passage, Paul speaks of the victory over death achieved through Christ's resurrection. He reflects on the transformation that will take place when the perishable is clothed with the imperishable, and mortality is clothed with immortality. This victory enables believers to stand firm, dedicating themselves fully to the work of the Lord, knowing that their labor is not in vain.

Reflection:

Paul's words are a powerful reminder of the hope we have in Christ. Through His resurrection, we are promised eternal life and victory over death. This assurance should inspire us to live faithfully, investing our time and energy in the work of the Lord. We are called to remain steadfast in our faith, knowing that our efforts are meaningful and will bear fruit in the kingdom of God.

Prayer:

Lord Jesus, thank You for the victory over death that You have won for us. Strengthen our resolve to serve You with unwavering faith and dedication. May we find joy and purpose in doing Your work, confident in the knowledge that our labor is not in vain. Keep us steadfast in hope, always trusting in Your promise of eternal life. Amen.

➢ Gospel: Luke 6: 39-45

In this passage, Jesus teaches through a series of parables, emphasizing the importance of self-awareness and the integrity of one's inner life. He warns against hypocrisy, urging His followers to first remove the "plank" from their own eye before addressing the "speck" in someone else's. Jesus also speaks about the connection between a person's heart and their actions, stating that "a good tree bears good fruit" and that "out of the overflow of the heart, the mouth speaks."

Reflection:

Jesus calls us to cultivate self-awareness and humility, reminding us that we cannot lead others well unless we have first attended to our own spiritual health. His analogy of the tree and its fruit challenges us to reflect on the kind of "fruit" our lives are producing. If our hearts are filled with God's love and truth, our actions and words will naturally reflect that goodness.

Prayer:
Lord, help us to live with integrity and humility. Teach us to examine our own hearts and lives before passing judgment on others. May Your love fill us, so that we may bear good fruit in all we do. Guide our words and actions, so that they may be true reflections of Your grace and truth. Amen.

Monday, March 3

- ❖ Monday of the Eighth week in Ordinary Time
- ❖ In the United States- Monday of the Eighth week in Ordinary Time
- ❖ Saint Katharine Drexel, virgin - Optional Memorial

➤ First Reading: Sirach 17: 20-24
➤ Responsorial Psalm: Psalms 32: 1-2, 5, 6, 7
➤ Alleluia: Second Corinthians 8: 9
➤ Gospel: Mark 10: 17-27
➤ Lectionary: 347

As we enter the Eighth Week in Ordinary Time, today's readings remind us of God's boundless mercy and the challenges of following Christ. The memorial of Saint Katharine Drexel, a woman known for her profound charity and commitment to justice, offers us a powerful example of how to live out the Gospel message.

➤ First Reading: Sirach 17: 20-24

In this passage, Sirach reflects on God's mercy towards those who have turned away from Him. Despite our failures and sins, God is always ready to offer forgiveness. He calls us to repentance, urging us to return to Him with sincere hearts. The reading emphasizes God's patience and His desire for all people to seek Him and live.

Reflection:
God's mercy is infinite and ever-present, ready to embrace us when we turn back to Him. This reading invites us to trust in His forgiveness and to repent with humility. No matter how far we may stray, God's love remains steadfast, and He eagerly awaits our return. Let us take this opportunity to renew our commitment to Him, confident in His mercy.

Prayer:
Merciful Father, thank You for Your endless compassion and readiness to forgive. Help us to turn our hearts back to You whenever we falter. May we always seek Your mercy and strive to live in Your grace. Guide us in repentance and draw us closer to Your loving embrace. Amen.

➤ Gospel: Mark 10: 17-27

In this Gospel passage, Jesus encounters a rich young man who desires to inherit eternal life. When Jesus tells him to sell all he has, give to the poor, and follow Him, the man leaves sorrowful because of his great wealth. Jesus then teaches His disciples about the difficulty for the rich to enter the Kingdom of God, but reassures them that with God, all things are possible.

Reflection:
Jesus challenges us to consider what we truly value. The rich young man could not let go of his wealth, revealing how deeply it held his heart. This passage asks us to reflect on the attachments in our own lives that may prevent us from fully following Christ. Jesus invites us to place our trust in God, who provides all we need and makes the impossible possible.

Prayer:
Lord Jesus, help us to recognize the attachments that keep us from fully following You. Give us the courage to let go of anything that hinders our relationship with You. May we trust in Your providence and seek first Your Kingdom, knowing that with You, all things are possible. Amen.

➤ Saint Katharine Drexel (Optional Memorial):

Saint Katharine Drexel devoted her life and her considerable inheritance to the service of marginalized communities, particularly Native Americans and African Americans. She founded the Sisters of the Blessed Sacrament and established schools and missions across the United States.

Reflection:
Saint Katharine Drexel's life is a testament to the power of using one's gifts for the service of others. Her deep faith and commitment to justice challenge us to consider how we can use our resources—be they financial, personal, or spiritual—in the service of God's kingdom. She reminds us that true wealth is found not in material possessions, but in the love and service of others.

Prayer:
Lord, through the intercession of Saint Katharine Drexel, inspire us to be generous with the gifts You have given us. May we use our resources to serve those in need, working for justice and spreading Your love. Help us to follow her example of faith and dedication to Your will. Amen.

Tuesday, March 4

- ❖ Tuesday of the Eighth week in Ordinary Time
- ❖ Saint Casimir - Optional Memorial

> ➢ First Reading: Sirach 35: 1-12
> ➢ Responsorial Psalm: Psalms 50: 5-6, 7-8, 14 and 23
> ➢ Alleluia: Matthew 11: 25
> ➢ Gospel: Mark 10: 28-31
> ➢ Lectionary: 348

Today, we reflect on the generosity of spirit that God calls us to embody. The readings encourage us to offer our lives, not just our material goods, in sincere service to God. The optional memorial of Saint Casimir, a prince who chose a life of prayer and humility over worldly power, serves as a model of how to live out this call.

> ➢ First Reading: Sirach 35: 1-12

In this passage, Sirach speaks about the importance of giving offerings to God with a sincere heart. The Lord does not need our material gifts; rather, He desires our righteousness, obedience, and love. Sacrifices made with a pure heart are pleasing to God, and He rewards those who honor Him with their actions.

Reflection:
Our offerings to God should be more than just ritual acts; they should be expressions of our genuine love and devotion. God values the intention behind our sacrifices, urging us to live righteously and serve Him with integrity. This reading challenges us to examine our motivations and ensure that our acts of worship are rooted in a deep commitment to God.

Prayer:
Heavenly Father, teach us to offer our lives to You with sincerity and love. May our actions reflect a true devotion to Your will, and may we serve You with pure hearts. Help us to live righteously, seeking to honor You in all we do. Amen.

> ➢ Gospel: Mark 10: 28-31

In this passage, Peter reminds Jesus that the disciples have left everything to follow Him. Jesus assures them that those who sacrifice for His sake will receive blessings in this life and eternal life in the age to come. However, He also warns that many who are first will be last, and the last will be first.

Reflection:
Jesus teaches us about the rewards of discipleship, but He also cautions us against seeking worldly recognition or status. True discipleship involves sacrifice, humility, and trust in God's promises. This passage invites us to reflect on what we are willing to give up for the sake of following Christ and to trust that God will reward our faithfulness in ways beyond our understanding.

Prayer:
Lord Jesus, help us to follow You with a willing heart, letting go of anything that holds us back. May we trust in Your promises and seek to serve You with humility and love. Grant us the grace to embrace the sacrifices of discipleship, knowing that You will bless us abundantly. Amen.

➤ Saint Casimir (Optional Memorial):

Saint Casimir, known for his piety, humility, and dedication to prayer, chose to live a life of virtue despite the temptations of power and wealth as a prince of Poland. He is remembered for his commitment to purity, justice, and the poor.

Reflection:
Saint Casimir's life reminds us that true nobility lies in living according to God's will, not in worldly power or prestige. His example encourages us to prioritize our spiritual lives and to serve others with humility and love, regardless of our status or position.

Prayer:
Lord, through the intercession of Saint Casimir, help us to live lives of humility and service. May we seek to please You above all else and remain steadfast in our commitment to Your will. Guide us to use our positions and resources to serve those in need and to honor You in all things. Amen.

Wednesday, March 5

- ❖ Day of Fast and Abstinance
- ❖ Ash Wednesday

- ➤ First Reading: Joel 2: 12-18
- ➤ Responsorial Psalm: Psalms 51: 3-4, 5-6ab, 12-13, 14 and 17
- ➤ Second Reading: Second Corinthians 5: 20 – 6:2
- ➤ Verse Before the Gospel: Psalms 95: 8
- ➤ Gospel: Matthew 6: 1-6, 16-18
- ➤ Lectionary: 219

Ash Wednesday marks the beginning of Lent, a season of penance, reflection, and fasting in preparation for Easter. The ashes we receive today are a powerful reminder of our mortality and our need for repentance. As we enter this sacred time, we are called to return to God with all our hearts, seeking His mercy and grace.

➢ First Reading: Joel 2: 12-18

In this passage, the prophet Joel calls the people to repentance, urging them to return to God with fasting, weeping, and mourning. The Lord is gracious and merciful, slow to anger and abounding in steadfast love. He calls His people to a sincere conversion, offering them forgiveness and the chance to renew their relationship with Him.

Reflection:

God's call to repentance is a call to come back to His loving embrace. Lent is a time to reflect on our lives, acknowledge our sins, and turn back to God with humility and sincerity. The ashes we receive today symbolize our repentance and our desire to renew our relationship with God. Let us take this opportunity to seek His forgiveness and allow His grace to transform our hearts.

Prayer:

Merciful God, we come before You with contrite hearts, seeking Your forgiveness and mercy. Help us to turn away from our sins and to embrace the path of repentance. May this Lenten season be a time of deep spiritual renewal, as we strive to grow closer to You. Amen.

➢ Second Reading: Second Corinthians 5: 20 – 6:2

Saint Paul reminds the Corinthians that they are ambassadors for Christ, called to be reconciled to God. He urges them not to receive God's grace in vain but to embrace this moment as the acceptable time for salvation. Paul emphasizes that now is the time for repentance and renewal, as God's grace is freely available to all who seek it.

Reflection:

Lent is the "acceptable time" for us to be reconciled with God. As ambassadors for Christ, we are called to live lives that reflect His love and mercy. This reading invites us to embrace the opportunity for conversion that Lent offers, recognizing that God's grace is at work in our lives, calling us to a deeper relationship with Him.

Prayer:

Lord, we thank You for the gift of Your grace and for the opportunity to be reconciled with You. Help us to respond to Your call with open hearts, embracing the chance for renewal and transformation. May we be faithful ambassadors of Your love, sharing Your mercy with others. Amen.

> Gospel: Matthew 6: 1-6, 16-18

In this passage, Jesus teaches about the importance of sincerity in our acts of piety. He warns against performing religious practices for the sake of being seen by others. Instead, Jesus calls us to pray, fast, and give alms in secret, seeking only the approval of our heavenly Father, who sees what is hidden.

Reflection:
The practices of prayer, fasting, and almsgiving are central to the Lenten journey. Jesus reminds us that these acts should be done with humility and sincerity, not for the sake of human praise. As we enter this season of Lent, let us focus on deepening our relationship with God, offering our sacrifices and prayers with pure hearts, and seeking to grow in holiness.

Prayer:
Heavenly Father, as we begin this Lenten season, help us to practice our faith with humility and sincerity. May our prayers, fasting, and almsgiving draw us closer to You and help us to grow in holiness. Teach us to seek Your approval above all else, and to serve You with a pure heart. Amen.

Thursday, March 6

❖ Thursday after Ash Wednesday

> First Reading: Deuteronomy 30: 15-20

> Responsorial Psalm: Psalms 1: 1-2, 3, 4 and 6

> Verse Before the Gospel: Matthew 4: 17

> Gospel: Luke 9: 22-25

> Lectionary: 220

As we continue our journey through Lent, today's readings invite us to reflect on the choices we make in life. We are called to choose the path of life, which leads to blessings, over the path of death, which leads to destruction. This is a time to align our lives with God's will and to follow the example of Christ, even when it involves sacrifice.

> First Reading: Deuteronomy 30: 15-20

In this passage, Moses presents the Israelites with a choice between life and death, blessing and curse. He urges them to love the Lord their God, obey His commandments, and hold fast to Him. Choosing life means walking in God's ways and receiving His blessings, while turning away from God leads to death and destruction.

Reflection:

Life is a series of choices, and God invites us to choose the path that leads to Him. This passage challenges us to examine our own lives and the choices we make daily. Are we choosing life by following God's commandments, or are we choosing a path that leads away from Him? Lent is a time to renew our commitment to God, choosing life and the blessings that come with it.

Prayer:

Lord, You have set before us the choice between life and death. Help us to choose life by following Your commandments and walking in Your ways. Give us the strength to turn away from sin and to embrace the path that leads to Your blessings. May our choices reflect our love for You and our desire to live according to Your will. Amen.

➢ Gospel: Luke 9: 22-25

In this passage, Jesus foretells His suffering, death, and resurrection, and calls His followers to take up their cross daily and follow Him. He warns that those who try to save their lives will lose them, but those who lose their lives for His sake will save them. Jesus challenges us to consider what we value most and to be willing to sacrifice everything for the sake of following Him.

Reflection:

The call to discipleship is a call to sacrifice. Jesus asks us to take up our cross daily, which means embracing the challenges and sufferings that come with following Him. Lent is a time to reflect on what we are willing to sacrifice for the sake of our faith. Are we holding on to things that keep us from fully following Christ? Let us use this season to let go of anything that hinders our relationship with God and to follow Jesus with our whole hearts.

Prayer:

Jesus, You call us to take up our cross and follow You. Help us to embrace the sacrifices that come with discipleship and to trust in Your promise of eternal life. Give us the courage to let go of anything that holds us back from fully following You. May we find true life by losing ourselves in Your love and service. Amen.

Friday, March 7

- ❖ First Friday
- ❖ Day of Abstinance
- ❖ Saints Perpetua and Felicity, martyrs - Commemoration

> First Reading: Isaiah 58: 1-9a
> Responsorial Psalm: Psalms 51: 3-4, 5-6ab, 18-19
> Verse Before the Gospel: Amos 5: 14
> Gospel: Matthew 9: 14-15
> Lectionary: 221

On this First Friday, a day of abstinence, we commemorate Saints Perpetua and Felicity, whose unwavering faith led them to martyrdom. Today's readings remind us of the true spirit of fasting and penance, calling us to a deeper relationship with God that goes beyond outward rituals. We are invited to examine our hearts and intentions as we continue our Lenten journey.

> First Reading: Isaiah 58: 1-9a

In this reading, the prophet Isaiah addresses the people of Israel, challenging their superficial fasting and rituals. God, through Isaiah, declares that true fasting is not merely about outward acts, but about living with justice, compassion, and love. He calls His people to care for the oppressed, share with the hungry, and clothe the naked. When they do this, their light will break forth like the dawn, and God will hear their prayers.

Reflection:
Lent calls us to look beyond the mere externals of fasting and to focus on the heart of the matter—our relationship with God and others. True fasting is about letting go of selfishness and embracing acts of kindness, justice, and mercy. As we abstain from certain foods today, let us also examine how we can better live out the love and compassion that God desires.

Prayer:
Lord, You desire mercy, not sacrifice. Help us to fast in a way that pleases You, by seeking justice, loving mercy, and walking humbly with You. May our Lenten practices draw us closer to You and transform us into people who reflect Your love and light in the world. Amen.

> Gospel: Matthew 9: 14-15

In this passage, the disciples of John the Baptist ask Jesus why His disciples do not fast. Jesus responds by explaining that as long as the bridegroom (Himself) is with them, they do not fast. However, the time will come when the bridegroom is taken away, and then they will fast. This highlights the importance of understanding the appropriate time and spirit for fasting.

Reflection:
Fasting is not just a religious obligation but a response to our relationship with Christ. When we fast, it should come from a place of longing for deeper union with Jesus, especially when we feel distant from Him. Today, let us fast not out of mere duty, but out of a desire to draw nearer to Christ, recognizing that fasting is a way to make room for God in our lives.

Prayer:
Jesus, You are the bridegroom of our souls. Help us to fast with the right intention, seeking to draw closer to You. May our fasting today be a sign of our love and devotion to You, and may it lead us to a deeper understanding of Your presence in our lives. Strengthen us in our Lenten journey, that we may grow in holiness and love. Amen.

Saturday, March 8

- ❖ Saturday after Ash Wednesday
- ❖ Saint John of God, religious - Commemoration

> First Reading: Isaiah 58: 9b-14

> Responsorial Psalm: Psalms 86: 1-2, 3-4, 5-6

> Verse Before the Gospel: Ezekiel 33: 11

> Gospel: Luke 5: 27-32

> Lectionary: 222

Today, as we continue our Lenten journey, we commemorate Saint John of God, a man who dedicated his life to serving the sick and the poor. The readings invite us to reflect on the call to true conversion—turning away from sin and embracing a life of compassion and service.

> First Reading: Isaiah 58: 9b-14

In this passage, the prophet Isaiah speaks of the blessings that follow true repentance and right living. If the people turn away from oppression, false accusations, and malicious speech, and instead serve those in need, God promises that their light will rise in the darkness. He will guide them continually, strengthen them, and make their lives fruitful. Observing the Sabbath and keeping it holy will bring delight in the Lord and blessings upon their land.

Reflection:
Isaiah reminds us that living a life of justice, compassion, and integrity is what God truly desires. Our Lenten practices should not only be about personal piety but about transforming our actions toward others. By caring for the marginalized, we allow God's light to shine through us, bringing healing and restoration to our world.

Prayer:
Lord, teach us to love as You love. Help us to turn away from all that harms others and instead, to live lives of kindness and mercy. May our actions reflect Your love and bring light to those who are in darkness. Guide us and strengthen us on our journey toward You. Amen.

➢ Gospel: Luke 5: 27-32

In this Gospel passage, Jesus calls Levi, a tax collector, to follow Him. Despite Levi's sinful reputation, Jesus sees beyond his past and offers him a new beginning. When criticized by the Pharisees for dining with sinners, Jesus responds that He has come not to call the righteous, but sinners to repentance.

Reflection:
Jesus' call to Levi reminds us that no one is beyond God's mercy. Lent is a time to recognize our own need for conversion and to respond to Jesus' invitation to follow Him more closely. Just as Levi left everything to follow Jesus, we too are called to leave behind anything that separates us from God and to embrace His grace.

Prayer:
Jesus, You came to seek and save the lost. We thank You for Your boundless mercy and love. Help us to respond to Your call with open hearts, leaving behind our sins and following You more closely each day. May we extend Your mercy to others, especially those who are most in need. Amen.

Sunday, March 9

❖ **First Sunday of Lent**

- ➤ First Reading: Deuteronomy 26: 4-10
- ➤ Responsorial Psalm: Psalms 91: 1-2, 10-11, 12-13, 14-15
- ➤ Second Reading: Romans 10: 8-13
- ➤ Verse Before the Gospel: Matthew 4: 4b
- ➤ Gospel: Luke 4: 1-13
- ➤ Lectionary: 24

On this First Sunday of Lent, the Church invites us to reflect on the themes of trust, obedience, and the power of God's Word. As we begin this season of penance and renewal, we are reminded of the importance of turning to God in times of temptation and placing our complete trust in His saving power.

➤ First Reading: Deuteronomy 26: 4-10

In this reading, Moses instructs the Israelites on the ritual of offering the first fruits to the Lord. As they present their offerings, they are to recount the story of God's deliverance—how He brought them out of slavery in Egypt, led them through the wilderness, and brought them to a land flowing with milk and honey. This act of remembrance is a powerful expression of gratitude and trust in God's faithfulness.

Reflection:
The Israelites' offering of first fruits serves as a reminder to us that everything we have comes from God. During this Lenten season, we are called to offer our own "first fruits"—our time, talents, and resources—in gratitude for God's many blessings. Let us also remember how God has been faithful in our own lives, especially in times of trial and need.

Prayer:
Gracious God, You have blessed us abundantly and guided us through every trial. As we begin this Lenten journey, help us to trust in Your providence and to offer our lives in service to You. May we always remember Your faithfulness and respond with grateful hearts. Amen.

➤ Second Reading: Romans 10: 8-13

In his letter to the Romans, Saint Paul emphasizes the importance of faith in Jesus Christ. He teaches that salvation is available to all who confess with their mouths and believe in their hearts that Jesus is Lord.

There is no distinction between Jew and Greek; the same Lord is Lord of all, and everyone who calls on the name of the Lord will be saved.

Reflection:
Paul's message reminds us that faith is both a personal and communal act. Our belief in Jesus Christ should be evident in both our words and actions. As we journey through Lent, let us deepen our faith and share the hope of salvation with those around us, knowing that God's mercy is available to all who seek it.

Prayer:
Lord Jesus, You are our Savior and Redeemer. Strengthen our faith so that we may boldly proclaim Your name and live according to Your will. Help us to trust in Your mercy and to share the Good News of Your salvation with all whom we meet. Amen.

➤ Gospel: Luke 4: 1-13

In the Gospel, we hear of Jesus' temptation in the wilderness. After fasting for forty days, Jesus is confronted by the devil, who tempts Him to misuse His divine power, to seek worldly authority, and to test God's protection. Jesus responds to each temptation by quoting Scripture, affirming His trust in God's Word and His commitment to His mission.

Reflection:
The temptation of Jesus in the wilderness is a powerful example for us as we begin our own Lenten journey. Like Jesus, we too will face temptations—whether they come in the form of doubts, desires, or distractions. Through prayer, fasting, and the study of Scripture, we can find the strength to resist these temptations and remain faithful to God's will.

Prayer:
Heavenly Father, as Jesus resisted the temptations in the wilderness, so too help us to resist the temptations we face. Grant us the grace to rely on Your Word, to trust in Your guidance, and to remain faithful to You in all things. May this Lent be a time of renewal and growth in our relationship with You. Amen.

Monday, March 10

❖ Monday of the First week of Lent

- ➢ First Reading: Leviticus 19: 1-2, 11-18
- ➢ Responsorial Psalm: Psalms 19: 8, 9, 10, 15
- ➢ Verse Before the Gospel: Second Corinthians 6: 2b
- ➢ Gospel: Matthew 25: 31-46
- ➢ Lectionary: 224

As we enter the first full week of Lent, today's readings call us to examine our relationships with others in light of God's commandments. We are reminded that holiness is not just about our relationship with God but also about how we treat our neighbors. Lent is a time to grow in love, compassion, and justice, following the example of Christ.

➢ First Reading: Leviticus 19: 1-2, 11-18

In this passage from Leviticus, the Lord speaks to Moses, instructing the people of Israel to be holy as He is holy. The reading outlines specific ways in which the Israelites are to live out this holiness: they must be honest, just, and loving in their interactions with one another. The passage culminates in the command, "You shall love your neighbor as yourself," which Jesus later identifies as one of the greatest commandments.

Reflection:
Holiness is not just about rituals and worship; it is also about our daily actions and attitudes toward others. This reading challenges us to reflect on how we treat those around us. Do we act with honesty, integrity, and kindness? As we journey through Lent, let us strive to embody the love and justice that God calls us to live out in our relationships.

Prayer:
Lord, You call us to be holy as You are holy. Help us to live out this call by treating others with love, honesty, and respect. May we always seek to love our neighbors as ourselves, reflecting Your goodness in all we do. Amen.

➢ Gospel: Matthew 25: 31-46

In this powerful passage, Jesus speaks of the final judgment, where the Son of Man will separate people as a shepherd separates the sheep from the goats. He reveals that our treatment of the least of His brothers and sisters—feeding the hungry, welcoming the stranger, clothing the naked, and visiting the sick and imprisoned—will be the basis of this judgment. Those who have served others in this way will inherit the kingdom, while those who have failed to do so will be sent away.

Reflection:

This Gospel reading reminds us that our faith is meant to be lived out in concrete acts of love and service. How we treat the most vulnerable among us is how we treat Christ Himself. As we continue our Lenten journey, let us examine how we are living out this call to love and serve others, especially those who are in need. May we respond to this challenge with open hearts and hands, recognizing Christ in every person we meet.

Prayer:

Jesus, You teach us that in serving others, we serve You. Open our eyes to see Your presence in those who are hungry, thirsty, lonely, and suffering. Give us the grace to respond to their needs with compassion and generosity, so that we may be counted among the righteous in Your kingdom. Amen.

Tuesday, March 11

❖ Tuesday of the First week of Lent

- ➢ First Reading: Isaiah 55: 10-11
- ➢ Responsorial Psalm: Psalms 34: 4-5, 6-7, 16-17, 18-19
- ➢ Verse Before the Gospel: Matthew 4: 4b
- ➢ Gospel: Matthew 6: 7-15
- ➢ Lectionary: 225

Today's readings invite us to contemplate the power of God's Word and the importance of prayer in our lives. We are reminded that God's Word always fulfills its purpose and that prayer is a powerful means of aligning our wills with His. As we continue our Lenten journey, these themes encourage us to trust in God's promises and to deepen our relationship with Him through sincere and persistent prayer.

- ➢ First Reading: Isaiah 55: 10-11

In this passage, the prophet Isaiah compares God's Word to the rain and snow that fall from the heavens, nourishing the earth and making it fruitful. Just as these waters bring forth life, so too does God's Word accomplish what it is sent to do. It never returns empty but always achieves the purpose for which God has spoken it.

Reflection:
God's Word is living and active, bringing about His will in our lives and in the world. This reading challenges us to trust in the power and efficacy of God's promises. During Lent, we are called to immerse ourselves more deeply in Scripture, allowing it to guide, nourish, and transform us. As we meditate on God's Word, let us trust that it will bear fruit in our lives, leading us closer to Him.

Prayer:
Heavenly Father, Your Word is powerful and true. Help us to receive it with open hearts and minds, trusting that it will accomplish Your will in our lives. May we be nourished by Your Word and bear fruit in all that we do. Amen.

➢ Gospel: Matthew 6: 7-15

In this passage, Jesus teaches His disciples how to pray, giving them the Lord's Prayer as a model. He emphasizes that prayer should not be about empty words or vain repetitions, but about a sincere and humble heart that seeks God's will. Jesus also underscores the importance of forgiveness, reminding us that our forgiveness from God is linked to our willingness to forgive others.

Reflection:
The Lord's Prayer is a perfect example of how we should approach God in prayer—with reverence, humility, and trust. It reminds us to seek God's will above our own, to rely on Him for our daily needs, and to forgive others as we have been forgiven. As we pray these words during Lent, let us reflect on their meaning and allow them to shape our relationship with God and with others.

Prayer:
Our Father, who art in heaven, hallowed be Thy name. Thy kingdom come, Thy will be done, on earth as it is in heaven. Give us this day our daily bread, and forgive us our trespasses, as we forgive those who trespass against us. Lead us not into temptation, but deliver us from evil. Amen.

Wednesday, March 12

❖ Wednesday of the First week of Lent

- ➢ First Reading: Jonah 3: 1-10
- ➢ Responsorial Psalm: Psalms 51: 3-4, 12-13, 18-19
- ➢ Verse Before the Gospel: Joel 2: 12-13
- ➢ Gospel: Luke 11: 29-32
- ➢ Lectionary: 226

Today's readings focus on the themes of repentance and the call to conversion. We are reminded of God's immense mercy and His desire for all people to turn back to Him. As we continue our Lenten journey, these passages encourage us to examine our hearts, repent of our sins, and seek God's forgiveness with a sincere and contrite spirit.

➢ First Reading: Jonah 3: 1-10

In this reading, the prophet Jonah is sent by God to the city of Nineveh with a message of impending judgment. To Jonah's surprise, the people of Nineveh, from the king to the common folk, respond to the warning with genuine repentance. They fast, put on sackcloth, and turn from their evil ways. Seeing their sincere contrition, God relents from the disaster He had planned to bring upon them.

Reflection:
The story of Jonah and Nineveh reminds us that no one is beyond the reach of God's mercy. When we turn to God with sincere hearts, He is always ready to forgive. During Lent, we are called to follow the example of the Ninevites by acknowledging our sins and making a sincere effort to change our ways. God's mercy is greater than our sins, and He eagerly awaits our return to Him.

Prayer:
Merciful God, You are always ready to forgive those who turn to You with sincere hearts. Help us to recognize our need for repentance and give us the grace to turn away from sin. May we experience the depth of Your mercy as we seek to live according to Your will. Amen.

➢ Gospel: Luke 11: 29-32

In this passage, Jesus addresses the crowds who are seeking a sign from Him. He points to the story of Jonah as a sign of God's call to repentance. Jesus then highlights the stark contrast between the people of Nineveh, who repented at Jonah's preaching, and the current generation, who fail to recognize the greater sign in Jesus Himself. He warns them that the Queen of the South and the Ninevites will rise in judgment against those who refuse to repent.

Reflection:
Jesus challenges us to recognize the signs of God's presence and action in our lives. The people of Nineveh repented at the preaching of Jonah, yet Jesus, who is greater than Jonah, is often met with resistance and indifference. This Gospel invites us to examine our own hearts and ask whether we are truly open to God's call to conversion. Lent is a time to heed this call, to turn away from sin, and to embrace the new life that Jesus offers.

Prayer:
Lord Jesus, You are the sign of God's love and mercy for all people. Open our hearts to Your call to repentance and help us to recognize the signs of Your presence in our lives. May we respond with faith and humility, seeking to follow You more closely each day. Amen.

Thursday, March 13

❖ Thursday of the First week of Lent

- First Reading: Esther C: 12, 14-16, 23-25
- Responsorial Psalm: Psalms 138: 1-2ab, 2cde-3, 7c-8
- Verse Before the Gospel: Psalms 51: 12a,14a
- Gospel: Matthew 7: 7-12
- Lectionary: 227

On this Lenten day, the readings highlight the power of prayer and trust in God. The story of Esther teaches us to approach God with faith, while Jesus' teaching in the Gospel reminds us of the assurance we have in God's response to our prayers. As we seek to deepen our relationship with God during Lent, these readings invite us to place our trust in His providence and love.

➢ First Reading: Esther C: 12, 14-16, 23-25

This passage presents the heartfelt prayer of Queen Esther, who finds herself in a desperate situation. Knowing the danger facing her people, she turns to God with fervent prayer, acknowledging her helplessness and placing her trust entirely in His mercy. Esther's prayer is one of humility and dependence, as she pleads for God's intervention and deliverance.

Reflection:
Esther's prayer is a powerful example of turning to God in times of distress. She doesn't rely on her own strength or wisdom but places her complete trust in God's ability to save her and her people. In our own lives, we are called to approach God with the same humility and trust, especially during the challenges and uncertainties we face. Lent is an opportune time to renew our prayer life, recognizing our need for God's grace and guidance.

Prayer:
Gracious God, like Queen Esther, we turn to You in our times of need, trusting in Your mercy and love. Strengthen our faith, especially when we face difficulties, and help us to rely on Your providence. May our prayers be filled with confidence in Your goodness, knowing that You always hear us and are ready to come to our aid. Amen.

> Gospel: Matthew 7: 7-12

In this passage, Jesus teaches about the power of persistent prayer. He encourages His followers to ask, seek, and knock, with the assurance that God will respond. Jesus emphasizes the goodness of God, comparing Him to a loving parent who desires to give good things to His children. He also highlights the Golden Rule, urging His followers to treat others as they would like to be treated.

Reflection:
Jesus' words remind us of the importance of perseverance in prayer and trust in God's generosity. God knows our needs and desires to provide for us, but He also invites us to actively seek Him through prayer. The assurance that God hears our prayers should encourage us to approach Him with confidence and trust. Additionally, the call to live by the Golden Rule challenges us to reflect God's love in our interactions with others, making our prayers not just words but actions of love and compassion.

Prayer:
Loving Father, we thank You for Your constant care and for always hearing our prayers. Teach us to pray with faith, knowing that You will answer according to Your perfect will. Help us to embody the love You show us by treating others with kindness and respect. May our lives reflect the goodness of Your heart. Amen.

Friday, March 14

❖ Day of Abstinance
❖ Friday of the First week of Lent

> First Reading: Ezekiel 18: 21-28
> Responsorial Psalm: Psalms 130: 1-2, 3-4, 5-6, 7-8
> Verse Before the Gospel: Ezekiel 18: 31
> Gospel: Matthew 5: 20-26
> Lectionary: 228

On this Friday of Lent, a day marked by abstinence and reflection, the readings call us to a deeper understanding of repentance and reconciliation. Ezekiel speaks of the transformative power of turning away from sin, while Jesus in the Gospel challenges us to seek reconciliation with others as a prerequisite for offering our gifts to God. This day invites us to reflect on our relationships with God and with others, urging us to embrace repentance and peace.

➢ First Reading: Ezekiel 18: 21-28

In this reading, the prophet Ezekiel presents a powerful message of hope and renewal. He emphasizes that if a wicked person turns away from their sins and follows God's commandments, they will live and not die. Conversely, if a righteous person turns away from righteousness and commits sin, they will face the consequences of their actions. This passage highlights God's justice and mercy, showing that each person is responsible for their choices, and that true repentance leads to life.

Reflection:
Ezekiel's message encourages us to reflect on our own lives and the choices we make. Lent is a time of conversion, a time to turn away from anything that separates us from God and to embrace the path of righteousness. This reading reassures us that no matter our past, God's mercy is always available to those who sincerely repent. It challenges us to examine our hearts and take concrete steps toward renewal and transformation.

Prayer:
Merciful God, You call us to turn from sin and embrace the fullness of life that You offer. Grant us the grace to recognize our failings and the courage to change our ways. May we always seek Your mercy and strive to live according to Your commandments, knowing that in You we find true life. Amen.

➢ Gospel: Matthew 5: 20-26

In this passage from the Sermon on the Mount, Jesus sets a high standard for His followers, teaching that righteousness must surpass that of the scribes and Pharisees. He warns against anger and calls for reconciliation, emphasizing that unresolved conflict with others hinders our relationship with God. Jesus teaches that we should be proactive in seeking peace, even if it means leaving our gifts at the altar to first be reconciled with our brother or sister.

Reflection:
Jesus' words remind us of the deep connection between our relationship with God and our relationships with others. Reconciliation is not just a nice idea; it is essential to our spiritual lives. This Gospel challenges us to examine our hearts for any lingering anger, grudges, or unresolved conflicts. Lent offers us the opportunity to seek forgiveness and to extend it to others, fostering a spirit of peace and harmony that reflects the love of God.

Prayer:
Lord Jesus, You call us to a higher standard of love and reconciliation. Help us to let go of anger and resentment, and to seek peace in our relationships. Give us the humility to ask for forgiveness when we have wronged others, and the grace to forgive those who have hurt us. May our lives be marked by the peace that only You can give. Amen.

Saturday, March 15

❖ **Saturday of the First week of Lent**

- First Reading: Deuteronomy 26: 16-19
- Responsorial Psalm: Psalms 119: 1-2, 4-5, 7-8
- Verse Before the Gospel: Second Corinthians 6: 2b
- Gospel: Matthew 5: 43-48
- Lectionary: 229

As we continue our Lenten journey, today's readings challenge us to consider the depth of our commitment to God's commandments and the radical love that Jesus calls us to embrace. The passage from Deuteronomy reminds us of the covenant relationship between God and His people, while Jesus in the Gospel challenges us to love our enemies, reflecting the perfect love of our Heavenly Father.

First Reading: Deuteronomy 26: 16-19

In this passage, Moses reminds the Israelites of their covenant with God. They are called to observe God's commandments with all their heart and soul. In return, God promises to set them high above all nations, making them a holy people, as He has promised. This reading emphasizes the mutual commitment between God and His people, highlighting the blessings that come from faithful adherence to His will.

Reflection:
This passage invites us to reflect on our own covenant with God. Lent is a time to renew our commitment to following His commandments with sincerity and devotion. God calls us to live as His chosen people, distinct in our faithfulness and love. This reading encourages us to embrace our identity as God's people and to strive to live according to His will, knowing that this path leads to true blessing and holiness.

Prayer:
Gracious God, You have called us to be Your holy people, set apart for Your purposes. Help us to live out this calling with wholehearted devotion. May we always seek to follow Your commandments and to honor the covenant You have made with us. Strengthen us in our resolve to live as Your faithful children, reflecting Your love and holiness in all that we do. Amen.

Gospel: Matthew 5: 43-48

In this Gospel passage, Jesus teaches one of His most challenging commandments: to love our enemies and pray for those who persecute us. He calls His followers to a love that goes beyond the ordinary, mirroring the perfect love of God, who causes the sun to rise on the evil and the good. Jesus concludes by urging His disciples to "be perfect, as your heavenly Father is perfect."

Reflection:

Jesus' call to love our enemies challenges us to go beyond our natural inclinations. True Christian love is not limited to those who love us in return; it extends even to those who oppose us. This radical love reflects the unconditional love of God, who loves all people without distinction. Lent is a time to grow in this perfect love, to forgive those who have wronged us, and to pray for those who are difficult to love. This Gospel calls us to expand our hearts, embracing the fullness of God's love and sharing it with others, even in the most difficult circumstances.

Prayer:

Lord Jesus, You have taught us the way of perfect love, a love that extends even to our enemies. Help us to love as You love, without reservation or condition. Give us the strength to forgive those who have hurt us and the grace to pray for those who oppose us. May we strive each day to reflect the perfect love of our Heavenly Father, becoming more like You in all that we do. Amen.

Sunday, March 16

❖ Second Sunday of Lent

- First Reading: Genesis 15: 5-12, 17-18
- Responsorial Psalm: Psalms 27: 1, 7-8, 8-9, 13-14
- Second Reading: Philippians 3: 17 – 4: 1 or 3: 20 – 4: 1
- Verse Before the Gospel: Matthew 17: 5
- Gospel: Luke 9: 28b-36
- Lectionary: 27

On this Second Sunday of Lent, we encounter the themes of covenant and transformation. The readings invite us to trust in God's promises, as exemplified in the covenant with Abram, and to open our hearts to the transforming power of Christ, who reveals His glory in the Transfiguration. As we continue our Lenten journey, we are called to deepen our faith and our commitment to following Jesus, even when the path is challenging.

- First Reading: Genesis 15: 5-12, 17-18

In this passage, God reassures Abram of His promise to make his descendants as numerous as the stars. Despite Abram's old age and the seeming impossibility of the promise, Abram believes, and God credits it to him as righteousness. The passage also describes the solemn covenant God makes with Abram, symbolized by the ritual of passing through the cut animals, a sign of God's unbreakable commitment to His promise.

Reflection:
Abram's faith in God's promise, despite the odds, is a powerful example for us during Lent. We are reminded that God is faithful, even when His promises seem beyond our understanding or experience. Lent invites us to renew our trust in God, believing that He is with us and will fulfill His promises in His perfect time. This reading encourages us to place our hope in God, who is always faithful to His word.

Prayer:
Faithful God, You made a covenant with Abram and promised him descendants as numerous as the stars. Strengthen our faith to trust in Your promises, even when the way ahead seems uncertain. Help us to walk in faithfulness to You, knowing that You are always true to Your word. May our lives be a testimony to Your unchanging love and faithfulness. Amen.

➢ Second Reading: Philippians 3: 17 – 4: 1 or 3: 20 – 4: 1

In this passage, Paul exhorts the Philippians to follow his example and to live as citizens of heaven, eagerly awaiting the return of the Lord Jesus Christ. He contrasts this heavenly mindset with those who live as "enemies of the cross of Christ," focused only on earthly matters. Paul encourages the believers to stand firm in the Lord, reminding them of the glorious transformation that awaits them in Christ.

Reflection:
Paul's message to the Philippians is a call to live with an eternal perspective. As we journey through Lent, we are reminded that our true citizenship is in heaven, and we are called to live in a way that reflects our identity as followers of Christ. This reading challenges us to focus on what truly matters—our relationship with God and our hope in the resurrection—rather than getting caught up in the distractions of the world. Lent is a time to realign our priorities and to live with our eyes fixed on Jesus, who will one day transform us into His glorious likeness.

Prayer:
Lord Jesus, help us to live as citizens of heaven, keeping our hearts and minds focused on You. May we not be swayed by the distractions of this world, but stand firm in our faith, eagerly awaiting the day when You will come again in glory. Transform our lives to reflect Your love and grace, that we may be a light to others and bring glory to Your name. Amen.

➢ Gospel: Luke 9: 28b-36

In this Gospel passage, Jesus takes Peter, James, and John up a mountain to pray. While He is praying, His appearance is transformed, and His clothes become dazzling white. Moses and Elijah appear with Him, speaking of His impending departure in Jerusalem. Peter, overwhelmed by the vision, suggests making three tents, but a cloud overshadows them, and a voice from the cloud says, "This is my chosen Son; listen to Him." The disciples are left in awe as the vision ends, and they keep silent about what they have seen.

Reflection:

The Transfiguration is a powerful revelation of Jesus' divine glory, offering the disciples a glimpse of His true identity. As we reflect on this mystery during Lent, we are reminded that our journey of faith is also a journey of transformation. Just as Jesus was transfigured before His disciples, we too are called to be transformed by His grace. This Gospel invites us to listen to Jesus, to follow Him closely, and to open our hearts to the changes He wants to work in us. The voice of the Father calls us to listen to His Son, to trust in His guidance, and to allow His light to shine through us.

Prayer:

Heavenly Father, in the Transfiguration of Your Son, You revealed His glory and called us to listen to Him. Open our hearts to hear His voice and to follow His will. Transform us by Your grace, that we may reflect the light of Christ in our lives. Help us to walk faithfully with Jesus, trusting in His love and guidance as we journey through Lent and beyond. Amen.

Monday, March 17

- Monday of the Second week of Lent
- Saint Patrick, bishop - Commemoration

- First Reading: Daniel 9: 4b-10
- Responsorial Psalm: Psalms 79: 8, 9, 11 and 13
- Verse Before the Gospel: John 6: 63c, 68c
- Gospel: Luke 6: 36-38
- Lectionary: 230

On this day, we commemorate Saint Patrick, the great missionary bishop who brought the Christian faith to Ireland. As we honor his legacy, our readings call us to reflect on God's mercy and our need for repentance. The themes of mercy and forgiveness resonate strongly as we continue our Lenten journey, seeking to align our hearts more closely with God's will.

- First Reading: Daniel 9: 4b-10

In this reading, Daniel offers a heartfelt prayer of confession and repentance on behalf of the people of Israel. Acknowledging their sins and disobedience, Daniel appeals to God's great mercy and compassion. He recognizes that despite their unfaithfulness, God remains faithful, and he humbly asks for forgiveness and restoration.

Reflection:

Daniel's prayer is a powerful reminder of the importance of repentance in our relationship with God. During Lent, we are called to examine our lives, acknowledge our sins, and seek God's forgiveness. Like Daniel, we can approach God with humility, confident in His mercy and willingness to forgive. This reading encourages us to turn back to God with sincere hearts, trusting that He is always ready to welcome us back with open arms.

Prayer:

Merciful God, like Daniel, we acknowledge our sins and shortcomings. We have not always followed Your commandments or lived according to Your will. Yet, we trust in Your great mercy and ask for Your forgiveness. Cleanse our hearts, renew our spirits, and draw us closer to You. Help us to live in a way that reflects Your love and faithfulness. Amen.

➤ Gospel: Luke 6: 36-38

In this Gospel passage, Jesus teaches about the importance of mercy, forgiveness, and generosity. He calls His followers to be merciful, just as their Heavenly Father is merciful. Jesus encourages us to avoid judgment and condemnation, and instead, to forgive and give freely. He assures us that the measure we use for others will be the measure we receive.

Reflection:

Jesus' words challenge us to reflect on how we treat others. Lent is a time to practice mercy and forgiveness, recognizing that we are all in need of God's grace. Jesus calls us to extend the same compassion and generosity to others that we desire for ourselves. This Gospel invites us to be mindful of our attitudes and actions, striving to embody the mercy of God in our relationships with others. It is a reminder that the way we treat others reflects our understanding of God's mercy toward us.

Prayer:

Lord Jesus, You have shown us the way of mercy and compassion. Help us to follow Your example by being merciful to others, forgiving those who have wronged us, and giving generously from the heart. Teach us to love as You love, without judgment or condemnation, and to reflect Your kindness in all that we do. May our lives be a testimony to Your boundless mercy. Amen.

Tuesday, March 18

- ❖ Tuesday of the Second week of Lent
- ❖ Saint Cyril of Jerusalem, bishop and doctor - Commemoration

> - First Reading: Isaiah 1: 10, 16-20
> - Responsorial Psalm: Psalms 50: 8-9, 16bc-17, 21 and 23
> - Verse Before the Gospel: Ezekiel 18: 31
> - Gospel: Matthew 23: 1-12
> - Lectionary: 231

Today, we honor Saint Cyril of Jerusalem, a great bishop and teacher of the early Church known for his catechetical lectures that deeply enriched the faith of the early Christian community. As we journey through Lent, the readings remind us of the call to genuine repentance and humility, guiding us to live out our faith with sincerity and integrity.

> - First Reading: Isaiah 1: 10, 16-20

In this reading, the prophet Isaiah delivers a powerful message from God, calling the people of Israel to repentance. God urges them to "wash yourselves clean" and "put away your misdeeds." He invites them to seek justice, correct oppression, and defend the vulnerable. God promises that though their sins are like scarlet, they shall become white as snow if they are willing to obey.

Reflection:
Isaiah's message speaks to the heart of our Lenten journey: the need for true repentance and a turning away from sin. God desires not just external observance of religious practices, but a deep, inner transformation that leads to justice and compassion in our lives. This reading challenges us to examine our hearts and actions, and to commit ourselves to living according to God's will. It reassures us that no matter how far we may have strayed, God's mercy is always available to those who return to Him with a sincere heart.

Prayer:
Loving God, You call us to genuine repentance and transformation. Help us to turn away from sin and to seek justice, mercy, and compassion in our lives. Cleanse our hearts and guide us to live in accordance with Your will. May we always trust in Your mercy and strive to reflect Your love in our actions. Amen.

> Gospel: Matthew 23: 1-12

In this Gospel passage, Jesus warns against hypocrisy and the desire for status and recognition. He criticizes the religious leaders of His time who impose heavy burdens on others but do not practice what they preach. Jesus teaches that greatness in the Kingdom of Heaven is found in humility and service, not in seeking titles or positions of honor.

Reflection:

Jesus' words remind us of the importance of humility and sincerity in our faith. He calls us to examine our motivations and to avoid the temptation of seeking recognition or power. Lent is a time to focus on serving others and living out our faith with genuine humility. Jesus teaches us that true greatness lies in being a servant to others, following His example of selfless love and service. This Gospel challenges us to put aside our pride and to approach our faith with a humble and contrite heart.

Prayer:

Lord Jesus, You taught us that true greatness comes from humility and service. Help us to resist the temptations of pride and hypocrisy. Grant us the grace to live our faith with sincerity, seeking to serve others and to follow Your example of love and humility. May our lives be a reflection of Your servant's heart, and may we always strive to put the needs of others before our own. Amen.

Wednesday, March 19

❖ Saint Joseph, Husband of Mary - Solemnity

> First Reading: Second Samuel 7: 4-5a, 12-14a, 16
> Responsorial Psalm: Psalms 89: 2-3, 4-5, 27 and 29
> Second Reading: Romans 4: 13, 16-18, 22
> Verse Before the Gospel: Psalms 84: 5
> Gospel: Matthew 1: 16, 18-21, 24 or Luke 2: 41-51a
> Lectionary: 543

Today, we celebrate the Solemnity of Saint Joseph, the husband of Mary and the foster father of Jesus. Saint Joseph is a model of faith, humility, and obedience to God's will. As we reflect on his life, we are invited to emulate his trust in God and his unwavering commitment to his family.

➢ First Reading: Second Samuel 7: 4-5a, 12-14a, 16

In this reading, the Lord speaks to King David through the prophet Nathan, promising that his kingdom will be established forever through his descendants. God assures David that his house and kingdom shall endure forever before Him, and his throne shall be established forever.

Reflection:

This passage reminds us of God's faithfulness to His promises. The prophecy to David finds its fulfillment in Jesus, who is born of the house of David and whose kingdom will never end. Saint Joseph, as a descendant of David, plays a crucial role in God's plan of salvation. His humble acceptance of God's will allows this promise to come to fruition. In our own lives, we are called to trust in God's promises, even when we do not fully understand His plans.

Prayer:

Faithful God, You fulfilled Your promise to David through the birth of Jesus, Your Son. Help us to trust in Your promises and to remain faithful to Your will. Like Saint Joseph, may we humbly accept our role in Your plan of salvation and serve You with a willing heart. Amen.

➢ Second Reading: Romans 4: 13, 16-18, 22

In this passage, Saint Paul reflects on the faith of Abraham, who believed in God's promises even when it seemed impossible. Paul emphasizes that it is through faith that we are made righteous and that this faith is open to all who believe, not just to those under the law. Abraham's faith was "credited to him as righteousness," and he became the father of many nations.

Reflection:

Saint Joseph, like Abraham, is a model of faith. He believed in God's promises and acted in faith, even in the face of uncertainty and challenges. His quiet, steadfast trust in God allowed him to protect and care for Mary and Jesus. This reading calls us to deepen our faith and trust in God's providence, knowing that righteousness comes through faith, not through our own efforts.

Prayer:

God of Abraham, You call us to a life of faith and trust in Your promises. Strengthen our faith, that we may follow the example of Saint Joseph in believing in Your word and acting with courage and humility. May our faith be a beacon of hope to those around us, as we live out our trust in Your unfailing love. Amen.

➢ Gospel: Matthew 1: 16, 18-21, 24 or Luke 2: 41-51a

In the Gospel reading from Matthew, we hear the story of Joseph's response to the angel's message in a dream. Despite his initial fear, Joseph takes Mary as his wife, in obedience to God's command, and becomes the earthly father of Jesus. Alternatively, in the Gospel from Luke, we hear of the episode when Jesus, at the age of twelve, stays behind in the temple, and Joseph and Mary search anxiously for Him. When they find Him, Jesus expresses His need to be in His Father's house, revealing His divine mission.

Reflection:

Both Gospel readings highlight Joseph's role as a protector and guardian of Jesus and Mary. His willingness to embrace God's plan, even when it was difficult and unclear, speaks to his deep faith and trust in God. Joseph's example teaches us the importance of obedience to God's will and the humility to accept our role in His greater plan. As we celebrate Saint Joseph today, we are reminded to be open to God's guidance in our lives and to fulfill our responsibilities with love and faithfulness.

Prayer:
Heavenly Father, we thank You for the example of Saint Joseph, who faithfully followed Your will and protected the Holy Family. Grant us the grace to be obedient to Your word and to trust in Your plans for our lives. May we, like Joseph, serve You with humility and love, always seeking to do Your will in all things. Amen.

Thursday, March 20

❖ Thursday of the Second week of Lent

- ➢ First Reading: Jeremiah 17: 5-10
- ➢ Responsorial Psalm: Psalms 1: 1-2, 3, 4 and 6
- ➢ Verse Before the Gospel: Luke 8: 15
- ➢ Gospel: Luke 16: 19-31
- ➢ Lectionary: 233

As we continue our Lenten journey, today's readings call us to reflect on where we place our trust and how we respond to the needs of others. We are invited to examine our hearts, to root out any reliance on worldly things, and to embrace the life-giving trust in God.

➢ First Reading: Jeremiah 17: 5-10

In this passage, the prophet Jeremiah contrasts two types of people: those who trust in human beings and turn away from the Lord, and those who trust in the Lord. Those who rely on human strength are like a barren bush in the desert, while those who trust in God are like a tree planted by the water, flourishing even in times of drought. The reading concludes with a reminder that the Lord alone knows the human heart and rewards each person according to their deeds.

Reflection:
Jeremiah's words challenge us to examine where we place our trust. Do we rely on our own abilities, wealth, or the approval of others, or do we place our trust in God? The image of the tree planted by the water is a powerful reminder that when we root our lives in God, we will thrive even in difficult times. Lent is a time to deepen our trust in God and to let go of anything that distracts us from His life-giving presence.

Prayer:

Lord, help us to trust in You with all our hearts. May we not rely on our own understanding or the ways of the world, but place our hope in You alone. Plant us by Your living waters, that we may bear fruit in every season and remain steadfast in faith, even in times of trial. Amen.

> ➢ Gospel: Luke 16: 19-31

In this Gospel passage, Jesus tells the parable of the rich man and Lazarus. The rich man lives in luxury, ignoring the poor man, Lazarus, who lies at his gate, hungry and covered in sores. After they both die, Lazarus is carried to Abraham's bosom, while the rich man suffers in Hades. The rich man pleads for relief and for Lazarus to warn his brothers, but Abraham tells him that they have already been warned through Moses and the prophets.

Reflection:

This parable is a stark reminder of the consequences of ignoring the needs of others and living a life focused solely on wealth and comfort. The rich man's fate serves as a warning that our earthly actions have eternal consequences. Jesus calls us to open our eyes to the suffering around us and to respond with compassion and generosity. Lent is a time to reflect on how we use our resources and whether we are truly living out the Gospel's call to love our neighbor.

Prayer:

Merciful Father, open our eyes to the needs of those around us. Give us hearts of compassion and the courage to act in love and generosity. Help us to see Your face in the poor and the suffering, and to respond to them as we would to You. May our lives be a reflection of Your mercy, and may we be found worthy of eternal life in Your presence. Amen.

Friday, March 21

❖ Day of Abstinance
❖ Friday of the Second week of Lent

> ➢ First Reading: Genesis 37: 3-4, 12-13a, 17b-28
> ➢ Responsorial Psalm: Psalms 105: 16-17, 18-19, 20-21
> ➢ Verse Before the Gospel: John 3: 16
> ➢ Gospel: Matthew 21: 33-43, 45-46
> ➢ Lectionary: 234

On this Lenten Friday, we are reminded of the challenges of living out our faith in a world that often rejects the message of the Gospel. Today's readings focus on themes of jealousy, betrayal, and the consequences of rejecting God's messengers. As we abstain from meat and practice self-denial, we are called to reflect on our own responses to God's call in our lives.

➤ First Reading: Genesis 37: 3-4, 12-13a, 17b-28

This reading recounts the story of Joseph, the beloved son of Jacob. Joseph's brothers, filled with jealousy because of their father's special love for him, conspire to kill him. Ultimately, they decide to sell him into slavery, and Joseph is taken to Egypt. This act of betrayal sets in motion a series of events that will eventually lead to the salvation of many, but it begins with a profound act of jealousy and rejection.

Reflection:
The story of Joseph and his brothers highlights the destructive power of jealousy and envy. The brothers' inability to accept their father's love for Joseph leads them to commit a grave sin. During Lent, we are called to examine our hearts for any traces of jealousy or envy that may be hindering our relationships with others and with God. Let us ask God for the grace to be content with what we have and to rejoice in the blessings of others.

Prayer:
Lord, free our hearts from jealousy and envy. Help us to recognize and celebrate the unique gifts and blessings You have given to each of us. May we never allow envy to lead us into sin, but instead, may we grow in love and understanding for one another. Amen.

➤ Gospel: Matthew 21: 33-43, 45-46

In this Gospel passage, Jesus tells the parable of the wicked tenants. A landowner plants a vineyard and leases it to tenants before going on a journey. When the time comes to collect the produce, the tenants beat, stone, and kill the landowner's servants and even his son. Jesus uses this parable to illustrate the rejection of the prophets and ultimately, of Himself. The parable ends with a stern warning that the kingdom of God will be taken away from those who reject it and given to those who bear its fruit.

Reflection:
The parable of the wicked tenants is a powerful reminder of the consequences of rejecting God's call. The tenants' refusal to give the landowner his due represents the hardness of heart that can develop when we turn away from God. During Lent, we are invited to soften our hearts and to be open to God's will in our lives. Let us reflect on how we can bear good fruit in our lives and avoid the pitfalls of pride and self-reliance.

Prayer:
Heavenly Father, grant us the humility to recognize Your presence in our lives and to respond to Your call with faith and obedience. May we never reject Your messengers or the promptings of Your Spirit. Help us to bear good fruit in all that we do, and to live lives that are pleasing to You. Amen.

Saturday, March 22

❖ **Saturday of the Second week of Lent**

> ➢ First Reading: Micah 7: 14-15, 18-20
> ➢ Responsorial Psalm: Psalms 103: 1-2, 3-4, 9-10, 11-12
> ➢ Verse Before the Gospel: Luke 15: 18
> ➢ Gospel: Luke 15: 1-3, 11-32
> ➢ Lectionary: 235

Today, as we continue our Lenten journey, we encounter themes of repentance, mercy, and forgiveness. The readings highlight God's unwavering love and forgiveness, even when we stray from His path. This Saturday invites us to reflect on the depth of God's mercy and our call to extend that mercy to others.

> ➢ **First Reading: Micah 7: 14-15, 18-20**

In this passage, the prophet Micah pleads with God to shepherd His people as He has done in the past. Micah emphasizes God's forgiveness and compassion, acknowledging that God is steadfast in love and mercy. The prophet also celebrates God's unique ability to cast sins into the depths of the sea and remain faithful to His covenant.

Reflection:
Micah's words remind us of God's infinite mercy and forgiveness. During Lent, it is important for us to remember that no matter how far we have strayed, God's love remains constant and His ability to forgive is boundless. Let us take this opportunity to seek reconciliation with God, trusting that He will embrace us with open arms, just as He has promised.

Prayer:
Lord God, we thank You for Your unending mercy and compassion. Help us to recognize Your love in our lives and to seek Your forgiveness with sincere hearts. May we reflect Your mercy to those around us and live in the light of Your grace. Amen.

> ➢ **Gospel: Luke 15: 1-3, 11-32**

The Gospel presents the parable of the Prodigal Son, a powerful story of repentance, forgiveness, and redemption. Jesus tells of a young man who demands his inheritance and squanders it in reckless living. When a famine strikes, he returns home, repentant and hoping to be treated as a hired servant. Instead, his father welcomes him back with joy and celebration. The parable also highlights the elder brother's resentment, revealing the struggles of those who feel left out of grace.

Reflection:
The parable of the Prodigal Son illustrates the boundless nature of God's forgiveness and the joy in Heaven over a single sinner who repents. It challenges us to reflect on our own attitudes towards forgiveness and grace. Are we like the prodigal son, seeking redemption and finding joy in God's mercy? Or are we like the elder brother, struggling with feelings of entitlement and resentment? This Lenten season calls us to embrace forgiveness and to celebrate the return of those who have been lost.

Prayer:
Father, we thank You for Your unending mercy and for welcoming us back when we stray. Help us to embrace the spirit of forgiveness and to celebrate the return of those who seek Your grace. May we reflect Your love and compassion in our dealings with others, and may our hearts be open to the joy of reconciliation. Amen.

Sunday, March 23

❖ Third Sunday of Lent

- First Reading: Exodus 3: 1-8a, 13-15
- Responsorial Psalm: Psalms 103: 1-2, 3-4, 6-7, 8, 11
- Second Reading: First Corinthians 10: 1-6, 10-12
- Verse Before the Gospel: Matthew 4: 17
- Gospel: Luke 13: 1-9
- Lectionary: 30

On this Third Sunday of Lent, we are invited to reflect on themes of divine encounter, repentance, and renewal. The readings focus on God's call to conversion and the need for spiritual growth and transformation. Today's liturgy encourages us to examine our own lives in light of God's covenant and to respond with repentance and commitment to His ways.

➤ First Reading: Exodus 3: 1-8a, 13-15

In this passage, Moses encounters God in the burning bush on Mount Horeb. God reveals Himself to Moses and commissions him to lead the Israelites out of Egypt. God's name is declared as "I AM WHO I AM," signifying His eternal and self-sufficient nature. This encounter marks a pivotal moment in the salvation history of Israel.

Reflection:

Moses' encounter with God reminds us that God is ever-present and active in our lives. Just as Moses was called to be a leader and bring freedom to his people, we too are called to respond to God's invitation in our own lives. This season of Lent is an opportunity to recognize God's presence and to heed His call for conversion and renewal.

Prayer:

Lord God, reveal Yourself to us as You did to Moses. Help us to recognize Your presence in our lives and to respond to Your call with faith and obedience. May this Lent be a time of deep renewal and transformation, as we seek to follow Your ways. Amen.

➢ Second Reading: First Corinthians 10: 1-6, 10-12

St. Paul reminds the Corinthians of the experiences of the Israelites in the desert, highlighting that their experiences serve as warnings for us. He emphasizes the importance of learning from the past and avoiding the pitfalls of disobedience and unbelief. The reading calls for vigilance and faithfulness in our walk with God.

Reflection:

Paul's message serves as a cautionary reminder of the need to stay faithful and avoid the errors of the past. During Lent, it is a time to reflect on our own lives and make adjustments where necessary. The call to repentance is not just a call to avoid mistakes but to actively pursue a life of faith and obedience.

Prayer:

Heavenly Father, guide us as we reflect on the lessons of the past. Help us to avoid the pitfalls of disobedience and to remain faithful to Your teachings. Strengthen our resolve to follow You wholeheartedly and to grow in our spiritual journey this Lent. Amen.

➢ Gospel: Luke 13: 1-9

In this Gospel passage, Jesus addresses questions about tragedy and suffering, using the parable of the fig tree to illustrate the necessity of repentance. The fig tree, though barren, is given another chance to bear fruit, symbolizing God's patience and the opportunity for renewal.

Reflection:

Jesus' parable challenges us to reflect on our own spiritual fruitfulness. Just as the fig tree was given another chance, we are called to examine our lives and seek genuine repentance. This Gospel reminds us of God's patience and His desire for us to bear good fruit. Lent is a time to cultivate our spiritual lives and make the necessary changes to bear fruit for His Kingdom.

Prayer:

Lord Jesus, thank You for Your patience and for giving us opportunities to renew our lives. Help us to bear fruit in keeping with Your call and to use this Lent as a time to cultivate our relationship with You. May we embrace Your call to repentance and grow in faith and virtue. Amen.

Monday, March 24

❖ **Monday of the Third week of Lent**

> ➢ First Reading: Second Kings 5: 1-15
> ➢ Responsorial Psalm: Psalms 42: 2, 3; 43: 3, 4
> ➢ Verse Before the Gospel: Psalms 130: 5, 7
> ➢ Gospel: Luke 4: 24-30
> ➢ Lectionary: 237

Today, we continue our Lenten journey with readings that highlight themes of healing, faith, and rejection. The readings challenge us to reflect on our openness to God's work in our lives and our willingness to embrace His message, even when it may not align with our expectations.

> ➢ **First Reading: Second Kings 5: 1-15**

In this passage, Naaman, a commander of the Syrian army, seeks healing from his leprosy. Directed by the prophet Elisha, Naaman initially struggles with the simplicity of the cure but eventually obeys and is healed. This story illustrates the power of faith and obedience in experiencing God's miracles.

Reflection:
Naaman's journey from skepticism to healing reflects our own struggles with faith and obedience. God's ways are often simple and profound, and our challenge is to trust and follow His directions even when they seem contrary to our expectations. Lent is a time to open our hearts to God's transformative power and embrace His call with humility and faith.

Prayer:
Lord, grant us the faith to trust in Your ways, even when they seem simple or unfamiliar. Help us to follow Your guidance with humility and openness, and to experience the healing and transformation You offer. May this Lent deepen our trust in Your plans for us. Amen.

> ➢ **Gospel: Luke 4: 24-30**

In this Gospel passage, Jesus refers to the rejection faced by prophets, including Himself. He recalls instances from the Old Testament where prophets were not accepted in their own towns. Jesus' words provoke anger among His listeners, leading them to attempt to throw Him off a cliff.

Reflection:

Jesus' experience of rejection underscores the difficulty of accepting and embracing the truth, especially when it challenges our preconceptions. The call to follow Jesus requires a willingness to listen to His message and accept Him fully, even when it disrupts our comfort zones. As we journey through Lent, let us reflect on our own openness to God's message and our readiness to follow Him despite challenges.

Prayer:

Lord Jesus, help us to embrace Your message with openness and courage. May we overcome any resistance or rejection in our hearts and be willing to follow You wherever You lead. Strengthen our resolve to accept Your truth and live according to Your teachings. Amen.

Tuesday, March 25

❖ Annunciation of the Lord - Solemnity

- First Reading: Isaiah 7: 10-14; 8: 10
- Responsorial Psalm: Psalms 40: 7-8a, 8b-9, 10, 11
- Second Reading: Hebrews 10: 4-10
- Verse Before the Gospel: John 1: 14ab
- Gospel: Luke 1: 26-38
- Lectionary: 545

Today, the Church celebrates the Solemnity of the Annunciation of the Lord, marking the moment when the Angel Gabriel announced to Mary that she would conceive the Son of God. This feast highlights the profound mystery of the Incarnation and the pivotal role of Mary's fiat (yes) in God's plan for salvation.

- First Reading: Isaiah 7: 10-14; 8: 10

In this reading, the prophet Isaiah conveys a message of hope to King Ahaz, revealing that a virgin will conceive and bear a son named Immanuel, which means "God is with us." This prophecy foretells the coming of Jesus and serves as a promise of God's presence and intervention in the world.

Reflection:

The prophecy in Isaiah underscores God's commitment to being with His people. The Annunciation fulfills this promise through the Incarnation of Jesus. As we celebrate this solemnity, we are reminded of God's intimate involvement in our lives and His desire to dwell among us. The announcement of Christ's coming invites us to reflect on the ways God is present and active in our own lives, encouraging us to respond with faith and openness.

Prayer:
Heavenly Father, we thank You for the incredible gift of Your Son, who was announced to Mary and came to dwell among us. Help us to recognize Your presence in our lives and respond with the same openness and trust as Mary. May we always seek to live in accordance with Your will and embrace Your promises with faith. Amen.

➢ Second Reading: Hebrews 10: 4-10

This passage from Hebrews highlights the inefficacy of the Old Testament sacrifices in achieving forgiveness and contrasts them with the ultimate sacrifice of Christ. Jesus' offering of Himself is described as a perfect and final sacrifice that sanctifies humanity and accomplishes God's will.

Reflection:
The reading from Hebrews emphasizes the transformative power of Christ's sacrifice. The Annunciation signifies the beginning of this redemptive act, as Jesus enters into our human condition to offer the ultimate sacrifice for our salvation. This solemnity invites us to appreciate the depth of Christ's love and the significance of His mission, as well as to reflect on our response to His sacrifice in our daily lives.

Prayer:
Lord Jesus, we thank You for Your sacrifice and for coming into our world to fulfill God's promise of salvation. Help us to live in gratitude for Your offering and to align our lives with the will of God. May we embrace Your grace and live out the joy of Your coming into our midst. Amen.

➢ Gospel: Luke 1: 26-38

The Gospel recounts the angel Gabriel's visit to Mary, announcing that she will conceive Jesus by the Holy Spirit. Mary's humble and obedient response, "I am the servant of the Lord; let it be done to me according to your word," demonstrates her faith and willingness to participate in God's plan.

Reflection:
The Annunciation is a profound moment of divine interaction and human cooperation. Mary's response exemplifies trust and surrender to God's will, setting a powerful example for us. As we celebrate this solemnity, let us reflect on our own openness to God's call and seek to imitate Mary's faithfulness and readiness to serve.

Prayer:
Blessed Mary, as we celebrate the Annunciation, we honor your willingness to accept God's will and bring forth the Savior of the world. Help us to respond with faith and openness to God's call in our lives. May your example inspire us to live with courage and trust in God's plans. Amen.

Wednesday, March 26

❖ Wednesday of the Third week of Lent

> ➢ First Reading: Deuteronomy 4:1, 5-9
> ➢ Responsorial Psalm: Psalms 147: 12-13, 15-16, 19-20
> ➢ Verse Before the Gospel: John 6: 63c, 68c
> ➢ Gospel: Matthew 5: 17-19
> ➢ Lectionary: 239

In today's liturgy, the readings focus on the importance of adhering to God's commandments and the role of Jesus in fulfilling the Law. As we continue our Lenten journey, these passages remind us of the enduring relevance of God's Word and our call to live in accordance with it.

➢ First Reading: Deuteronomy 4:1, 5-9

Moses speaks to the Israelites, urging them to observe and follow God's laws faithfully. He emphasizes that adherence to God's commandments will ensure their well-being and highlight their wisdom and understanding to the nations. Moses also recounts the importance of remembering the great acts of God and teaching them to future generations.

Reflection:
This reading underscores the importance of obedience to God's commandments and the wisdom that comes from living in accordance with His Word. In the context of Lent, it invites us to reflect on our own commitment to God's teachings and the ways we can more faithfully live out His commandments. Remembering God's past actions and teachings can inspire us to deepen our spiritual practice and commitment.

Prayer:
Lord, help us to follow Your commandments with sincerity and devotion. As we journey through Lent, may we remember Your past deeds and teachings, and be inspired to live in accordance with Your will. Strengthen our commitment to Your Word and guide us in our efforts to reflect Your wisdom in our lives. Amen.

➢ Gospel: Matthew 5: 17-19

In this passage, Jesus clarifies that He has not come to abolish the Law or the Prophets but to fulfill them. He stresses that not the smallest letter or stroke of the pen will disappear from the Law until everything is accomplished. Jesus also emphasizes that those who practice and teach the commandments will be called great in the Kingdom of Heaven.

Reflection:
Jesus' words affirm the ongoing relevance and fulfillment of the Law through Him. He embodies the complete realization of God's commandments and invites us to live by them fully. This passage encourages us to view the Law not as something outdated but as a guide that finds its ultimate meaning in Christ. Lent is a time to renew our commitment to living out these teachings and to embodying the values of the Kingdom of Heaven.

Prayer:
Jesus, we thank You for fulfilling the Law and revealing its true meaning. As we observe Lent, help us to understand and live out Your commandments more deeply. Teach us to practice and uphold Your Word in our daily lives, and to embody the values of Your Kingdom. May our actions reflect Your love and grace. Amen.

Thursday, March 27

❖ Thursday of the Third week of Lent

- First Reading: Jeremiah 7: 23-28
- Responsorial Psalm: Psalms 95: 1-2, 6-7, 8-9
- Verse Before the Gospel: Joel 2: 12-13
- Gospel: Luke 11: 14-23
- Lectionary: 240

Today's readings challenge us to reflect on our response to God's commands and the presence of His kingdom among us. They call us to examine our hearts and our readiness to embrace and live out the transformative power of God's Word.

First Reading: Jeremiah 7: 23-28

In this passage, the Lord speaks through the prophet Jeremiah, reminding the people of Israel of His command to obey Him and walk in His ways. God warns them of the consequences of their disobedience and their failure to heed His voice. The reading highlights the stark contrast between those who listen to God and those who persist in their rebellious ways.

Reflection:
This reading invites us to consider our own responsiveness to God's voice. Are we attentive to His

guidance, or do we ignore His commands in favor of our own desires? Lent is a time for introspection and conversion. This passage encourages us to renew our commitment to listening to God and following His ways, recognizing that our choices have significant consequences for our relationship with Him.

Prayer:

Lord, we ask for the grace to hear and respond to Your Word with open hearts. Help us to follow Your commands faithfully and to turn away from our own rebellious tendencies. During this Lenten season, guide us in our journey of repentance and renewal. May we align our lives with Your will and grow in our relationship with You. Amen.

➢ Gospel: Luke 11: 14-23

In this Gospel passage, Jesus performs an exorcism, casting out a demon from a mute man. Some in the crowd accuse Him of casting out demons by the power of Beelzebul, but Jesus refutes this claim, explaining that a kingdom divided against itself cannot stand. He emphasizes that His power comes from God and that His work represents the arrival of God's kingdom.

Reflection:

Jesus' words and actions in this passage underscore the reality of His divine authority and the presence of God's kingdom among us. The power of Jesus to overcome evil is a sign of the breaking in of God's reign. This passage challenges us to recognize the presence of God's kingdom in our midst and to align ourselves with His work rather than opposing it. It calls us to be allies in God's mission to bring healing and transformation to the world.

Prayer:

Jesus, we thank You for revealing the power of God's kingdom through Your works. Help us to recognize and support the presence of Your kingdom in our lives and in the world around us. Strengthen us to stand against the forces of evil and to be instruments of Your healing and grace. As we journey through Lent, may we grow closer to You and more committed to Your mission. Amen.

Friday, March 28

❖ Day of Abstinance
❖ Friday of the Third week of Lent

> ➢ First Reading: Hosea 14: 2-10
> ➢ Responsorial Psalm: Psalms 81: 6c-8a, 8bc-9, 10-11ab, 14 and 17
> ➢ Verse Before the Gospel: Matthew 4: 17
> ➢ Gospel: Mark 12: 28-34
> ➢ Lectionary: 241

Today's readings emphasize the importance of repentance and love. We are invited to reflect on our relationship with God and with others, recognizing that true repentance leads to a renewal of heart and a deeper commitment to loving God and our neighbors.

➢ First Reading: Hosea 14: 2-10

In this passage, the prophet Hosea calls Israel to repentance and promises God's healing and restoration. Hosea invites the people to return to the Lord with sincere hearts, acknowledging their need for God's mercy. He assures them that God will heal their waywardness and love them freely.

Reflection:
Hosea's call to repentance is both a reminder of God's faithfulness and an invitation to genuine transformation. During Lent, this passage challenges us to examine our own lives and return to God with humility and sincerity. It assures us that no matter how far we may have strayed, God's love and mercy are always available to heal and restore us.

Prayer:
Lord, we come before You with repentant hearts, seeking Your mercy and forgiveness. Help us to return to You with sincerity and faith, trusting in Your promise of healing and restoration. As we continue our Lenten journey, may we be open to Your grace and live according to Your will. Amen.

➢ Gospel: Mark 12: 28-34

In this Gospel, a scribe asks Jesus which commandment is the greatest. Jesus responds by summarizing the entire law with two commands: to love God with all one's heart, soul, mind, and strength, and to love one's neighbor as oneself. He emphasizes that these two commandments are the foundation of all the teachings and laws.

Reflection:
Jesus' teaching on the greatest commandment highlights the essence of our faith: love. Loving God and loving our neighbor are interconnected and central to living out our Christian vocation. This passage calls us to evaluate how well we embody this love in our daily lives. It challenges us to prioritize love in our interactions with others and in our relationship with God.

Prayer:
Jesus, You have taught us that love is the greatest commandment. Help us to love You with our whole being and to love our neighbors as ourselves. As we observe this Lenten season, guide us in living out this commandment in practical ways, and deepen our commitment to embodying Your love in all that we do. Amen.

Saturday, March 29

❖ Saturday of the Third week of Lent

- First Reading: Hosea 6: 1-6
- Responsorial Psalm: Psalms 51: 3-4, 18-19, 20-21ab
- Verse Before the Gospel: Psalms 95: 8
- Gospel: Luke 18: 9-14
- Lectionary: 242

As we approach the end of the third week of Lent, today's readings invite us to reflect on true repentance and humility. The messages emphasize the importance of sincere repentance over mere ritual and highlight the value of humility in our relationship with God.

- **First Reading: Hosea 6: 1-6**

Hosea speaks of God's desire for genuine repentance rather than empty ritualistic practices. The prophet urges the people to return to God, acknowledging their faults and seeking His healing. He emphasizes that God desires steadfast love and knowledge of Him more than sacrifices.

Reflection:
Hosea's message underscores that true repentance involves more than just external acts; it requires a sincere change of heart. God desires a relationship marked by genuine love and faithfulness, rather than

mere compliance with rituals. This Lent, we are called to examine our own repentance and ensure it is rooted in sincere love and commitment to God.

Prayer:
Heavenly Father, we come before You seeking true repentance and transformation. Help us to move beyond mere external practices and cultivate a heart that desires Your love and mercy. May our Lenten observances reflect a genuine commitment to You and a deeper relationship with You. Amen.

> ➤ **Gospel: Luke 18: 9-14**

In this parable, Jesus contrasts the prayers of a Pharisee and a tax collector. The Pharisee boasts of his righteousness and religious practices, while the tax collector humbly acknowledges his sinfulness and pleads for mercy. Jesus concludes that the tax collector, who approaches God with humility and repentance, is justified rather than the Pharisee.

Reflection:
This parable highlights the importance of humility in our relationship with God. True righteousness is not about self-righteousness or comparison with others but about recognizing our own need for God's mercy and approaching Him with a humble heart. This Lenten season, we are invited to embrace humility and seek God's grace sincerely.

Prayer:
Lord Jesus, teach us to approach You with humility and honesty, recognizing our need for Your mercy. Help us to avoid self-righteousness and to cultivate a heart that seeks Your forgiveness and grace. As we continue this Lent, may we grow in humility and align our lives more closely with Your will. Amen.

Sunday, March 30

❖ **Fourth Sunday of Lent**

> ➤ First Reading: Joshua 5: 9a, 10-12
> ➤ Responsorial Psalm: Psalms 34: 2-3, 4-5, 6-7
> ➤ Second Reading: Second Corinthians 5: 17-21
> ➤ Verse Before the Gospel: Luke 15: 18
> ➤ Gospel: Luke 15: 1-3,11-32
> ➤ Lectionary: 33

The Fourth Sunday of Lent, often called "Laetare Sunday," is a day of rejoicing and renewal as we progress through the Lenten season. Today's readings highlight themes of restoration, reconciliation, and the boundless mercy of God, inviting us to rejoice in the new life we have in Christ.

➤ First Reading: Joshua 5: 9a, 10-12

The Israelites celebrate the Passover and eat the produce of the land after their long journey through the desert. The manna that sustained them in the wilderness ceases as they begin to enjoy the abundance of the Promised Land. This marks a new chapter of fulfillment and blessing for the people of Israel.

Reflection:
The transition from the wilderness to the Promised Land symbolizes a journey from hardship to fulfillment. As we journey through Lent, we are invited to reflect on how God provides for us and leads us to spiritual abundance. This passage reminds us to recognize and give thanks for the blessings we receive as we move closer to Easter.

Prayer:
Lord God, we thank You for Your provision and the blessings You bestow upon us. As we continue our Lenten journey, help us to recognize the abundance You offer and guide us toward deeper faith and gratitude. May we embrace Your promises and live out our call to holiness with joy. Amen.

➤ Second Reading: Second Corinthians 5: 17-21

Paul speaks of the new creation in Christ, emphasizing that through Christ's reconciling work, we are transformed and made new. He calls us to be ambassadors of reconciliation, sharing the message of God's grace and forgiveness with the world.

Reflection:
This passage emphasizes the transformative power of Christ's work in our lives. As new creations in Him, we are called to live out our faith with a spirit of reconciliation and grace. This Lent, let us embrace our identity as new creations and actively work to embody and share the message of reconciliation that Christ has entrusted to us.

Prayer:
Gracious Father, thank You for the new life we have in Christ and the ministry of reconciliation You have given us. Help us to live out this new identity with faithfulness and joy. Empower us to be ambassadors of Your love and grace, sharing Your message of redemption with those around us. Amen.

➤ Gospel: Luke 15: 1-3, 11-32

In the parable of the Prodigal Son, Jesus tells of a young man who squanders his inheritance but is welcomed back by his father with open arms, while the older brother struggles with jealousy and resentment. The parable illustrates God's boundless mercy and the joy of reconciliation.

Reflection:

The parable of the Prodigal Son beautifully illustrates the depth of God's love and forgiveness. It calls us to reflect on our own experiences of forgiveness and to embrace God's mercy with humility. It also challenges us to extend that mercy to others, recognizing that God's grace is for everyone, regardless of their past.

Prayer:

Merciful Father, we thank You for Your endless love and forgiveness, as shown in the parable of the Prodigal Son. Help us to embrace Your mercy with humility and to extend that grace to others in our lives. As we rejoice in Your forgiveness, may we also become instruments of Your reconciliation in the world. Amen.

Monday, March 31

❖ Monday of the Fourth week of Lent

- ➢ First Reading: Isaiah 65: 17-21
- ➢ Responsorial Psalm: Psalms 30: 2 and 4, 5-6, 11-12a and 13b
- ➢ Verse Before the Gospel: Amos 5: 14
- ➢ Gospel: John 4: 43-54
- ➢ Lectionary: 244

As we progress through Lent, today's readings encourage us to anticipate the new creation that God promises and to deepen our trust in His power to heal and transform. The focus is on God's promise of renewal and the healing power of faith.

- ➢ First Reading: Isaiah 65: 17-21

In this passage, God promises to create a new heaven and a new earth, where former troubles will be forgotten and joy will abound. This vision of renewal and transformation highlights the hope and peace that God intends for His people.

Reflection:

Isaiah's vision of a new creation serves as a powerful reminder of God's ability to transform our lives and our world. As we continue our Lenten journey, let us focus on the promise of renewal that God offers us. This passage encourages us to trust in His ability to bring about profound change and to look forward to the joy and peace He intends for us.

Prayer:

Lord God, You have promised to create a new heaven and a new earth, where joy and peace will abound. As we journey through this season of Lent, help us to trust in Your promises and to open our hearts to the renewal You offer. May we embrace the transformation You bring and live in anticipation of the new creation You have prepared for us. Amen.

➤ Gospel: John 4: 43-54

In this Gospel, Jesus returns to Galilee and heals the son of a royal official who had requested His help. Jesus' healing of the boy from a distance demonstrates the power of faith and the authority of His word.

Reflection:

The story of the royal official's faith and the healing of his son underscores the importance of believing in Jesus' power and authority. It challenges us to deepen our own faith, trusting that Jesus can bring about healing and transformation in our lives. This passage invites us to approach Jesus with confidence and to trust in His promises, even when we do not see immediate results.

Prayer:

Lord Jesus, we are grateful for the healing power You have shown in the Gospel and the example of the royal official's faith. Increase our own faith and trust in Your word. Help us to believe in Your power to heal and transform our lives. As we continue through Lent, may we rely on Your promises and experience the renewal You bring. Amen.

April 2025

Tuesday, April 1

❖ Tuesday of the Fourth week of Lent

- First Reading: Ezekiel 47: 1-9, 12
- Responsorial Psalm: Psalms 46: 2-3, 5-6, 8-9
- Verse Before the Gospel: Psalms 51: 12a, 14a
- Gospel: John 5: 1-16
- Lectionary: 245

Today's readings draw our attention to the life-giving power of water, a symbol of the grace and healing that flow from God. As we continue our Lenten journey, we are invited to reflect on how God's grace renews and restores us, bringing us healing and new life.

First Reading: Ezekiel 47: 1-9, 12

In this vision, the prophet Ezekiel sees water flowing from the Temple, bringing life and healing wherever it goes. The water transforms the barren land into a fertile and vibrant place, teeming with life. Trees along the riverbanks bear fruit every month, and their leaves serve for healing.

Reflection:
Ezekiel's vision of water flowing from the Temple is a powerful symbol of God's grace. Just as water brings life to the earth, so does God's grace bring life and healing to our souls. During this Lenten season, let us allow God's grace to flow into our hearts, cleansing us and giving us new life. May we be open to the transforming power of His grace, which has the ability to heal our wounds and bring forth abundant fruit in our lives.

Prayer:
Lord God, we thank You for the gift of Your grace, which flows like living water into our lives. Help us to open our hearts to this grace, allowing it to cleanse and renew us. May Your healing waters restore what is broken and bring forth new life within us. As we journey through Lent, let Your grace guide us toward greater holiness and fruitfulness. Amen.

Gospel: John 5: 1-16

In this passage, Jesus heals a man who had been ill for thirty-eight years at the pool of Bethesda. Despite the man's long illness and inability to reach the healing waters of the pool, Jesus heals him with just a word, demonstrating His power and mercy.

Reflection:

The healing of the man at the pool of Bethesda reminds us that no matter how long we have been suffering or how impossible our situation may seem, Jesus has the power to heal and restore us. His mercy is not bound by time or circumstance. As we reflect on this passage, let us approach Jesus with confidence, knowing that He is always ready to heal us and to offer us new life. We are also reminded of the importance of not letting fear or doubt prevent us from receiving the healing grace that Jesus offers.

Prayer:

Lord Jesus, we are in awe of Your power to heal and restore. Just as You healed the man at the pool of Bethesda, we ask You to heal the areas of our lives that are in need of Your touch. Strengthen our faith so that we may trust in Your mercy and approach You with confidence, knowing that You desire to bring us new life. May we never let fear or doubt keep us from experiencing the fullness of Your grace. Amen.

Wednesday, April 2

- ❖ Wednesday of the Fourth week of Lent
- ❖ Saint Francis of Paola, hermit - Commemoration

- ➢ First Reading: Isaiah 49: 8-15
- ➢ Responsorial Psalm: Psalms 145: 8-9, 13cd-14, 17-18
- ➢ Verse Before the Gospel: John 11: 25a, 26
- ➢ Gospel: John 5: 17-30
- ➢ Lectionary: 246

As we honor Saint Francis of Paola today, a model of humility and simplicity, we are reminded of God's unwavering faithfulness. The readings invite us to reflect on God's compassion and the depth of His love for His people, even in times of difficulty and uncertainty.

- ➢ First Reading: Isaiah 49: 8-15

In this passage, the Lord assures His people that He has not forgotten them. Even though they may feel abandoned, God promises to restore them, to lead them with compassion, and to provide for them. The imagery of a mother caring for her child highlights the depth of God's love and commitment to His people.

Reflection:

Isaiah's words remind us that God's love for us is greater than any human love. Just as a mother cannot forget her child, so too God cannot forget us, even when we feel distant or forsaken. In the midst of our struggles, we are invited to trust in God's enduring love and to believe that He will guide us through every difficulty. This passage encourages us to hold on to hope, knowing that God is always with us, leading us toward His promises.

Prayer:
Loving Father, we thank You for Your unchanging love and faithfulness. Help us to trust in Your promises, especially in moments when we feel abandoned or alone. May we always remember that Your love for us is deeper than we can comprehend. Guide us with Your compassion and lead us to the fullness of life that You desire for us. Amen.

> Gospel: John 5: 17-30

In this Gospel passage, Jesus speaks of His unique relationship with the Father and the authority given to Him to give life and to judge. Jesus emphasizes that He works in perfect unity with the Father, bringing life to those who hear His word and believe.

Reflection:
Jesus' words reveal the profound mystery of His divine identity and mission. He is the source of life, the one who has been given all authority by the Father. As we listen to Jesus, we are invited to enter into a deeper relationship with Him, to trust in His words, and to receive the life that He offers. This passage calls us to reflect on our faith in Jesus and our openness to the life He wants to give us—a life that begins now and extends into eternity.

Prayer:
Lord Jesus, we praise You for the life You give us through Your word and Your love. Help us to grow in faith and to trust in the life-giving power of Your presence. May we listen to Your voice and follow You, knowing that You are leading us to eternal life. Strengthen our relationship with You, so that we may always remain close to You and experience the fullness of life that You offer. Amen.

Thursday, April 3

❖ Thursday of the Fourth week of Lent

> First Reading: Exodus 32: 7-14
> Responsorial Psalm: Psalms 106: 19-20, 21-22, 23
> Verse Before the Gospel: John 3: 16
> Gospel: John 5: 31-47
> Lectionary: 247

As we continue our Lenten journey, today's readings call us to reflect on our relationship with God and our response to His love. The first reading from Exodus reminds us of the dangers of turning away from God, while the Gospel challenges us to recognize and accept the testimony of Jesus. Let us open our hearts to God's call and seek to grow in faith and obedience.

➤ First Reading: Exodus 32: 7-14

In this passage, God tells Moses about the Israelites' sin of idolatry, as they turn away from Him to worship a golden calf. God's anger is kindled against His people, but Moses intercedes on their behalf, reminding God of His promises to Abraham, Isaac, and Israel. In response to Moses' plea, God relents and does not bring disaster upon His people.

Reflection:
This reading highlights the importance of faithfulness to God and the power of intercession. The Israelites' quick turn to idolatry serves as a warning against the temptations that can lead us away from God. Yet, it also shows God's mercy and willingness to forgive when we repent and turn back to Him. Moses' intercession is a powerful example of how prayer can change hearts and situations. We are called to be faithful to God, to avoid the idols of our time, and to trust in His mercy.

Prayer:
Merciful God, we confess that we sometimes turn away from You and follow our own desires. Forgive us for the times we have been unfaithful and help us to remain steadfast in our love for You. Grant us the grace to intercede for others, just as Moses did, and to trust in Your mercy and compassion. May we always seek to return to You, knowing that You are always ready to forgive and embrace us. Amen.

➤ Gospel: John 5: 31-47

In this passage, Jesus speaks to the Jews about the testimony that confirms His identity and mission. He explains that His works, the testimony of John the Baptist, the Scriptures, and the voice of the Father all bear witness to Him. Despite this, many fail to believe in Him because they seek glory from one another rather than from God.

Reflection:
Jesus challenges us to examine our hearts and our willingness to accept the truth. The people of His time struggled to recognize Him because their hearts were closed to the testimony that pointed to Him. This can also happen to us when we allow pride, fear, or the pursuit of worldly approval to cloud our vision. We are invited to open our hearts to the truth of Jesus, to seek God's glory rather than human praise, and to let His words transform our lives.

Prayer:
Lord Jesus, we thank You for the many ways You reveal Yourself to us. Help us to be open to the testimony of Your works, Your word, and Your Spirit. May we seek Your glory above all else and allow Your truth to guide our lives. Give us the grace to believe in You more deeply and to live in a way that reflects our faith in You. Amen.

Friday, April 4

- ❖ First Friday
- ❖ Day of Abstinance
- ❖ Friday of the Fourth week of Lent
- ❖ Saint Isidore, bishop and doctor - Commemoration

> First Reading: Wisdom 2: 1a, 12-22
> Responsorial Psalm: Psalms 34: 17-18, 19-20, 21 and 23
> Verse Before the Gospel: Matthew 4: 4b
> Gospel: John 7: 1-2, 10, 25-30
> Lectionary: 248

Today's readings bring us closer to the suffering of Christ as we approach the end of Lent. The first reading from the Book of Wisdom foreshadows the persecution of the just, while the Gospel of John shows the growing tension between Jesus and those who reject Him. As we honor Saint Isidore, a bishop and doctor of the Church, let us ask for his intercession to grow in wisdom and understanding of our faith.

> First Reading: Wisdom 2: 1a, 12-22

In this reading, the wicked plot against the righteous, mocking their faithfulness and planning to test the just man's patience and integrity. They believe that if the just man truly is God's child, God will protect him. However, the reading reveals that the wicked are blinded by their malice, unable to understand the mysteries of God and the reward for the faithful.

Reflection:
This passage is a prophetic reflection on the suffering of Christ, who was unjustly condemned by those who failed to recognize His divinity. It also speaks to the experience of many who suffer for righteousness' sake. The just person is often misunderstood and persecuted by those who do not see the value in a life of virtue. Yet, this reading reminds us that God's wisdom surpasses human understanding, and the faithful will ultimately be vindicated. In our own lives, we are called to remain steadfast in faith, even when faced with opposition or misunderstanding.

Prayer:
Lord God, grant us the grace to remain faithful in the face of trials and to trust in Your wisdom and justice. May we, like the just man in today's reading, hold fast to our integrity and live in a way that honors You. Help us to forgive those who persecute us and to pray for their conversion. Strengthen us in our

commitment to follow Your path, even when it is difficult, and let us find comfort in Your promise of eternal life. Amen.

> Gospel: John 7: 1-2, 10, 25-30

In this Gospel passage, Jesus moves discreetly to Jerusalem for the Feast of Tabernacles, aware of the growing threat to His life. Despite the plots against Him, He continues to teach openly in the temple, revealing His divine mission. The people are divided in their opinion of Him, with some recognizing Him as the Christ and others rejecting Him.

Reflection:
Jesus' courage and determination to fulfill His mission, even in the face of danger, is a powerful example for us. He knows that His time has not yet come, but He remains faithful to His calling, trusting in the Father's plan. This passage also highlights the division that Jesus' presence causes among the people, as they struggle to understand who He is. We too may encounter division and confusion in our journey of faith, but like Jesus, we are called to trust in God's timing and to persevere in our mission.

Prayer:
Lord Jesus, thank You for Your example of courage and faithfulness in the face of opposition. Help us to follow Your example, trusting in God's plan for our lives, even when we face uncertainty or danger. Give us the strength to stand firm in our faith and to proclaim Your truth with boldness and love. May we, like You, seek to do the Father's will in all things, knowing that His timing is perfect. Amen.

Saturday, April 5

- ❖ First Saturday
- ❖ Saturday of the Fourth week of Lent
- ❖ Saint Vincent Ferrer, priest - Commemoration

> First Reading: Jeremiah 11: 18-20
> Responsorial Psalm: Psalms 7: 2-3, 9bc-10, 11-12
> Verse Before the Gospel: Luke 8: 15
> Gospel: John 7: 40-53
> Lectionary: 249

Today, as we honor Saint Vincent Ferrer, known for his powerful preaching and missionary work, the readings remind us of the challenges faced by those who proclaim God's truth. The prophet Jeremiah and

Jesus both experience rejection and danger as they carry out their divine missions. As we reflect on their experiences, we are called to deepen our commitment to living out the Gospel in our own lives.

➢ First Reading: Jeremiah 11: 18-20

In this passage, the prophet Jeremiah reveals how the Lord made him aware of a plot against his life. Despite the danger, Jeremiah remains steadfast, entrusting his cause to God, whom he describes as a just judge who tests the heart and mind. He prays for the Lord's vengeance against his enemies, confident that God will vindicate him.

Reflection:

Jeremiah's experience is one of betrayal and danger, a reality often faced by those who stand up for truth and justice. His unwavering trust in God's justice is a powerful example for us. When we encounter hostility or opposition because of our faith, we too can turn to God, trusting that He sees our hearts and will ultimately bring about justice. Like Jeremiah, we are invited to place our confidence in God, who is our protector and our judge.

Prayer:

O God of justice, when we face opposition and danger for standing up for Your truth, help us to remain steadfast in our faith. Like Jeremiah, may we trust in Your wisdom and justice, knowing that You see our hearts and will vindicate us in Your time. Give us the courage to continue speaking Your truth with love, even when it is difficult, and protect us from those who seek to harm us. Amen.

➢ Gospel: John 7: 40-53

This Gospel passage recounts the division among the people regarding the identity of Jesus. Some recognize Him as the Prophet or the Christ, while others doubt, arguing that the Christ could not come from Galilee. The religious leaders, particularly the Pharisees, are resistant to believing in Jesus, even dismissing Nicodemus, who suggests that they give Jesus a fair hearing.

Reflection:

The division and confusion surrounding Jesus in this passage reflect the challenges of faith. Many were unable to see beyond their preconceptions and prejudices to recognize the truth of who Jesus was. Today, we still encounter resistance and division when it comes to matters of faith. Jesus calls us to be open to the truth, even when it challenges our understanding or requires us to step out in faith. Like Nicodemus, we are encouraged to seek the truth and to approach it with humility and openness.

Prayer:

Lord Jesus, in a world full of division and confusion, help us to seek and recognize the truth of who You are. Give us the grace to be open to Your teachings, even when they challenge our preconceptions or require us to step out of our comfort zones. Like Nicodemus, may we approach You with humility and a sincere desire to understand and follow Your will. Strengthen our faith and help us to be witnesses of Your love and truth in the world. Amen.

Sunday, April 6

❖ Fifth Sunday of Lent

- First Reading: Isaiah 43: 16-21
- Responsorial Psalm: Psalms 126: 1-2ab, 2cd-3, 4-5, 6
- Second Reading: Philippians 3: 8-14
- Verse Before the Gospel: Joel 2: 13
- Gospel: John 8: 1-11
- Lectionary: 36

As we enter the fifth Sunday of Lent, we are invited to reflect on God's mercy and the promise of new life. The readings today speak of God's power to transform our lives, to make a way where there seems to be no way, and to call us forward into a future filled with hope. As we prepare our hearts for the culmination of Lent in Holy Week, we are encouraged to let go of the past and press on toward the goal of Christ's love.

First Reading: Isaiah 43: 16-21

In this passage, the prophet Isaiah speaks of God as the one who makes a way through the sea and a path in the mighty waters. God reminds His people not to dwell on the past but to recognize the new things He is doing. He is creating streams in the wasteland and providing for His people in the desert.

Reflection:
God is always at work in our lives, even when we cannot see it. This reading invites us to trust in God's ability to bring about new beginnings, even in the most barren places. Just as He led the Israelites through the Red Sea, He is leading us through our own challenges and struggles. We are called to perceive the new things God is doing in our lives, to let go of the past, and to embrace the future He has prepared for us.

Prayer:
O Lord, You are the God who makes a way where there is no way. Help us to trust in Your power to transform our lives and our circumstances. Give us eyes to see the new things You are doing in our midst and the courage to step into the future You have prepared for us. May we always remember that with You, nothing is impossible. Amen.

➤ Second Reading: Philippians 3: 8-14

In his letter to the Philippians, Paul speaks of the surpassing worth of knowing Christ Jesus as his Lord. He considers everything else as loss compared to this. Paul strives to forget what lies behind and presses on toward the goal for the prize of God's heavenly call in Christ Jesus.

Reflection:
Paul's single-minded focus on Christ challenges us to examine our own priorities. What are we holding onto that keeps us from fully embracing Christ? Like Paul, we are called to let go of anything that hinders our relationship with God and to press on toward the goal of knowing and following Christ. This passage encourages us to keep our eyes fixed on Jesus, the source of our hope and strength, and to run the race of faith with perseverance.

Prayer:
Lord Jesus, help us to value nothing more than knowing You. Give us the grace to let go of anything that holds us back from fully following You. Strengthen our resolve to press on toward the goal of eternal life with You. May we run this race with our eyes fixed on You, trusting in Your love and grace to sustain us. Amen.

➤ Gospel: John 8: 1-11

This Gospel passage recounts the story of the woman caught in adultery. The scribes and Pharisees bring her before Jesus, hoping to trap Him, but Jesus responds with mercy. He challenges those without sin to cast the first stone, and when they all leave, He tells the woman that He does not condemn her and instructs her to go and sin no more.

Reflection:
This powerful encounter reveals the depth of God's mercy and forgiveness. Jesus does not condone the woman's sin, but neither does He condemn her. Instead, He offers her a new beginning, free from the judgment of others. This story reminds us that no one is beyond the reach of God's mercy. We are all sinners in need of forgiveness, and Jesus calls us to extend that same mercy to others. As we reflect on this passage, we are invited to examine our own hearts and to seek God's forgiveness for our sins, trusting in His boundless love.

Prayer:
Merciful Jesus, we thank You for the gift of Your forgiveness. Help us to recognize our own need for Your mercy and to extend that mercy to others. May we never be quick to judge, but always ready to forgive, as You have forgiven us. Teach us to live in the freedom of Your love, and guide us to follow Your command to go and sin no more. Amen.

Monday, April 7

❖ Saint John Baptist de la Salle, priest - Commemoration

- ➢ First Reading: Daniel 13: 1-9, 15-17, 19-30, 33-62 or Daniel 13: 41c-62
- ➢ Responsorial Psalm: Psalms 23: 1-3a, 3b-4, 5, 6
- ➢ Verse Before the Gospel: Ezekiel 33: 11
- ➢ Gospel: John 8: 12-20
- ➢ Lectionary: 251

Today, we commemorate Saint John Baptist de la Salle, a priest known for his dedication to the education of the poor and for founding the Institute of the Brothers of the Christian Schools. His life was a testament to the transformative power of education and faith. The readings for today invite us to reflect on integrity, light, and truth, qualities that Saint John Baptist de la Salle embodied in his life and ministry.

➢ First Reading: Daniel 13: 1-9, 15-17, 19-30, 33-62 or Daniel 13: 41c-62

The story of Susanna is one of integrity and courage. Accused falsely by corrupt elders, Susanna stands firm in her innocence, trusting in God's justice. God hears her prayer, and through the wisdom of the young prophet Daniel, her innocence is proven, and the wicked elders are condemned.

Reflection:
This reading emphasizes the importance of standing firm in righteousness, even in the face of false accusations and adversity. Susanna's faith in God and her refusal to yield to the pressure of her accusers is an example for all who seek to live a life of integrity. The story also reminds us that God is the ultimate judge who sees all and will bring justice to those who are faithful to Him.

Prayer:
O God of justice, grant us the strength to stand firm in our convictions and to trust in Your righteous judgment. Help us to live lives of integrity, even when we face challenges and opposition. May we always seek to do what is right in Your eyes, and may Your truth prevail in our hearts and in our world. Amen.

➢ Gospel: John 8: 12-20

In this passage, Jesus declares, "I am the light of the world. Whoever follows me will not walk in darkness, but will have the light of life." The Pharisees challenge Jesus, questioning His authority and testimony. Jesus responds by affirming His divine origin and mission, pointing to the Father as His witness.

Reflection:
Jesus, the light of the world, invites us to follow Him and walk in His light. In a world filled with darkness and confusion, His light brings clarity, truth, and life. This Gospel challenges us to examine the areas of our lives where we may still be walking in darkness and to invite Jesus' light into those places. As we follow Him, we are called to reflect His light to others, becoming beacons of hope and truth in a world that desperately needs it.

Prayer:
Lord Jesus, You are the light of the world. Shine Your light into our hearts, dispelling all darkness and leading us into the fullness of life. Help us to follow You faithfully, trusting in Your guidance and truth. May we reflect Your light in our words and actions, bringing hope and clarity to those around us. Amen.

Tuesday, April 8

❖ Tuesday of the Fifth week of Lent

- First Reading: Numbers 21: 4-9
- Responsorial Psalm: Psalms 102: 2-3, 16-18, 19-21
- Gospel: John 8: 21-30
- Lectionary: 252

As we journey through the fifth week of Lent, today's readings bring to mind the theme of salvation and redemption. In both the First Reading and the Gospel, we see the powerful imagery of being lifted up, a symbol of healing and salvation that ultimately points to Christ on the cross.

- First Reading: Numbers 21: 4-9

In this reading, the Israelites, frustrated by their journey in the wilderness, speak against God and Moses. In response, God sends fiery serpents among them, and many are bitten and die. When the people repent, God instructs Moses to make a bronze serpent and set it on a pole. Anyone who looks at the bronze serpent is healed from the serpent's bite.

Reflection:
The bronze serpent lifted up on a pole is a powerful symbol of healing and redemption, foreshadowing the crucifixion of Christ. Just as the Israelites were healed by looking at the bronze serpent, we are healed and saved by looking to Jesus, who was lifted up on the cross for our sins. This reading calls us to recognize our need for repentance and to turn our gaze towards Christ, trusting in His power to heal and save us.

Prayer:
Merciful God, we acknowledge our sinfulness and our need for Your healing touch. As we reflect on the

Israelites' journey, help us to turn away from all that separates us from You and to look upon Christ, our Savior. May we find healing, forgiveness, and new life in His sacrifice on the cross. Amen.

➤ Gospel: John 8: 21-30

In this Gospel passage, Jesus continues His teaching in the temple, speaking of His coming departure and warning the Pharisees that they will die in their sins if they do not believe in Him. He reveals that when He is "lifted up," they will know that He is the one sent by the Father.

Reflection:
Jesus' words about being "lifted up" clearly refer to His crucifixion, where His true identity as the Son of God will be revealed. This passage reminds us of the gravity of rejecting Christ, but also of the immense grace available to those who believe in Him. As we approach the final days of Lent, this Gospel challenges us to deepen our faith in Jesus and to recognize Him as the one sent by the Father for our salvation.

Prayer:
Lord Jesus, You were lifted up on the cross to bring salvation to the world. Open our hearts to believe in You more deeply and to trust in Your saving power. May we never turn away from the grace You offer, but always look to You with faith and gratitude. Lead us into a deeper understanding of Your love and the mystery of Your sacrifice. Amen.

Wednesday, April 9

❖ Wednesday of the Fifth week of Lent

- ➤ First Reading: Daniel 3: 14-20, 91-92, 95
- ➤ Responsorial Psalm: Daniel 3: 52, 53, 54, 55, 56
- ➤ Verse Before the Gospel: Luke 8: 15
- ➤ Gospel: John 8: 31-42
- ➤ Lectionary: 253

Today's readings offer a profound reflection on the power of faith and the freedom found in following Christ. As we continue our Lenten journey, we are encouraged to deepen our commitment to God, trusting in His protection and the truth that sets us free.

➤ First Reading: Daniel 3: 14-20, 91-92, 95

In this passage, King Nebuchadnezzar confronts Shadrach, Meshach, and Abednego, demanding that they worship the golden statue he has set up. When they refuse, professing their unwavering faith in God, the king orders them to be thrown into a blazing furnace. Miraculously, they are unharmed, and the king sees a fourth figure in the fire, "like a son of God." Astonished, Nebuchadnezzar praises the God of Israel, acknowledging His power to save.

Reflection:
The courage of Shadrach, Meshach, and Abednego in the face of death is a testament to the power of faith. Their story reminds us that God is with us even in the most trying circumstances, protecting and delivering us. Their refusal to compromise their faith, even under threat of death, challenges us to remain steadfast in our beliefs, trusting that God will be with us in our own trials and tribulations.

Prayer:
Almighty God, give us the strength and courage of Shadrach, Meshach, and Abednego. Help us to stand firm in our faith, even when faced with challenges and persecution. May we always trust in Your presence and protection, knowing that You are with us in every trial. May our lives be a witness to Your saving power. Amen.

➤ Gospel: John 8: 31-42

In today's Gospel, Jesus addresses the Jews who had believed in Him, telling them that if they remain in His word, they will truly be His disciples, and they will know the truth, and the truth will set them free. The people misunderstand, claiming they are descendants of Abraham and have never been enslaved. Jesus clarifies that anyone who commits sin is a slave to sin, but He, as the Son, can set them free.

Reflection:
Jesus' words highlight the distinction between physical and spiritual freedom. While the people took pride in their lineage, Jesus points to the deeper bondage of sin. True freedom, He teaches, comes not from heritage or external status but from embracing His teachings and allowing His truth to transform us. As we reflect on this passage, we are called to examine the areas in our lives where sin may still hold us captive and to seek the freedom that only Christ can give.

Prayer:
Lord Jesus, You offer us true freedom through Your word and Your sacrifice. Help us to remain in Your word and to be open to the transforming power of Your truth. Free us from the bondage of sin and lead us into the fullness of life that You desire for us. May we always seek Your truth and live as Your faithful disciples. Amen.

Thursday, April 10

❖ **Thursday of the Fifth week of Lent**

> ➢ First Reading: Genesis 17: 3-9
> ➢ Responsorial Psalm: Psalms 105: 4-5, 6-7, 8-9
> ➢ Verse Before the Gospel: Psalms 95: 8
> ➢ Gospel: John 8: 51-59
> ➢ Lectionary: 254

As we approach the end of our Lenten journey, today's readings invite us to reflect on God's covenant with His people and the identity of Jesus as the eternal Word. We are called to deepen our understanding of God's promises and to recognize the profound truth of Jesus' divinity.

> ➢ **First Reading: Genesis 17: 3-9**

In this passage, God renews His covenant with Abram, promising that he will be the father of many nations. God changes Abram's name to Abraham, signifying his new identity and role in salvation history. The covenant is an everlasting bond between God and Abraham's descendants, a promise of blessing and a call to faithfulness.

Reflection:
The covenant between God and Abraham is foundational to our faith, marking the beginning of God's plan to gather a people unto Himself. Abraham's name change reflects the transformation that comes from being in a covenantal relationship with God. We, too, are called to live as heirs of this covenant, embracing our identity as God's people and responding with faith and obedience to His promises.

Prayer:
Heavenly Father, You established Your covenant with Abraham, promising to be with him and his descendants forever. Help us to live as true children of this covenant, faithful to Your commands and trusting in Your promises. May our lives be a testimony to Your faithfulness, and may we always walk in Your ways. Amen.

> ➢ **Gospel: John 8: 51-59**

In today's Gospel, Jesus makes a profound declaration about His identity, telling the Jews that whoever keeps His word will never see death. The people are confused and challenge Him, questioning how He could say such a thing. Jesus responds by revealing that He existed before Abraham, using the divine name

"I AM" to affirm His eternal existence. This claim leads the crowd to attempt to stone Him, but Jesus evades them.

Reflection:
Jesus' declaration of "I AM" is a powerful affirmation of His divinity, directly connecting Him to the God who revealed Himself to Moses in the burning bush. This passage challenges us to confront the mystery of Jesus' identity and to acknowledge Him not just as a teacher or prophet, but as the eternal Son of God. His words also remind us of the promise of eternal life for those who keep His word, offering us hope and assurance as we follow Him.

Prayer:
Lord Jesus, You are the eternal Word, existing before all time and offering us the promise of eternal life. Help us to keep Your word and to recognize You as the "I AM," the one true God. Strengthen our faith, especially when we face doubts or challenges, and lead us into the fullness of life that You promise. May we always honor You as Lord and God, living in the light of Your truth. Amen.

Friday, April 11

- ❖ Day of Abstinance
- ❖ Friday of the Fifth week of Lent
- ❖ Saint Stanislaus, Bishop and martyr - Commemoration

> First Reading: Jeremiah 20: 10-13
>
> Responsorial Psalm: Psalms 18: 2-3a, 3bc-4, 5-6, 7
>
> Verse Before the Gospel: John 6: 63c, 68c
>
> Gospel: John 10: 31-42
>
> Lectionary: 255

As we continue our Lenten journey, today's readings focus on the prophetic courage of Jeremiah and the profound claims of Jesus. We are invited to reflect on the suffering endured for faith and the call to recognize and respond to Jesus as the source of eternal life.

> First Reading: Jeremiah 20: 10-13

In this passage, Jeremiah, the prophet, expresses his anguish over the rejection and threats he faces from those he is called to serve. Despite his suffering, he remains steadfast, trusting in God's justice and deliverance. He prays for rescue from his enemies and proclaims his trust in God's strength and salvation.

Reflection:
Jeremiah's suffering as a prophet highlights the cost of following God's call and speaking His truth. His unwavering trust in God, despite personal anguish, is a model for us as we face our own challenges. It reminds us that faithfulness often involves struggle and opposition but that God is always our refuge and deliverer.

Prayer:
Lord God, You called Jeremiah to be Your prophet in difficult times. Grant us the courage to speak Your truth boldly, even when faced with opposition. Strengthen our faith and trust in Your deliverance, and help us to remain steadfast in our commitment to You. May we always find solace in Your presence and support in our times of need. Amen.

> Gospel: John 10: 31-42

In this Gospel passage, Jesus faces hostility from the Jewish leaders who accuse Him of blasphemy for claiming to be one with the Father. Jesus responds by pointing to His works as evidence of His divine mission and authority. Despite their rejection, many come to believe in Him, recognizing the truth of His words and deeds.

Reflection:
Jesus' defense of His divine identity underscores the profound mystery of the Trinity and the unity of His mission with the Father. His works testify to His divine authority and the truth of His claims. This passage challenges us to recognize Jesus as the true Son of God and to respond with faith and acceptance of His message, even in the face of doubt and opposition.

Prayer:
Lord Jesus, You revealed Your divine identity through Your words and works. Open our hearts to recognize You as the true Son of God and to believe in Your message. Help us to stand firm in our faith and to witness to Your truth in our lives. Strengthen us to follow You with courage and conviction, trusting in Your promise of eternal life. Amen.

Saturday, April 12

❖ Saturday of the Fifth week of Lent

> First Reading: Ezekiel 37: 21-28
> Responsorial Psalm: Jeremiah 31: 10, 11-12, 13
> Verse Before the Gospel: Ezekiel 18: 31
> Gospel: John 11: 45-56
> Lectionary: 256

As we approach the final days of Lent, today's readings invite us to contemplate God's promise of restoration and unity, as well as the growing tension surrounding Jesus' mission. We are called to reflect on the fulfillment of God's plan and our response to His work in our lives.

➢ First Reading: Ezekiel 37: 21-28

In this passage, the Lord speaks through the prophet Ezekiel, promising to gather the scattered people of Israel and bring them back to their own land. God pledges to unite them under one king and make a covenant of peace with them. He assures them that they will be His people, and He will dwell among them forever.

Reflection:
Ezekiel's prophecy of the reunification and restoration of Israel is a powerful reminder of God's faithfulness to His promises. It foreshadows the coming of Christ, who unites all people under His kingship. This passage invites us to trust in God's plan for our lives and to embrace the unity and peace that He offers through Jesus.

Prayer:
O God of restoration, You promised to gather Your people and dwell among them forever. Unite our hearts in Your love and peace. May we live as Your faithful people, trusting in Your covenant and following Your Son, our King. Help us to recognize Your presence in our lives and to be instruments of unity and peace in our world. Amen.

➢ Gospel: John 11: 45-56

In this Gospel passage, following the raising of Lazarus, the tension surrounding Jesus reaches a critical point. The miraculous sign leads many to believe in Him, but it also intensifies the opposition from the religious leaders. Fearing the loss of their power and the potential destruction of their nation, they plot to put Jesus to death, not realizing that His death would indeed bring about the salvation of all.

Reflection:
The plot against Jesus highlights the tragic irony of the religious leaders' actions. In their attempt to preserve their nation, they unwittingly set in motion the events that would bring about the fulfillment of God's redemptive plan. This passage calls us to recognize Jesus as the source of true life and to reflect on how we respond to His presence and works in our lives.

Prayer:
Lord Jesus, in the face of opposition, You remained faithful to Your mission of love and redemption. Help us to recognize You as the source of true life and to trust in Your saving power. May we follow You with unwavering faith, even when we face challenges or opposition. Strengthen our resolve to live according to Your will and to witness to Your love in all that we do. Amen.

Sunday, April 13

❖ Passion (Palm) Sunday

- Procession: Luke 19: 28-40
- First Reading: Isaiah 50: 4-7
- Responsorial Psalm: Psalms 22: 8-9, 17-18, 19-20, 23-24
- Second Reading: Philippians 2:6-11
- Verse Before the Gospel: Philippians 2: 8-9
- Gospel: Luke 22: 14 – 23: 56
- Lectionary: 37/38

On this solemn day, we begin Holy Week, the most sacred time of the liturgical year. Passion (Palm) Sunday marks Jesus' triumphal entry into Jerusalem, where He is welcomed as a king, only to be later rejected and crucified. Today's liturgy invites us to journey with Christ through His Passion, reflecting on His immense love and sacrifice for humanity.

➢ Procession: Luke 19: 28-40

In this passage, Jesus enters Jerusalem riding on a colt, fulfilling the prophecy of the humble King. The crowds joyfully welcome Him, spreading their cloaks on the road and praising God for all the miracles they have seen. Yet, Jesus knows that these same people will soon turn against Him.

Reflection:
The crowds' cheers and the waving of palms remind us of the fleeting nature of human approval. While the people welcome Jesus with joy, their understanding of His kingship is incomplete. This moment invites us to consider how we receive Christ in our lives—are we ready to accept Him as He truly is, even when it challenges us?

Prayer:
Lord Jesus, as You entered Jerusalem, You were met with shouts of joy and praise. Help us to welcome You into our hearts with true understanding and commitment. May we follow You with steadfast faith, especially when the journey becomes difficult. Strengthen our resolve to remain faithful to You, our humble King. Amen.

➢ First Reading: Isaiah 50: 4-7

The prophet Isaiah speaks of the Suffering Servant who willingly accepts suffering and humiliation. Despite being struck and spat upon, He remains steadfast, trusting in God's help and refusing to be disgraced.

Reflection:
Isaiah's portrayal of the Suffering Servant points directly to Jesus, who endured unimaginable pain and suffering for our salvation. His unwavering trust in the Father, even in the face of rejection and abuse, challenges us to deepen our own trust in God, especially in times of trial.

Prayer:
O Lord, in Your Passion, You bore the weight of our sins with humility and trust in the Father. Teach us to embrace our own crosses with the same trust and to find strength in Your example. May our faith remain strong, even in the face of suffering, knowing that You are always with us. Amen.

➢ Second Reading: Philippians 2: 6-11

This passage from St. Paul's letter to the Philippians captures the profound mystery of Christ's humility and exaltation. Jesus, though divine, emptied Himself, becoming human and obedient to death on a cross. Because of this, God exalted Him, and every knee shall bow at His name.

Reflection:
Paul's hymn of Christ's humility and exaltation invites us to reflect on the paradox of the cross. Jesus' ultimate act of love—His death on the cross—becomes the very means of His glorification. We are called to imitate this humility in our own lives, trusting that in losing ourselves for Christ, we will find true life.

Prayer:
Lord Jesus, You humbled Yourself to become one of us, and You obeyed the Father even unto death. Teach us to follow Your example of humility and self-giving love. May we seek not our own glory but Yours alone, and may we be united with You in Your victory over sin and death. Amen.

➢ Gospel: Luke 22: 14 – 23: 56

The Passion narrative in Luke recounts the events from the Last Supper to Jesus' crucifixion and burial. It is a profound and emotional journey through Jesus' suffering, betrayal, and death, highlighting His mercy, forgiveness, and ultimate sacrifice for humanity.

Reflection:
As we listen to the Passion narrative, we are invited to enter deeply into the mystery of Christ's suffering and death. Each moment—from the agony in the garden to the final words on the cross—reveals the depth of God's love for us. This is a time for profound reflection and gratitude, as we contemplate the cost of our redemption.

Prayer:
Lord Jesus, as we journey with You through Your Passion, open our hearts to the depths of Your love and sacrifice. Help us to stand with You in Your suffering, to seek forgiveness for our sins, and to embrace the

new life You offer through Your death and resurrection. May Your Passion inspire us to live lives of greater love, mercy, and service to others. Amen.

Monday, April 14

❖ Monday of Holy Week

- First Reading: Isaiah 42: 1-7
- Responsorial Psalm: Psalms 27: 1, 2, 3, 13-14
- Gospel: John 12: 1-11
- Lectionary: 257

As we enter into the heart of Holy Week, the readings today draw us closer to the profound mystery of Christ's Passion. Monday of Holy Week focuses on the anointing of Jesus at Bethany, a symbolic preparation for His burial. The passages today invite us to reflect on the servanthood of Jesus and the selfless love that underpins His journey to the cross.

First Reading: Isaiah 42: 1-7

This passage from Isaiah introduces the first of the "Servant Songs," describing God's chosen servant who will bring forth justice to the nations. The servant is gentle, steadfast, and filled with God's Spirit. He will open the eyes of the blind and set captives free, establishing a covenant for the people.

Reflection:
Isaiah's Servant Song paints a picture of a Messiah who is both powerful and gentle. Jesus, the Servant of God, embodies this prophecy perfectly. He is the light to the nations, bringing hope and justice through His sacrificial love. As we reflect on these words, we are called to recognize Christ as the true Servant who liberates us from the darkness of sin and guides us into the light of God's love.

Prayer:
Lord Jesus, You are the Servant of God who brings justice and peace to the world. Help us to follow Your example of humility and service. Open our eyes to see the needs of those around us, and grant us the courage to serve others with the same love and compassion that You have shown us. Amen.

Gospel: John 12: 1-11

In this Gospel passage, Jesus is anointed by Mary at Bethany, just days before His crucifixion. Mary's act of anointing Jesus' feet with expensive perfume is an expression of deep love and devotion. Meanwhile, Judas criticizes her, but Jesus defends Mary's action, recognizing it as a preparation for His burial.

Reflection:

Mary's act of anointing Jesus with costly perfume is a powerful gesture of love and reverence. It signifies her understanding of Jesus' impending death and her desire to honor Him. Judas' reaction, however, highlights a stark contrast between selfless devotion and self-serving motives. As we meditate on this passage, we are invited to consider our own attitudes towards Jesus—are we willing to give Him our best, or do we hold back out of fear or selfishness?

Prayer:

Lord Jesus, as Mary anointed Your feet with love and devotion, teach us to give ourselves fully to You. May we not hold back in our love for You, but offer You our whole hearts, knowing that You gave everything for us. Help us to resist the temptations of selfishness and to embrace a spirit of generosity and service. Amen.

Tuesday, April 15

❖ Tuesday of Holy Week

➤ First Reading: Isaiah 49: 1-6
➤ Responsorial Psalm: Psalms 71: 1-2, 3-4a, 5ab-6ab, 15 and 17
➤ Gospel: John 13: 21-33, 36-38
➤ Lectionary: 258

On this Tuesday of Holy Week, we delve deeper into the events leading to Jesus' Passion. The readings today present us with the growing tension and betrayal that Jesus faces as He moves closer to the cross. In the first reading, we hear of the Servant of God, whose mission seems to be in vain, but who remains confident in God's plan. In the Gospel, Jesus reveals the impending betrayal by one of His own disciples, underscoring the sorrow and loneliness that accompany His journey.

➤ First Reading: Isaiah 49: 1-6

In this second Servant Song, the prophet Isaiah speaks of a servant called by God from the womb, destined to be a light to the nations. Despite apparent failure and discouragement, the servant places trust in God's plan, knowing that his mission extends far beyond the restoration of Israel to include all peoples.

Reflection:

The Servant in Isaiah expresses a deep sense of purpose, even in the face of apparent failure. This mirrors Jesus' own experience as He approaches His Passion. Although His mission appears to be heading towards defeat, Jesus remains steadfast, trusting in the Father's will. We are reminded that in moments of doubt and discouragement, our faith should rest in God's greater plan, which often surpasses our understanding.

Prayer:
Lord, in times of doubt and discouragement, help us to trust in Your plan. Like Your servant, may we be lights to those around us, reflecting Your love and hope even when the path seems uncertain. Strengthen our resolve to fulfill the mission You have entrusted to us, knowing that our efforts are never in vain when offered to You. Amen.

> ➤ Gospel: John 13: 21-33, 36-38

In this passage from John's Gospel, Jesus, during the Last Supper, becomes troubled and reveals that one of His disciples will betray Him. The disciples are shocked, and Peter, in his eagerness, promises to follow Jesus even unto death. Yet, Jesus predicts Peter's denial, illustrating the frailty of human commitment in the face of fear.

Reflection:
The foretelling of Judas's betrayal and Peter's denial brings to light the complexities of human weakness and the pain of betrayal that Jesus experiences. Despite knowing the hearts of His disciples, Jesus continues to love and lead them. This challenges us to examine our own faithfulness to Christ. Do we remain steadfast in our commitment, or do we falter when trials arise? Jesus' response to both Judas and Peter teaches us about the depth of His mercy and the call to repentance.

Prayer:
Lord Jesus, You faced betrayal and denial from those closest to You, yet You continued to love them. Help us to remain faithful to You in all circumstances. When we falter, give us the grace to repent and return to Your embrace. May our love for You be steadfast, grounded in a deep trust in Your unending mercy. Amen.

Wednesday, April 16

❖ **Wednesday of Holy Week**

> ➤ First Reading: Isaiah 50: 4-9a
> ➤ Responsorial Psalm: Psalms 69: 8-10, 21-22, 31 and 33-34
> ➤ Gospel: Matthew 26: 14-25
> ➤ Lectionary: 259

As we reach the midpoint of Holy Week, traditionally known as "Spy Wednesday," our readings draw us deeper into the unfolding drama of Jesus' Passion. The first reading from Isaiah reflects on the suffering servant who is steadfast despite persecution. In the Gospel, we witness Judas making the fateful decision to betray Jesus, setting in motion the final events leading to the crucifixion. Today's readings invite us to contemplate the weight of betrayal and the steadfastness required to follow God's will, even in the face of suffering.

➢ First Reading: Isaiah 50: 4-9a

This passage is part of the third Servant Song in Isaiah, where the servant of the Lord speaks of his role as a disciple who listens and obeys. Despite suffering, humiliation, and rejection, the servant remains resolute, trusting in the Lord's help and justice. The passage ends with a declaration of confidence in God's vindication, leaving no room for shame.

Reflection:
The Servant in Isaiah exemplifies unwavering faith in God amidst persecution. His willingness to endure suffering without retaliation is a profound lesson in humility and trust. This foreshadows Jesus' own Passion, where He too will endure mockery and abuse without resistance, trusting entirely in the Father's plan. We are challenged to reflect on our own reactions to adversity—do we respond with faith and patience, or do we let fear and anger guide us?

Prayer:
Lord, grant us the courage and strength to endure trials with the same faith and trust as Your servant. When we face challenges and opposition, may we not falter, but rather lean on Your promises and stand firm in Your love. Help us to be faithful disciples, listening to Your voice and following wherever You lead. Amen.

➢ Gospel: Matthew 26: 14-25

In this Gospel passage, Judas Iscariot goes to the chief priests and agrees to betray Jesus for thirty pieces of silver. At the Last Supper, Jesus, fully aware of the betrayal, shares this knowledge with His disciples, causing great distress among them. Judas, in a moment of profound duplicity, asks, "Surely it is not I, Rabbi?" and Jesus affirms that it is indeed him.

Reflection:
The betrayal of Judas is one of the most poignant moments in the Gospel narrative. For thirty pieces of silver, Judas chooses to betray his teacher and friend, setting the stage for Jesus' arrest and crucifixion. This act of betrayal forces us to examine our own lives—how often do we, in smaller ways, betray our relationship with Christ? Whether through neglect, sin, or failing to stand up for our faith, we too can betray the love and trust Jesus has placed in us. Yet, even in this moment of deep betrayal, Jesus does not lash out but instead continues His journey to the cross, offering us a powerful example of forgiveness and grace.

Prayer:
Lord Jesus, in the face of betrayal, You remained steadfast in love and mercy. Help us to recognize the ways we may betray You in our daily lives, and grant us the grace to repent and return to Your embrace. May we always value our relationship with You above all else, staying true to Your call even when tempted by the allure of worldly gain. Amen.

Thursday, April 17

❖ Holy Thursday

- ➢ First Reading: Exodus 12: 1-8, 11-14
- ➢ Responsorial Psalm: Psalms 116: 12-13, 15-16bc, 17-18
- ➢ Second Reading: First Corinthians 11: 23-26
- ➢ Verse Before the Gospel: John 13: 34
- ➢ Gospel: John 13: 1-15
- ➢ Lectionary: 39

Holy Thursday marks the beginning of the sacred Triduum, the three most solemn days in the Christian calendar. On this day, we commemorate the Last Supper, where Jesus instituted the Eucharist and washed the feet of His disciples, setting an example of humble service. The readings today invite us to reflect on the profound mysteries of our faith—the sacrifice of the Lamb, the institution of the Eucharist, and the call to love one another through humble service.

➢ First Reading: Exodus 12: 1-8, 11-14

In this passage, God instructs Moses and Aaron regarding the Passover, the night when the Israelites were to be delivered from slavery in Egypt. The Israelites were to sacrifice a lamb, eat it with unleavened bread and bitter herbs, and mark their doorposts with its blood. This act of faith and obedience would protect them from the final plague and signal the beginning of their journey to freedom.

Reflection:
The Passover lamb foreshadows Christ, the Lamb of God, who would be sacrificed for our deliverance from sin and death. Just as the blood of the lamb protected the Israelites, the blood of Christ protects and redeems us. On Holy Thursday, as we recall the institution of the Eucharist, we are reminded that every Mass is a participation in this great mystery of our salvation. We are invited to partake in the Body and Blood of Christ, the true Lamb who takes away the sins of the world.

Prayer:
O God of deliverance, as You saved the Israelites through the Passover, so too have You saved us through the sacrifice of Your Son, Jesus Christ. Help us to approach the Eucharistic table with hearts full of gratitude and reverence, recognizing the great gift of Your love. May we live our lives as a continual offering of thanksgiving, sharing in Christ's mission of love and service. Amen.

➢ Second Reading: First Corinthians 11: 23-26

In this reading, Saint Paul recounts the words of Jesus at the Last Supper, instituting the Eucharist. Jesus took bread, gave thanks, broke it, and said, "This is my body that is for you. Do this in remembrance of me." He then took the cup and declared, "This cup is the new covenant in my blood. Do this, as often as you drink it, in remembrance of me." Saint Paul reminds the faithful that by eating the bread and drinking the cup, they proclaim the Lord's death until He comes.

Reflection:

The institution of the Eucharist is central to our faith. In the simple elements of bread and wine, Jesus offers us His Body and Blood, a perpetual memorial of His sacrifice and a source of grace for our lives. Each time we celebrate the Eucharist, we are drawn into the mystery of Christ's death and resurrection, renewing our covenant with God and one another. This sacrament not only nourishes us spiritually but also calls us to be Christ's presence in the world, living out His command to love one another as He has loved us.

Prayer:

Lord Jesus, in the gift of the Eucharist, You have given us the greatest sign of Your love. As we receive Your Body and Blood, may we be transformed by Your grace and strengthened to follow Your example of selfless love. Help us to become more like You, offering ourselves in service to others and proclaiming Your love in all we do. Amen.

➢ Gospel: John 13: 1-15

In this Gospel passage, Jesus washes the feet of His disciples during the Last Supper, a gesture of profound humility and service. After washing their feet, Jesus instructs them, saying, "If I, therefore, the master and teacher, have washed your feet, you ought to wash one another's feet. I have given you a model to follow, so that as I have done for you, you should also do."

Reflection:

Jesus' act of washing the feet of His disciples is a powerful symbol of the servant leadership to which all Christians are called. It challenges us to reconsider our notions of power and greatness, reminding us that true leadership is found in humble service to others. On Holy Thursday, as we remember this act of humility, we are invited to follow Christ's example in our own lives. Whether through small acts of kindness or significant sacrifices, we are called to serve one another with love and humility, just as Christ has served us.

Prayer:

Lord Jesus, You have shown us the true meaning of love and leadership through Your example of humble service. Help us to follow in Your footsteps, embracing the call to serve others with love and humility. May our lives reflect Your love, and may we always seek to lift up those in need, washing their feet with the same love and compassion You have shown us. Amen.

Friday, April 18

- ❖ Day of Fast and Abstinance
- ❖ Good Friday

> First Reading: Isaiah 52: 13 – 53: 12
> Responsorial Psalm: Psalms 31: 2, 6, 12-13, 15-16, 17, 25
> Second Reading: Hebrews 4: 14-16; 5: 7-9
> Verse Before the Gospel: Philippians 2: 8-9
> Gospel: John 18: 1 – 19: 42
> Lectionary: 40

Good Friday is the most solemn day of the Christian calendar, marking the crucifixion and death of our Lord Jesus Christ. The readings of today take us through the Suffering Servant's prophecy in Isaiah, the depth of Christ's obedience in Hebrews, and the Passion narrative in John's Gospel. This day is a profound reminder of the sacrifice Jesus made for the salvation of humanity, inviting us to contemplate the immense love that led Him to the cross.

> First Reading: Isaiah 52: 13 – 53: 12

This passage, often referred to as the Song of the Suffering Servant, is a prophetic description of the Messiah's suffering and the redemption that would come through His pain and sacrifice. The Servant is described as one who bears the iniquities of others, is despised and rejected, and yet, through His suffering, brings healing and salvation to many.

Reflection:
The Suffering Servant in Isaiah is a powerful prefiguration of Christ's Passion. It reminds us that Jesus, though innocent, took upon Himself the sins of the world. His suffering was not in vain; it was redemptive, bringing healing and peace to all who believe. As we meditate on this prophecy, we are called to a deeper understanding of the cost of our salvation and the boundless love of God, who did not spare His own Son but gave Him up for us all.

Prayer:
O suffering Christ, through Your wounds, we are healed. In Your pain, we find our salvation. As we reflect on Your Passion, help us to comprehend the depth of Your love and the magnitude of the sacrifice You made for us. May this knowledge lead us to live lives worthy of Your gift, embracing our crosses with faith and trust in Your redemptive power. Amen.

➢ Second Reading: Hebrews 4: 14-16; 5: 7-9

In this passage from Hebrews, we are reminded of Jesus as the great High Priest, who, though sinless, fully shared in our humanity and suffering. Through His obedience and His prayers, even in the face of death, He became the source of eternal salvation for all who obey Him.

Reflection:

Jesus, the great High Priest, understands our weaknesses and sufferings because He has experienced them Himself. His obedience, even unto death, is a model for us to follow. In moments of suffering and temptation, we can approach Him with confidence, knowing that He intercedes for us with compassion and mercy. Good Friday calls us to unite our own sufferings with those of Christ, trusting that through them, God can bring about our sanctification and the salvation of others.

Prayer:

Merciful Jesus, our great High Priest, You understand the depth of our struggles because You have endured them Yourself. Help us to turn to You in our moments of need, confident in Your compassion and mercy. Strengthen us to follow Your example of obedience, even in the face of suffering, and make us instruments of Your salvation in the world. Amen.

➢ Gospel: John 18: 1 – 19: 42

John's Gospel gives us the narrative of the Passion of Christ, from His arrest in the Garden of Gethsemane to His crucifixion and burial. This detailed account reveals the betrayal, trials, suffering, and ultimate death of Jesus on the cross. It is a story of profound love, sacrifice, and the fulfillment of God's redemptive plan.

Reflection:

The Passion narrative in John's Gospel invites us to walk with Jesus through His final hours, witnessing His steadfast love and unwavering commitment to the Father's will. It is a call to remember that His suffering was borne out of love for each one of us. As we contemplate the cross, we see the ultimate act of love and the complete gift of self. Today, as we venerate the cross, let us not only recall the events of Good Friday but allow them to transform us, inspiring us to live lives rooted in the love and sacrifice of Christ.

Prayer:

Lord Jesus, as we stand before the cross, we are overwhelmed by the depth of Your love for us. You embraced the cross out of love for humanity, and through Your death, You have given us life. Help us to carry our crosses with courage and to love others as You have loved us. May Your Passion inspire us to live lives of selfless love, bearing witness to the power of Your sacrifice. Amen.

Saturday, April 19

❖ Holy Saturday

- First Reading: Genesis 1: 1 – 2: 2 or 1: 1, 26-31a
- Responsorial Psalm: Psalms 104: 1-2, 5-6, 10, 12, 13-14, 24, 35 or Psalms 33: 4-5, 6-7, 12-13, 20 and 22
- Second Reading: Genesis 22: 1-18 or 22: 1-2, 9a, 10-13, 15-18
- Responsorial Psalm: Psalms 16: 5, 8, 9-10, 11
- Third Reading: Exodus 14: 15 – 15: 1
- Responsorial Psalm: Exodus 15: 1-2, 3-4, 5-6, 17-18
- Fourth Reading: Isaiah 54: 5-14
- Responsorial Psalm: Psalms 30: 2, 4, 5-6, 11-12, 13
- Fifth Reading: Isaiah 55: 1-11
- Responsorial Psalm: Isaiah 12: 2-3, 4, 5-6
- Sixth Reading: Baruch 3: 9-15, 32 – 4: 4
- Responsorial Psalm: Psalms 19: 8, 9, 10, 11
- Seventh Reading: Ezekiel 36: 16-17a, 18-28
- Responsorial Psalm: Psalms 42: 3, 5; 43: 3, 4 or Isaiah 12: 2-3, 4bcd, 5-6 or Psalms 51:12-13, 14-15, 18-19
- Epistle Reading: Romans 6: 3-11
- Responsorial Psalm: Psalms 118: 1-2, 16-17, 22-23
- Gospel: Luke 24: 1-12
- Lectionary: 41

Holy Saturday is a day of waiting, a day of deep silence, as the Church contemplates the mystery of Christ's descent into the realm of the dead. It is a time of reflection on the immense sacrifice of Jesus, who has died for our sins and lies in the tomb. The solemn readings of the Easter Vigil, which begins after sunset, trace the history of salvation, leading us from the creation of the world to the resurrection of Christ, the new creation.

➢ First Reading: Genesis 1: 1 – 2: 2 or 1: 1, 26-31a

The account of creation in Genesis reminds us of God's immense power and His deliberate intention in creating the world and humanity. Everything God created was good, and humanity, made in God's image, was declared very good. This reading is a reminder of the original goodness of creation, which God desires to restore through Christ.

Reflection:
As we contemplate the creation story, we are reminded of the original harmony between God and creation, a harmony that was disrupted by sin. Holy Saturday invites us to reflect on the new creation brought about by Christ's resurrection. Through His victory over sin and death, Jesus restores the goodness and dignity of humanity, calling us to live as new creations in Him.

Prayer:
Creator God, You made all things good and fashioned humanity in Your image. As we reflect on the mystery of creation, help us to recognize the beauty of Your work and to live in harmony with Your will. May we embrace the new life that Christ offers and reflect His image in our daily lives. Amen.

➢ Second Reading: Genesis 22: 1-18 or 22: 1-2, 9a, 10-13, 15-18

The story of Abraham's willingness to sacrifice his son Isaac is a profound act of faith and obedience. It prefigures God's ultimate sacrifice of His own Son, Jesus, for the salvation of the world. Abraham's trust in God and God's provision of a ram as a substitute for Isaac point to the sacrificial love of Christ.

Reflection:
Abraham's test of faith is a powerful reminder of the trust and obedience that God asks of us. Just as God provided a ram in place of Isaac, He provided His own Son as the Lamb of God who takes away the sins of the world. On this Holy Saturday, we are called to deepen our faith in God's providence and to recognize the sacrifice of Jesus as the ultimate act of love and redemption.

Prayer:
Faithful God, as we remember Abraham's trust in You, help us to deepen our own faith and obedience. We thank You for the gift of Jesus, the Lamb of God who takes away our sins. May we respond to Your love with gratitude and a willingness to follow wherever You lead. Amen.

➢ Third Reading: Exodus 14: 15 – 15: 1

The crossing of the Red Sea is a powerful moment of deliverance for the Israelites, marking their liberation from slavery in Egypt. This reading is a central part of the Easter Vigil, symbolizing the passage from death to life, from slavery to freedom, that is accomplished through Christ's resurrection.

Reflection:
The Israelites' passage through the Red Sea is a foreshadowing of our own baptism, where we pass from the slavery of sin into the freedom of new life in Christ. Holy Saturday calls us to remember our own deliverance through the waters of baptism and to live as people who have been set free by Christ's victory over death.

Prayer:
O God of deliverance, You led Your people through the waters of the Red Sea, freeing them from slavery and bringing them into a new life. As we recall this great act of salvation, help us to live in the freedom that Christ has won for us, rejoicing in the new life we have through our baptism. Amen.

➢ Fourth Reading: Isaiah 54: 5-14

This passage from Isaiah speaks of God's enduring love for His people, despite their unfaithfulness. It is a message of hope and restoration, promising that God will gather His people back to Himself with compassion and steadfast love.

Reflection:
Isaiah's prophecy reminds us of God's unfailing love and His desire to restore His people to a relationship with Him. On this Holy Saturday, as we await the joy of Easter, we are called to trust in God's promises and to embrace the new covenant of love and mercy that He offers us through Christ.

Prayer:
Merciful God, Your love for us is steadfast and unchanging, even when we stray from You. As we reflect on Your promise of restoration, help us to trust in Your mercy and to return to You with all our hearts. May we experience the fullness of Your love in the new life of Christ. Amen.

➢ Fifth Reading: Isaiah 55: 1-11

In this reading, God invites all who are thirsty to come to the waters and be satisfied. It is a call to seek the Lord and to receive His abundant mercy. The passage emphasizes the power of God's word to accomplish His purposes, bringing life and renewal to all who listen.

Reflection:
Isaiah's invitation to come to the waters is a powerful reminder of God's desire to satisfy our deepest longings with His grace and mercy. Holy Saturday invites us to seek the Lord with all our hearts, trusting in the life-giving power of His word. As we prepare for the joy of Easter, let us open our hearts to the transformative power of God's love.

Prayer:
Loving God, You invite us to come to You and find life. As we reflect on Your word, help us to seek You with all our hearts and to trust in the power of Your promises. May we be renewed by Your grace and filled with the joy of Your salvation. Amen.

➢ Sixth Reading: Baruch 3: 9-15, 32 – 4: 4

Baruch calls God's people to return to the source of wisdom and to walk in the way of light. It is a call to recognize the greatness of God's wisdom and to live according to His commandments, which lead to life and peace.

Reflection:

The reading from Baruch emphasizes the importance of seeking God's wisdom and walking in His ways. Holy Saturday is a time to reflect on the wisdom of the cross, where God's love and justice meet. As we prepare for the resurrection, let us commit ourselves to living according to the wisdom that comes from God, which leads to true and lasting peace.

Prayer:

God of wisdom, You call us to walk in the light of Your truth. As we reflect on Your word, help us to seek Your wisdom and to live according to Your commandments. May we find life and peace in following Your ways and grow in our love for You each day. Amen.

➢ Seventh Reading: Ezekiel 36: 16-17a, 18-28

Ezekiel's prophecy speaks of God's promise to cleanse His people, to give them a new heart and a new spirit, and to bring them back to their land. It is a message of renewal and transformation, pointing to the new covenant established through Christ.

Reflection:

Ezekiel's promise of a new heart and a new spirit finds its fulfillment in the resurrection of Christ. On this Holy Saturday, as we await the joy of Easter, we are called to open our hearts to the transforming power of the Holy Spirit. Let us embrace the new life that God offers us, allowing His Spirit to renew and guide us each day.

Prayer:

Renewing God, You promise to cleanse us and to give us a new heart and a new spirit. As we reflect on this promise, help us to open our hearts to the work of Your Spirit in our lives. May we be transformed by Your love and live as new creations in Christ. Amen.

➢ Epistle Reading: Romans 6: 3-11

Paul's letter to the Romans reminds us that through baptism, we have been united with Christ in His death and resurrection. Just as Christ was raised from the dead, we too are called to walk in newness of life, living as people who have been brought from death to life.

Reflection:

Paul's words in Romans challenge us to live in the reality of our baptism. On this Holy Saturday, we are reminded that we have died with Christ and have been raised to new life with Him. As we prepare to celebrate His resurrection, let us commit ourselves to living as people who have been set free from sin, walking in the light of Christ's victory.

Prayer:

Risen Lord, through baptism, we have been united with You in Your death and resurrection. Help us to live as people who have been raised to new life, walking in the light of Your victory over sin and death. May our lives be a testimony to the power of Your resurrection and a beacon of hope to others. Amen.

> Gospel: Luke 24: 1-12

Luke's account of the resurrection describes the women finding the empty tomb and the angel's announcement that Jesus is not among the dead but has risen. This is the central proclamation of the Christian faith: Christ is risen! The disciples' initial disbelief turns to amazement as they begin to understand the reality of the resurrection.

Reflection:
The discovery of the empty tomb is the turning point in the story of salvation. The resurrection of Jesus is the foundation of our faith, the source of our hope, and the reason for our joy. On this Holy Saturday, we stand on the threshold of Easter, ready to proclaim with the Church throughout the ages: Christ is risen! As we meditate on the Gospel, let us renew our commitment to live as witnesses of the resurrection, bringing the light of Christ to a world in need.

Prayer:
Lord of life, we rejoice in the victory of Your resurrection. As we contemplate the empty tomb, fill our hearts with the joy and hope of Easter. Help us to live as witnesses to Your resurrection, proclaiming the good news of Your victory over sin and death to all we meet. Amen.

Sunday, April 20

❖ Easter Sunday - Solemnity

> First Reading: Acts 10: 34a, 37-43

> Responsorial Psalm: Psalms 118: 1-2, 16-17, 22-23

> Second Reading: Colossians 3: 1-4 or First Corinthians 5: 6b-8

> Alleluia: First Corinthians 5: 7b-8a

> Gospel: John 20: 1-9 or Matthew 28: 1-10 or, at an afternoon or evening Mass, Luke 24: 13-35

> Lectionary: 42

Easter Sunday is the pinnacle of the Christian liturgical year, the day we celebrate the resurrection of our Lord Jesus Christ. It is a day of immense joy and triumph, marking the victory of life over death, light over darkness. Through the resurrection, Jesus has opened the way to eternal life, and we are called to live as people of the resurrection, filled with hope, joy, and love.

➤ First Reading: Acts 10: 34a, 37-43

In this passage from Acts, Peter proclaims the good news of Jesus' resurrection. He recounts the life, death, and resurrection of Jesus, emphasizing that Jesus is the one appointed by God to judge the living and the dead. Peter's testimony affirms that everyone who believes in Jesus receives forgiveness of sins through His name.

Reflection:
Peter's proclamation is a powerful reminder of the universality of the resurrection. Jesus' victory over death is not just for a select few but for all who believe in Him. On this Easter Sunday, we are called to join in this proclamation, sharing the good news of Christ's resurrection with the world and inviting others to experience the forgiveness and new life that He offers.

Prayer:
Risen Lord, through Your resurrection, You have opened the way to eternal life for all who believe. Help us to proclaim this good news with boldness and joy, inviting others to experience the new life that You offer. May our lives be a testimony to the power of Your resurrection and a reflection of Your love. Amen.

➤ Second Reading: Colossians 3: 1-4

Paul exhorts the Colossians to set their hearts on things above, where Christ is seated at the right hand of God. He reminds them that their lives are hidden with Christ in God and that when Christ, who is their life, appears, they will also appear with Him in glory.

Reflection:
Paul's message to the Colossians calls us to live with a heavenly perspective, focusing not on the things of this world but on the things that are eternal. On this Easter Sunday, we are reminded that our true life is in Christ, and we are called to live as people who have been raised with Him, seeking the things above and reflecting His glory in our lives.

Prayer:
Heavenly Father, help us to set our hearts on things above, where Christ is seated at Your right hand. As we celebrate His resurrection, may we live as people who have been raised with Him, seeking the things that are eternal and reflecting His glory in all that we do. Amen.

➤ Gospel: John 20: 1-9

John's account of the resurrection begins with Mary Magdalene discovering the empty tomb. She informs Peter and the beloved disciple, who then run to the tomb and find it empty, with the burial cloths lying there. The beloved disciple sees and believes, though they do not yet fully understand the scripture that Jesus must rise from the dead.

Reflection:
The empty tomb is the first sign of the resurrection, and the beloved disciple's belief marks the beginning of a new understanding of Jesus' mission. On this Easter Sunday, we are invited to enter into the mystery

of the resurrection with faith, even when we do not fully understand it. Like the beloved disciple, we are called to see and believe, trusting in the promise of new life in Christ.

Prayer:
Lord Jesus, as we gaze upon the empty tomb, fill our hearts with faith and hope in Your resurrection. Help us to believe, even when we do not fully understand, and to live in the light of Your victory over death. May the joy of Easter fill our hearts and overflow into our lives, as we share the good news of Your resurrection with all we meet. Amen.

➤ Alternate Gospel: Matthew 28: 1-10

Matthew's account of the resurrection describes the appearance of an angel who rolls back the stone and announces to the women that Jesus has risen. Jesus Himself then appears to them, instructing them to tell His disciples to go to Galilee, where they will see Him.

Reflection:
The appearance of the risen Jesus to the women is a powerful moment of joy and reassurance. Jesus' first words to them are "Do not be afraid," a message that resonates throughout the Easter season. On this Easter Sunday, we are reminded that the resurrection of Jesus dispels all fear and fills us with hope and joy. We, too, are called to go and tell others the good news of Jesus' resurrection, bringing His message of hope to a world in need.

Prayer:
Risen Jesus, Your resurrection fills us with joy and dispels all fear. Help us to hear Your words, "Do not be afraid," and to live with the confidence that comes from knowing that You are alive. May we be bold in sharing the good news of Your resurrection with others, bringing hope and joy to those around us. Amen.

➤ Alternate Gospel: Luke 24: 13-35 (for an afternoon or evening Mass)

Luke's account of the road to Emmaus describes how two disciples, walking and discussing the events of Jesus' death, are joined by the risen Christ, though they do not recognize Him at first. It is only in the breaking of the bread that their eyes are opened, and they recognize Him.

Reflection:
The road to Emmaus is a story of gradual recognition and revelation. The disciples' hearts burn within them as Jesus speaks, and their eyes are finally opened in the breaking of the bread. On this Easter Sunday, we are reminded that the risen Christ walks with us on our journey, even when we do not recognize Him. He reveals Himself to us in the scriptures and in the Eucharist, inviting us to deeper faith and communion with Him.

Prayer:
Risen Lord, as You walked with the disciples on the road to Emmaus, walk with us on our journey of faith. Open our eyes to recognize You in the breaking of the bread and in the events of our daily lives. May our hearts burn with love for You, and may we share the joy of Your resurrection with others. Amen.

Monday, April 21

❖ Monday of Easter Week

- ➤ First Reading: Acts 2: 14, 22-33
- ➤ Responsorial Psalm: Psalms 16: 1-2a and 5, 7-8, 9-10, 11
- ➤ Alleluia: Psalms 118: 24
- ➤ Gospel: Matthew 28: 8-15
- ➤ Lectionary: 261

In the octave of Easter, the Church continues to celebrate the joy of the Resurrection. This first week of Easter is a time to deepen our understanding and appreciation of the resurrection of Jesus. The readings for today highlight the early Christian proclamation of the Resurrection and the spreading of the Good News despite opposition.

➤ First Reading: Acts 2: 14, 22-33

In this passage, Peter delivers a powerful sermon to the people, explaining that Jesus, whom they had crucified, was raised from the dead by God. Peter cites the prophecy of David to affirm that Jesus' resurrection was foretold and that He is now exalted at the right hand of God, pouring out the Holy Spirit.

Reflection:
Peter's sermon is a bold declaration of the core message of Christianity: Jesus has risen from the dead. This proclamation is not just a historical event but a declaration of God's power and faithfulness. Peter's use of Scripture to explain the Resurrection reminds us that Jesus' resurrection fulfills ancient promises and reveals the new reality of God's Kingdom. As we begin the Easter season, we are invited to reflect on the profound significance of Jesus' resurrection and its implications for our faith and life.

Prayer:
Lord Jesus, Your resurrection is the fulfillment of Your promises and the foundation of our faith. As Peter boldly proclaimed the Good News, grant us the courage and conviction to live in the light of Your Resurrection and to share this message with others. May Your Spirit guide us in our witness and deepen our understanding of the hope and joy found in Your victory over death. Amen.

➤ Gospel: Matthew 28: 8-15

The Gospel recounts how the women, after encountering the angel at the tomb, go to tell the disciples about Jesus' resurrection. On their way, they encounter the risen Jesus, who instructs them to inform the disciples to go to Galilee. Meanwhile, the guards report the resurrection to the chief priests, who conspire to spread a false story about the disciples stealing the body.

Reflection:

The Gospel of Matthew presents a dramatic contrast between the faithfulness of the women who encounter the risen Jesus and the deceit of those who seek to deny the resurrection. The women's encounter with Jesus is a moment of profound joy and commissioning, while the chief priests' plot reveals their attempt to suppress the truth. As we celebrate the Easter season, we are called to be witnesses of the Resurrection, embracing the truth and joy of the risen Christ amidst a world that may seek to obscure it.

Prayer:

Risen Lord, we rejoice in Your appearance to the women and the message of Your Resurrection. Help us to be faithful witnesses of Your victory over sin and death. Strengthen us to stand firm in the truth of Your resurrection, and guide us in sharing this joy with others. May we, like the women, be filled with Your peace and go forth to proclaim the Good News of Your rising. Amen.

Tuesday, April 22

❖ Tuesday of Easter Week

- ➢ First Reading: Acts 2: 36-41
- ➢ Responsorial Psalm: Psalms 33: 4-5, 18-19, 20 and 22
- ➢ Alleluia: Psalms 118: 24
- ➢ Gospel: John 20: 11-18
- ➢ Lectionary: 262

The Easter season continues to unfold, focusing on the immediate aftermath of Christ's resurrection. Today's readings highlight the impact of the Resurrection on the early Christian community and the personal encounter of Mary Magdalene with the risen Lord. These passages invite us to reflect on the transformative power of the Resurrection in our own lives.

➢ First Reading: Acts 2: 36-41

In this passage, Peter addresses the crowd in Jerusalem, proclaiming that Jesus, whom they crucified, is both Lord and Christ. He calls for repentance and baptism in the name of Jesus Christ for the forgiveness of sins, promising the gift of the Holy Spirit. About three thousand people accept his message and are baptized.

Reflection:

Peter's proclamation in Acts is a turning point in the early Church. His message is clear: Jesus' resurrection confirms His divine authority and His role as the promised Messiah. The call to repentance and baptism is an invitation to transformation and new life. The large number of people who responded indicates the powerful impact of the Resurrection message. As we reflect on this passage, we are encouraged to examine our own response to the Gospel and to embrace the new life offered through Christ's resurrection.

Prayer:

Lord Jesus, Your resurrection is the foundation of our faith and the source of our hope. We thank You for the gift of the Holy Spirit and the invitation to repentance and renewal. Help us to respond to Your call with open hearts and to live as witnesses of Your resurrection. May our lives reflect the transformation You bring, and may we share the Good News with others through our words and actions. Amen.

➢ Gospel: John 20: 11-18

This Gospel passage describes Mary Magdalene's encounter with the risen Jesus. After finding the empty tomb, she weeps outside and encounters Jesus, though she does not immediately recognize Him. Jesus calls her by name, and she then recognizes Him. Jesus instructs her to go to His brothers and tell them that He is ascending to His Father.

Reflection:

Mary Magdalene's encounter with the risen Jesus is a profound moment of personal recognition and commissioning. Her experience underscores the intimate and personal nature of Jesus' resurrection. Jesus' calling of Mary by name and her subsequent role as the first witness to the Resurrection highlight the importance of personal encounters with Christ and the role of women in the early Church. As we reflect on this passage, we are reminded of the personal call Jesus extends to each of us and the invitation to share our encounter with others.

Prayer:

Risen Lord, we rejoice in Mary Magdalene's encounter with You and her role as the first witness to Your Resurrection. Like Mary, help us to recognize Your presence in our lives and to respond with faith and joy. Guide us in our mission to proclaim Your Resurrection to the world and to live as witnesses of Your love and grace. Amen.

Wednesday, April 23

❖ Wednesday of Easter Week

- First Reading: Acts 3: 1-10
- Responsorial Psalm: Psalms 105: 1-2, 3-4, 6-7, 8-9
- Alleluia: Psalms 118: 24
- Gospel: Luke 24: 13-35
- Lectionary: 263

As we continue to celebrate the Easter season, today's readings focus on the early effects of the Resurrection in the lives of the apostles and the profound encounter with the risen Christ on the road to Emmaus. These passages invite us to recognize the transformative power of the Resurrection in our own lives and in the community of believers.

First Reading: Acts 3: 1-10

In this passage, Peter and John heal a man who had been lame from birth. The healing takes place at the Beautiful Gate of the Temple, and it leads to a great crowd gathering, astonished by the miracle. Peter seizes the opportunity to preach about Jesus and His resurrection, explaining that the healing was done in the name of Jesus Christ of Nazareth.

Reflection:
The healing of the lame man is a powerful sign of the continuing work of Jesus through His apostles. It demonstrates the transformative power of the Resurrection, not just in spiritual terms but in tangible, everyday life. The miracle serves as a powerful testimony to the power of Jesus' name and an opportunity for Peter to proclaim the Gospel. As we reflect on this passage, we are reminded of the ways in which the Resurrection brings healing and renewal, urging us to recognize and act upon the ways Christ is working in our own lives and communities.

Prayer:
Lord Jesus, we thank You for the power of Your resurrection, which brings healing and transformation. As Peter and John were instruments of Your grace, help us to be witnesses of Your love and power in our own lives. Strengthen our faith and embolden us to share the Good News of Your resurrection with others. May we be agents of Your healing and renewal in the world. Amen.

> Gospel: Luke 24: 13-35

This Gospel recounts the story of two disciples on the road to Emmaus. They are discussing the recent events of Jesus' crucifixion and the reports of His resurrection. Jesus joins them, but they do not recognize Him. He explains the Scriptures concerning Himself and breaks bread with them. It is in the breaking of the bread that their eyes are opened, and they recognize Him. They return to Jerusalem to share their encounter with the other disciples.

Reflection:
The Emmaus story is a profound testament to the ways in which Jesus meets us in our journeys, even when we fail to recognize Him. The disciples' realization comes through the breaking of the bread, which points to the importance of the Eucharist in recognizing and encountering the risen Christ. This passage encourages us to recognize Jesus in the breaking of the bread and in our daily lives, as well as to share our experiences of His presence with others.

Prayer:
Risen Lord, we thank You for the way You revealed Yourself to the disciples on the road to Emmaus. Open our eyes to recognize You in the breaking of the bread and in our daily encounters. As we journey through life, help us to be aware of Your presence and to share the joy of Your resurrection with others. Strengthen our faith and our commitment to living as Your disciples. Amen.

Thursday, April 24

❖ Thursday of Easter Week

> First Reading: Acts 3: 11-26
> Responsorial Psalm: Psalms 8: 2ab and 5, 6-7, 8-9
> Alleluia: Psalms 118: 24
> Gospel: Luke 24: 35-48
> Lectionary: 264

As we continue to celebrate the joy of Easter, today's readings focus on the proclamation of the Resurrection and the affirmation of Jesus' identity and mission. We are invited to deepen our understanding of the Resurrection's implications and to recognize Christ's presence in our midst.

> First Reading: Acts 3: 11-26

In this passage, Peter addresses the crowd following the healing of the lame man at the Temple. He explains that the healing was done in the name of Jesus Christ, whom the people had rejected. Peter calls for repentance and conversion, asserting that Jesus is the fulfillment of God's promises to the patriarchs and the one who brings healing and salvation.

Reflection:
Peter's speech is a powerful testimony to the reality of the Resurrection and its significance. He emphasizes that Jesus, who was crucified, has been raised from the dead and is the cornerstone of God's plan of salvation. This passage challenges us to reflect on our own response to Jesus. Are we, like the crowd, surprised by His power and work, or do we recognize Him as the fulfillment of God's promises? Peter's call to repentance reminds us of the need for ongoing conversion in our own lives.

Prayer:
Lord Jesus, we are grateful for the gift of Your resurrection and the healing it brings. Help us to recognize You as the fulfillment of God's promises and to respond with true repentance and faith. May we be transformed by Your grace and empowered to share the Good News with others. Strengthen our commitment to living as Your disciples and witnesses to Your resurrection. Amen.

➢ Gospel: Luke 24: 35-48

In this Gospel passage, Jesus appears to the disciples and confirms His resurrection. He shows them His hands and feet, eats with them, and explains how His suffering and resurrection fulfill the Scriptures. Jesus also commissions them to be witnesses of these events and to proclaim repentance and forgiveness to all nations.

Reflection:
The encounter on Easter evening underscores the reality of Jesus' resurrection and His physical presence. By eating with the disciples, Jesus emphasizes His real, bodily resurrection and affirms that His mission is now their mission. This passage invites us to recognize Jesus in the breaking of the bread, to understand the fulfillment of Scriptures in His resurrection, and to embrace our role as witnesses of His resurrection and messengers of repentance and forgiveness.

Prayer:
Risen Lord, we rejoice in the reality of Your resurrection and the fulfillment of Your promises. As You appeared to the disciples and commissioned them, strengthen us to be faithful witnesses of Your resurrection. Open our hearts to understand the Scriptures and empower us to proclaim Your message of repentance and forgiveness. May we live as true disciples, reflecting Your love and grace in all that we do. Amen.

Friday, April 25

❖ Saint Mark, evangelist - Feast

> First Reading: Acts 4: 1-12
> Responsorial Psalm: Psalms 118: 1-2 and 4, 22-24, 25-27a
> Alleluia: Psalms 118: 24
> Gospel: John 21: 1-14
> Lectionary: 265

Today, the Church celebrates the feast of Saint Mark, the Evangelist, who is traditionally credited with writing the Gospel of Mark. This day honors his contributions to the early Christian community and his role in spreading the message of Jesus Christ. The readings for this feast highlight the importance of proclaiming the Good News and the witness of the apostles.

> First Reading: Acts 4: 1-12

In this passage, Peter and John are confronted by the Jewish authorities for their preaching about Jesus and His resurrection. Despite being arrested, Peter boldly proclaims that Jesus, whom they crucified, has been raised from the dead and is the only name by which salvation can be found. This reading underscores the transformative power of the resurrection and the apostles' commitment to preaching the Gospel.

Reflection:
Peter's courage and conviction in the face of opposition reflect the impact of his encounter with the risen Christ. His proclamation that Jesus is the sole source of salvation emphasizes the centrality of Christ in the Christian faith. As followers of Christ, we are invited to boldly proclaim the Gospel, trusting in the power of Jesus' name and being unafraid of the challenges that may come our way.

Prayer:
Lord Jesus, we thank You for the witness of Saint Mark and the courage of Peter and John. Grant us the boldness to proclaim Your name with the same conviction and trust in Your power. Strengthen us in our mission to share the Good News and to stand firm in the face of opposition. May we live our lives as true witnesses of Your love and salvation. Amen.

> Gospel: John 21: 1-14

In this Gospel passage, the risen Jesus appears to the disciples by the Sea of Tiberias. After a night of unsuccessful fishing, Jesus instructs them to cast their nets on the right side of the boat, leading to a miraculous catch of fish. Jesus then shares a meal with them, reaffirms Peter's role, and commissions him to feed His sheep.

Reflection:
This post-resurrection appearance of Jesus is a powerful reminder of His ongoing presence and provision. The miraculous catch of fish symbolizes the abundance of the harvest that will come from the disciples' future ministry. Jesus' act of sharing a meal with the disciples emphasizes His intimate relationship with them and His continued guidance. For Peter, it is a moment of restoration and commissioning, reinforcing his role as a leader in the early Church.

Prayer:
Risen Lord, we rejoice in Your continued presence among us and Your provision for our needs. Thank You for the miraculous catch of fish and the way You affirm and restore us. Help us to heed Your call and follow Your guidance, knowing that You are with us in our mission to spread the Good News. May we be faithful in our service to You and in nurturing those entrusted to our care. Amen.

Saturday, April 26

❖ Saturday of Easter Week

- ➢ First Reading: Acts 4: 13-21
- ➢ Responsorial Psalm: Psalms 118: 1 and 14-15ab, 16-18, 19-21
- ➢ Alleluia: Psalms 118: 24
- ➢ Gospel: Mark 16: 9-15
- ➢ Lectionary: 266

On this Saturday of Easter Week, the Church continues to celebrate the joy of Christ's resurrection. The readings reflect the apostles' boldness in proclaiming the risen Lord and the mission entrusted to them by Jesus. They highlight the call to continue the work of spreading the Gospel despite opposition.

- ➢ First Reading: Acts 4: 13-21

In this passage, Peter and John are brought before the Sanhedrin for healing a lame man and proclaiming Jesus' resurrection. The Jewish leaders are astonished by their boldness and realize that these men had been with Jesus. Despite threats, Peter and John refuse to be silenced, declaring that they cannot stop speaking about what they have seen and heard. The reading underscores the apostles' unwavering commitment to their mission and their courage in the face of persecution.

Reflection:

The apostles' determination to proclaim the Gospel, even under threat, demonstrates the power of their conviction and the transformative effect of their encounter with the risen Christ. Their boldness serves as an example for us, encouraging us to speak the truth of our faith and live out our call to be witnesses of Jesus, regardless of the challenges we may face.

Prayer:

Lord Jesus, we thank You for the bold witness of Peter and John. Grant us the same courage and conviction in sharing our faith and living according to Your teachings. Help us to remain steadfast in our mission to spread the Good News, and strengthen us to face any opposition with faith and grace. May our lives reflect Your love and truth to those around us. Amen.

➢ Gospel: Mark 16: 9-15

In this passage, the risen Jesus appears first to Mary Magdalene, who then announces His resurrection to the disciples. Jesus later appears to two disciples walking in the countryside, and finally, He appears to the eleven apostles. Jesus rebukes them for their lack of faith and commissions them to go into the whole world and preach the Gospel to all creation. This commissioning highlights the global scope of the mission entrusted to the disciples.

Reflection:

Jesus' appearances and commissioning of the disciples signify the fulfillment of His promise and the beginning of the Church's mission to the world. His rebuke of the disciples' disbelief emphasizes the need for faith and readiness to bear witness to His resurrection. The call to preach the Gospel to all creation is a reminder of the universal mission of the Church and our role in sharing the message of salvation with all people.

Prayer:

Risen Lord, we rejoice in Your victory over death and Your commission to spread the Gospel. Help us to overcome our doubts and fears, and empower us to boldly proclaim Your message to all people. May our words and actions be a testament to Your resurrection and the hope it brings. Strengthen us in our mission and guide us as we seek to live out our call to evangelize and serve others. Amen.

Sunday, April 27

❖ Second Sunday of Easter

- First Reading: Acts 5: 12-16
- Responsorial Psalm: Psalms 118: 2-4, 13-15, 22-24
- Second Reading: Revelation 1: 9-11a, 12-13, 17-19
- Alleluia: John 20: 29
- Gospel: John 20:19-31
- Lectionary: 45

The Second Sunday of Easter, also known as Divine Mercy Sunday, focuses on the themes of faith and mercy. The readings emphasize the early Christian community's witness to the resurrection and the role of faith in experiencing the fullness of Christ's victory over sin and death. It is a day to reflect on the mercy of God and the importance of faith in our journey as disciples.

First Reading: Acts 5: 12-16

In this passage, the apostles perform many signs and wonders among the people, leading to increased respect and admiration from the community. The early Christian community grows rapidly as many are healed and added to the faith. This reading highlights the power and grace at work through the apostles and the growing influence of the early Church.

Reflection:
The signs and wonders performed by the apostles demonstrate the continuing presence and power of Jesus through the Holy Spirit. The growth of the early Christian community reflects the transformative impact of faith in the risen Lord. We are called to witness to God's power in our own lives and to participate in the mission of building up the Church and serving others through acts of love and healing.

Prayer:
Lord Jesus, we praise You for the miracles and signs performed by Your apostles and for the growth of the early Church. Help us to recognize and respond to Your power in our lives and in the world around us. Strengthen our faith and guide us in our mission to be witnesses of Your love and mercy. May we be instruments of Your healing and peace in our communities. Amen.

➢ Second Reading: Revelation 1: 9-11a, 12-13, 17-19

In this passage from Revelation, John describes his vision of the risen Christ, who appears to him in glory. John is instructed to write down what he sees and hears. The vision of Christ, the Alpha and Omega, emphasizes His eternal nature and authority over all things. This revelation serves to encourage the faithful to remain steadfast in their faith.

Reflection:
The vision of Christ in glory reveals His divine majesty and eternal reign. It reassures us of His power and presence in our lives and throughout history. This reading encourages us to trust in Christ's sovereignty and to remain faithful even amidst challenges and uncertainties. It invites us to see beyond our immediate struggles and to live with the hope and assurance of Christ's ultimate victory.

Prayer:
Risen Lord, we are in awe of Your glorious vision revealed to John. Help us to see Your power and majesty in our daily lives and to trust in Your eternal reign. Strengthen our faith and encourage us to remain steadfast in our commitment to You. May Your vision inspire us to live with hope and to share the message of Your victory with others. Amen.

➢ Gospel: John 20:19-31

In this passage, Jesus appears to His disciples on the evening of His resurrection, offering them peace and commissioning them to continue His work. He shows them His wounds and breathes on them, giving them the Holy Spirit and the authority to forgive sins. Thomas, who was not present, doubts the resurrection until he sees Jesus and touches His wounds. Jesus blesses those who believe without seeing, highlighting the importance of faith.

Reflection:
Jesus' appearance to the disciples and His gift of the Holy Spirit mark the beginning of their mission to continue His work. Thomas's doubt and subsequent confession of faith underscore the importance of belief in the resurrection. Jesus' words to Thomas remind us that faith is a gift and that those who believe without seeing are blessed. This passage calls us to embrace faith in Christ and to be witnesses of His resurrection.

Prayer:
Lord Jesus, we are grateful for Your presence among us and for the gift of the Holy Spirit. Help us to overcome our doubts and to deepen our faith in Your resurrection. May we be empowered by Your Spirit to live as Your witnesses and to proclaim the message of Your mercy and forgiveness to all. Strengthen us in our journey of faith and guide us in sharing Your love with the world. Amen.

Monday, April 28

- ❖ Monday of the Second week of Easter
- ❖ Saint Peter Chanel, priest and martyr - Optional Memorial
- ❖ Saint Louis Mary de Montfort, priest - Optional Memorial

> ➢ First Reading: Acts 4: 23-31
> ➢ Responsorial Psalm: Psalms 2: 1-3, 4-6, 7-9
> ➢ Alleluia: Colossians 3: 1
> ➢ Gospel: John 3: 1-8
> ➢ Lectionary: 267

Today's readings reflect the early Church's resilience and the transformative power of the Holy Spirit, echoing the life and legacy of Saint Peter Chanel, a martyr who exemplified unwavering faith, and Saint Louis Mary de Montfort, known for his profound devotion to the Blessed Virgin Mary.

> ➢ First Reading: Acts 4: 23-31

After their release from imprisonment, Peter and John return to their community and report what happened. The believers pray for courage to continue their mission despite threats. The place where they are gathered is shaken, and they are all filled with the Holy Spirit and speak the word of God with boldness.

Reflection:
This passage underscores the power of communal prayer and the role of the Holy Spirit in strengthening the Church's mission. The believers' unity and boldness in proclaiming the gospel, even under threat, inspire us to rely on God's strength and courage in our own witness.

Prayer:
Lord, grant us the courage and boldness of the early Church. Fill us with Your Spirit that we may speak Your truth fearlessly and live as witnesses of Your love. Through Christ our Lord. Amen.

> ➢ Gospel: John 3: 1-8

In this passage, Nicodemus, a Pharisee, comes to Jesus by night seeking understanding. Jesus speaks to him about the necessity of being born again of water and the Spirit to enter the Kingdom of God. He explains that the Spirit is like the wind—mysterious and uncontrollable—but essential for new birth in faith.

Reflection:
Jesus' conversation with Nicodemus emphasizes the profound transformation required to enter God's Kingdom. Being "born again" means embracing a new life in the Spirit, marked by a radical change in how we see and live our faith. This spiritual rebirth is a gift that empowers us to live as true children of God.

Prayer:
Heavenly Father, we ask for the renewal of our hearts and minds through the Holy Spirit. Help us to embrace the new life You offer and to live in a way that reflects Your love and grace. Through Christ our Lord. Amen.

Tuesday, April 29

❖ Saint Catherine of Siena, virgin and doctor - Memorial

- First Reading: Acts 4: 32-37
- Responsorial Psalm: Psalms 93: 1ab, 1cd-2, 5
- Alleluia: John 3: 14-15
- Gospel: John 3: 7b-15
- Lectionary: 268

Today, we honor Saint Catherine of Siena, a Doctor of the Church and a mystic known for her profound spiritual writings and her influential role in the Church's history. Her life of intense prayer and action inspires us to seek a deeper relationship with God and to live out our faith with zeal and commitment.

- First Reading: Acts 4: 32-37

The early Christians are united in heart and mind, sharing everything they have. The apostles continue to testify to the resurrection of Jesus with great power, and abundant grace is upon them all. Joseph, also called Barnabas, sells a field and lays the proceeds at the apostles' feet, an example of selfless generosity.

Reflection:
This passage highlights the unity and generosity of the early Christian community. The believers' willingness to share their resources reflects their deep commitment to one another and to the mission of spreading the Gospel. It challenges us to examine how we live out our call to be a community of love and support.

Prayer:
Lord, we thank You for the example of the early Church and for the life of Saint Catherine of Siena. Help

us to live in unity and generosity, following the example of those who have gone before us. Strengthen us in our commitment to Your mission and to one another. Through Christ our Lord. Amen.

> ➤ Gospel: John 3: 7b-15

Jesus tells Nicodemus that one must be born again of the Spirit to see the Kingdom of God. He compares the Spirit's work to the wind—unseen but powerful. Jesus explains that just as Moses lifted up the serpent in the desert, so must the Son of Man be lifted up, that everyone who believes in Him may have eternal life.

Reflection:

Jesus' message to Nicodemus emphasizes the necessity of spiritual rebirth and the role of faith in obtaining eternal life. The reference to Moses lifting up the serpent points to Jesus' crucifixion as the means of salvation. Our belief in Jesus and His sacrifice brings us new life and hope.

Prayer:

Lord Jesus, we thank You for the gift of new life through the Holy Spirit. Help us to embrace the transformative power of Your grace and to live in faith and hope. May Your Spirit guide us as we seek to follow You more closely. Through Christ our Lord. Amen.

Wednesday, April 30

- ❖ Wednesday of the Second week of Easter
- ❖ Saint Pius V, pope - Optional Memorial

> ➤ First Reading: Acts 5: 17-26
> ➤ Responsorial Psalm: Psalms 34: 2-3, 4-5, 6-7, 8-9
> ➤ Alleluia: John 3: 16
> ➤ Gospel: John 3: 16-21
> ➤ Lectionary: 269

Saint Pius V, a Pope known for his role in implementing the reforms of the Council of Trent, is remembered today for his dedication to the Church's renewal and his commitment to the purity of the liturgy. His leadership was instrumental in shaping the post-Reformation Church, and his example calls us to remain steadfast in our faith and devotion.

➢ First Reading: Acts 5: 17-26

The high priest and the Sadducees arrest the apostles and put them in jail for preaching about Jesus. An angel of the Lord frees them during the night, instructing them to continue speaking in the temple. The next day, when the authorities seek them, they find the apostles teaching as commanded. The authorities are perplexed but recognize the power of their witness.

Reflection:
This passage illustrates the apostles' unwavering commitment to their mission despite opposition. The miraculous release from prison highlights the divine support for their efforts and the continued growth of the Church despite human obstacles. It encourages us to trust in God's guidance and remain faithful in our witness to Christ.

Prayer:
Heavenly Father, we thank You for the example of Saint Pius V and the courage of the apostles. Grant us the strength to proclaim Your Word boldly and to trust in Your guidance in times of trial. Help us to follow the path of faithfulness and dedication. Through Christ our Lord. Amen.

➢ Gospel: John 3: 16-21

In this passage, Jesus explains the purpose of His coming into the world. He states that God loved the world so much that He gave His only Son, so that everyone who believes in Him might not perish but have eternal life. Jesus came not to condemn but to save. Those who live by the truth come to the light, while those who do evil avoid it.

Reflection:
John 3:16 is one of the most famous verses, encapsulating the essence of the Gospel message: God's profound love and the promise of eternal life through faith in Jesus. This passage calls us to examine how we respond to God's love and to live in the light of truth, allowing our lives to reflect His grace.

Prayer:
Lord Jesus, we are grateful for Your sacrifice and the boundless love of God the Father. Help us to live in the light of Your truth and to share Your love with others. Strengthen our faith and guide us as we seek to live out the promise of eternal life. Through Christ our Lord. Amen.

May 2025

Thursday, May 1

- ❖ Thursday of the Second week of Easter
- ❖ Saint Joseph the Worker - Optional Memorial

> First Reading: Acts 5: 27-33
> Responsorial Psalm: Psalms 34: 2 and 9, 17-18, 19-20
> Alleluia: John 20: 29
> Gospel: John 3: 31-36, Proper Gospel for Joseph: Matthew 13: 54-58
> Lectionary: 270

Today, we honor Saint Joseph the Worker, whose feast was established to highlight the dignity of labor and the example of Saint Joseph as a hardworking and righteous man. His life of dedication to his family and work reflects the values of industriousness and faithfulness, reminding us of the sanctity of everyday work.

> First Reading: Acts 5: 27-33

The apostles are brought before the Sanhedrin for preaching about Jesus, despite the orders to stop. They boldly declare that they must obey God rather than human authorities. Peter and the apostles witness to the resurrection of Jesus and emphasize the forgiveness of sins through Him. The council members are furious, but Gamaliel, a respected Pharisee, advises caution, suggesting that if their work is of God, it cannot be stopped.

Reflection:
This reading highlights the apostles' commitment to their mission and their reliance on divine authority over human power. Their willingness to endure suffering for the sake of the Gospel exemplifies true faith. It invites us to reflect on our own commitment to God's will, even when faced with challenges or opposition.

Prayer:
Lord God, grant us the courage and strength of the apostles as we strive to live according to Your will. Help us to remain steadfast in our faith and to follow Your guidance in all that we do. May we always prioritize Your commands over worldly pressures. Through Christ our Lord. Amen.

➢ Gospel: John 3: 31-36

In this passage, John the Baptist speaks about the superiority of Jesus, who comes from heaven and speaks the words of God. He contrasts Jesus with himself, acknowledging that he is from the earth and speaks from an earthly perspective. Jesus, being above all, offers eternal life to those who believe in Him. The passage emphasizes the importance of accepting Jesus' testimony and believing in Him for eternal life.

Reflection:
This Gospel reading underscores the divine authority of Jesus and the significance of His role in offering eternal life. It encourages us to trust in His words and to recognize His supreme authority in our lives. Belief in Jesus is presented as the key to receiving God's promises and blessings.

Prayer:
Heavenly Father, we thank You for the gift of Your Son, Jesus, who brings us the promise of eternal life. Help us to fully accept His testimony and to trust in His divine authority. Guide us in living according to His teachings and sharing His love with others. Through Christ our Lord. Amen.

➢ Proper Gospel for Saint Joseph the Worker: Matthew 13: 54-58

This Gospel recounts how Jesus returns to His hometown and teaches in the synagogue. The people are astonished at His wisdom and miracles but struggle to believe that someone they know so well could be the Messiah. Jesus remarks that a prophet is not without honor except in his own country and among his own kin. Due to their lack of faith, Jesus performs few miracles there.

Reflection:
This reading emphasizes the challenge of recognizing and accepting the divine in familiar settings. It reflects on the difficulty of overcoming preconceived notions and biases that can hinder our recognition of God's work in our lives and those around us. It also highlights the importance of faith in receiving the fullness of God's grace.

Prayer:
Lord Jesus, help us to recognize and honor Your presence and work in our lives, even when it comes from familiar or unexpected sources. Strengthen our faith and open our hearts to the ways You are present and active among us. Through Christ our Lord. Amen.

Friday, May 2

- ❖ First Friday
- ❖ Saint Athanasius, bishop and doctor - Memorial

- ➢ First Reading: Acts 5: 34-42
- ➢ Responsorial Psalm: Psalms 27: 1, 4, 13-14
- ➢ Alleluia: Matthew 4: 4b
- ➢ Gospel: John 6: 1-15
- ➢ Lectionary: 271

Today we celebrate Saint Athanasius, a key figure in the early Church known for his staunch defense of Trinitarian doctrine and his role in combating Arianism. His unwavering commitment to the truth and his theological writings have made a lasting impact on Christian doctrine. His feast invites us to reflect on the importance of defending our faith and upholding the truth of the Gospel.

- ➢ First Reading: Acts 5: 34-42

In this passage, Gamaliel, a respected Pharisee, advises the Sanhedrin to be cautious in dealing with the apostles. He suggests that if their movement is from God, it cannot be stopped. The council agrees, and the apostles are flogged but continue to preach and teach about Jesus with joy, rejoicing that they were counted worthy to suffer for His name.

Reflection:
Gamaliel's counsel highlights the idea that if something is truly of God, it will prevail despite opposition. The apostles' reaction to their suffering—with joy rather than despair—demonstrates a profound faith and commitment to their mission. This passage encourages us to view challenges in our faith journey as opportunities to witness to the power and truth of God's work in our lives.

Prayer:
Heavenly Father, we thank You for the example of Saint Athanasius and the apostles, who faced trials with unwavering faith and joy. Help us to remain steadfast in our commitment to Your truth and to find strength in adversity. May we always be courageous in our witness to Your love and grace. Through Christ our Lord. Amen.

> Gospel: John 6: 1-15

In this Gospel passage, Jesus performs the miracle of feeding the five thousand with five loaves and two fish. The people are amazed and begin to recognize Him as the Prophet who is to come into the world. Jesus withdraws to a mountain to be alone when He realizes they want to make Him king by force.

Reflection:
The miracle of the loaves and fish is a profound demonstration of Jesus' compassion and divine power. It teaches us about God's ability to provide abundantly and to meet our needs in ways that surpass our expectations. This passage also challenges us to recognize Jesus' true mission and to avoid misinterpreting His purpose for our own desires.

Prayer:
Lord Jesus, we thank You for Your miraculous provision and for the way You meet our needs with abundance. Help us to recognize Your true mission and to trust in Your plan for our lives. May we be inspired by Your example of compassion and generosity to serve others with love and faith. Through Christ our Lord. Amen.

Saturday, May 3

- ❖ First Saturday
- ❖ Saints Philip and James, apostles - Feast

> First Reading: First Corinthians 15: 1-8
> Responsorial Psalm: Psalms 19: 2-3, 4-5
> Alleluia: John 14: 6b, 9c
> Gospel: John 14: 6-14
> Lectionary: 561

Today we honor Saints Philip and James, two of the twelve apostles who played significant roles in spreading the message of Jesus. Philip was known for bringing Nathanael to Jesus and for his questions that revealed deep insights into Christ's teachings. James, often referred to as James the Less or James the Just, was a key figure in the early Church and is traditionally considered the first bishop of Jerusalem. Their feast reminds us of the foundational role of the apostles in the Church and their commitment to the mission of Christ.

➢ First Reading: 1 Corinthians 15: 1-8

Saint Paul recounts the core of the Gospel message: that Christ died for our sins, was buried, and rose on the third day. He emphasizes the importance of the resurrection as the foundation of Christian faith and lists the witnesses who saw the risen Christ, including himself.

Reflection:

This passage highlights the centrality of the resurrection in the Christian faith. The resurrection is not just an event but the cornerstone of our belief, affirming that Jesus has conquered death and offers new life to all who believe. The witnesses of the resurrection, including Paul, underscore the reality and significance of this event. This reflection calls us to live with the conviction that Christ's resurrection transforms our lives and our understanding of our faith.

Prayer:

Lord Jesus, we thank You for the gift of the resurrection and for the witnesses who have testified to Your victory over death. Strengthen our faith in Your promise of new life and help us to live with the hope and joy that Your resurrection brings. May the example of Saints Philip and James inspire us to boldly proclaim Your truth and follow Your example. Through Christ our Lord. Amen.

➢ Gospel: John 14: 6-14

In this passage, Jesus declares Himself as "the way, the truth, and the life," emphasizing that no one comes to the Father except through Him. He reassures His disciples that through belief in Him, they will see and do even greater works than He has done. This statement is a profound declaration of His divinity and His unique role as the mediator between humanity and God.

Reflection:

Jesus' declaration about being "the way, the truth, and the life" is central to our understanding of Him as the sole path to salvation and truth. This passage challenges us to reflect on our own relationship with Christ and our commitment to following Him. It also assures us of the power of His name and the promise that those who believe in Him will be empowered to carry out His work in the world.

Prayer:

Lord Jesus, we believe that You are the way, the truth, and the life. Help us to follow You faithfully and to trust in Your guidance. May we be empowered by Your Spirit to continue Your work in the world and to live out the truth of Your resurrection. Through Christ our Lord. Amen.

Sunday, May 4

❖ **Third Sunday of Easter**

> First Reading: Acts 5: 27-32, 40b-41
> Responsorial Psalm: Psalms 30: 2 and 4, 5-6, 11-12, 13
> Second Reading: Revelation 5: 11-14
> Gospel: John 21: 1-19
> Lectionary: 48

As we continue to celebrate the Easter season, today's readings remind us of the joy and strength that come from being witnesses to the risen Christ. The apostles, despite facing persecution, boldly proclaim the Good News. The heavenly vision in Revelation points us to the worship of the Lamb, and the Gospel recounts a powerful encounter between the risen Jesus and His disciples, particularly Peter, who is restored and commissioned to lead.

> **First Reading: Acts 5: 27-32, 40b-41**

The apostles are brought before the Sanhedrin and ordered to stop teaching in the name of Jesus. Peter and the apostles respond courageously, saying, "We must obey God rather than men." Despite being flogged and threatened, they leave rejoicing that they were found worthy to suffer for the name of Jesus.

Reflection:
The boldness of the apostles in the face of persecution is a powerful testimony to the transformative power of the resurrection. They are not deterred by threats or suffering because they have encountered the risen Christ, who has filled them with courage and joy. This reading challenges us to reflect on our own faith and witness. Are we willing to stand firm in our belief in Christ, even when it is difficult or costly?

Prayer:
Lord, grant us the courage and conviction of the apostles. Help us to stand firm in our faith and to rejoice in whatever trials we may face for Your name. May our witness be a testimony to the power of Your resurrection. Through Christ our Lord. Amen.

> **Second Reading: Revelation 5: 11-14**

John shares a vision of heavenly worship, where countless angels and all creatures in heaven and on earth give praise to the Lamb who was slain. The Lamb is declared worthy to receive power, wealth, wisdom, strength, honor, glory, and praise.

Reflection:

This passage draws us into the grandeur of heavenly worship, where all creation acknowledges the worthiness of Christ, the Lamb of God. It reminds us that our worship on earth is a participation in the eternal worship of heaven. This vision calls us to a deeper reverence and awe in our own worship, recognizing that in Christ, we encounter the One who is truly worthy of all honor and glory.

Prayer:

Worthy are You, O Lamb of God, to receive all our praise and worship. May our hearts be lifted in adoration and may our lives reflect Your glory. Help us to join in the heavenly chorus, praising You with all that we are. Through Christ our Lord. Amen.

➢ Gospel: John 21: 1-19

In this post-resurrection appearance, Jesus reveals Himself to the disciples by the Sea of Tiberias. After a miraculous catch of fish, He shares a meal with them. Jesus then asks Peter three times, "Do you love me?" Each time Peter affirms his love, Jesus commissions him to "feed my sheep," restoring him after his denial.

Reflection:

This Gospel passage is a poignant reminder of Jesus' mercy and His desire to restore and commission us, even when we have failed. Peter's threefold denial is met with a threefold opportunity to express his love for Jesus, highlighting the depth of Christ's forgiveness. This encounter invites us to experience the mercy of Jesus in our own lives, to be renewed in our love for Him, and to embrace the mission He entrusts to us.

Prayer:

Lord Jesus, thank You for Your mercy and for restoring us when we fall. Help us to love You more deeply and to faithfully carry out the mission You have given us. May we feed Your sheep with the love and grace You have shown us. Through Christ our Lord. Amen.

Monday, May 5

❖ Monday of the Third week of Easter

> ➢ First Reading: Acts 6: 8-15
> ➢ Responsorial Psalm: Psalms 119: 23-24, 26-27, 29-30
> ➢ Alleluia: Matthew 4: 4b
> ➢ Gospel: John 6: 22-29
> ➢ Lectionary: 273

As we journey through the Easter season, today's readings call us to reflect on the unwavering faith of early disciples like Stephen, who was filled with grace and power, and on Jesus' teaching about the true bread from heaven. We are invited to deepen our understanding of Christ as the source of eternal life.

> ➢ First Reading: Acts 6: 8-15

Stephen, one of the first deacons, is described as being filled with grace and power. He performs great wonders and signs among the people. However, some who oppose him begin to argue with him, and unable to defeat his wisdom, they falsely accuse him of blasphemy. Stephen is brought before the council, where his face shines like that of an angel.

Reflection:
Stephen's unwavering faith and courage in the face of opposition are a model for us. Even when falsely accused and threatened, Stephen remains steadfast, filled with the Holy Spirit. His shining face symbolizes his closeness to God and his unshakable confidence in the truth. This passage reminds us that when we stand for Christ, even in adversity, God strengthens us with His grace and fills us with His peace.

Prayer:
Lord, give us the grace and courage of Stephen to stand firm in our faith, even when we face opposition. May our lives radiate Your presence and truth in every situation. Through Christ our Lord. Amen.

> ➢ Gospel: John 6: 22-29

After the miracle of the loaves, the crowd seeks Jesus, and He challenges them not to work for food that perishes but for the food that endures to eternal life. Jesus tells them that the work of God is to believe in the one He has sent.

Reflection:

This passage invites us to reflect on the deeper hunger within us that only Christ can satisfy. The crowd was focused on material needs, but Jesus redirects them to the spiritual nourishment that leads to eternal life. Faith in Jesus is the work God desires from us—the belief that He alone is the Bread of Life, the source of our eternal sustenance.

Prayer:

Lord Jesus, help us to seek You above all else, trusting that You are the Bread of Life who satisfies our deepest hunger. Strengthen our faith and lead us to the eternal life You offer. Through Christ our Lord. Amen.

Tuesday, May 6

❖ Tuesday of the Third week of Easter

- First Reading: Acts 7: 51-60
- Responsorial Psalm: Psalms 31: 3cd-4, 6 and 7b and 8a, 17 and 21ab
- Alleluia: John 6: 35ab
- Gospel: John 6: 30-35
- Lectionary: 274

Today's readings present us with the profound faith and ultimate sacrifice of Stephen, the first Christian martyr, and the deep spiritual truth that Jesus is the Bread of Life. We are invited to contemplate the cost of discipleship and the life-giving sustenance that only Christ can provide.

- First Reading: Acts 7: 51-60

Stephen continues his defense before the Sanhedrin, boldly accusing them of resisting the Holy Spirit, just as their ancestors did. Enraged, they drag him out of the city and stone him. Stephen, filled with the Holy Spirit, gazes into heaven and sees the glory of God and Jesus standing at the right hand of God. As he is being stoned, he prays for his attackers, saying, "Lord, do not hold this sin against them." With these words, Stephen dies, becoming the first martyr of the Christian faith.

Reflection:

Stephen's martyrdom is a powerful testimony to the depth of his faith and his Christ-like love, even for his enemies. His vision of Jesus standing at the right hand of God reassures us of the glory that awaits those who are faithful to the end. Stephen's prayer for his persecutors challenges us to forgive and love others, even in the face of injustice and suffering.

Prayer:
Lord, grant us the courage and faith of Stephen, to stand firm in the truth and to love others as You have loved us, even in the midst of trials. May we always seek Your glory and trust in Your promise of eternal life. Through Christ our Lord. Amen.

> ➢ Gospel: John 6: 30-35

The crowd asks Jesus for a sign so that they may believe in Him, recalling how their ancestors received manna in the desert. Jesus responds by revealing that the true bread from heaven is not like the manna their ancestors ate but is the Bread of Life that gives life to the world. He declares, "I am the bread of life; whoever comes to me will never hunger, and whoever believes in me will never thirst."

Reflection:
In this passage, Jesus reveals Himself as the Bread of Life, the true sustenance that satisfies our deepest spiritual hunger. Unlike the manna that temporarily fed the Israelites, Jesus offers eternal nourishment. By coming to Him and believing in Him, we receive the life-giving sustenance that only He can provide. This is an invitation to deepen our relationship with Jesus, trusting in His promise to fulfill our every need.

Prayer:
Lord Jesus, You are the Bread of Life who satisfies our deepest longings. Help us to come to You with open hearts, trusting in Your promise of eternal life. Nourish our souls with Your love and grace, that we may never hunger or thirst again. Through Christ our Lord. Amen.

Wednesday, May 7

❖ Wednesday of the Third week of Easter

> ➢ First Reading: Acts 8: 1b-8
> ➢ Responsorial Psalm: Psalms 66: 1-3a, 4-5, 6-7a
> ➢ Alleluia: John 6: 40
> ➢ Gospel: John 6: 35-40
> ➢ Lectionary: 275

Today's readings continue to reveal the spread of the early Church through both persecution and proclamation. As we reflect on the courage of the early Christians, we are also reminded by Jesus in the Gospel that He is the Bread of Life, the source of our hope and eternal life.

➢ First Reading: Acts 8: 1b-8

After the martyrdom of Stephen, a severe persecution breaks out against the Church in Jerusalem, scattering the believers throughout Judea and Samaria. Despite this, the scattered believers continue to preach the word. Philip goes to a city in Samaria and proclaims the Christ there. The crowds, seeing the signs and hearing the message, are filled with joy, and many are healed and delivered from unclean spirits.

Reflection:

The early Christians faced intense persecution, yet their faith did not waver. Instead, they saw every challenge as an opportunity to spread the Gospel. Philip's mission to Samaria shows that God's work cannot be confined or stopped by human opposition. The joy and healing experienced by the Samaritans remind us that the Good News brings freedom and joy wherever it is received. We, too, are called to proclaim Christ with courage, trusting that God will work through us to bring light and hope to others.

Prayer:

Lord, in the face of challenges and trials, may we be like the early Christians, steadfast in faith and bold in proclaiming Your word. Fill us with the joy of Your salvation and use us as instruments of Your healing and peace. Through Christ our Lord. Amen.

➢ Gospel: John 6: 35-40

Jesus continues His discourse on the Bread of Life, declaring that whoever comes to Him will never hunger, and whoever believes in Him will never thirst. He emphasizes that He has come down from heaven to do the will of the Father, which is that everyone who believes in Him may have eternal life, and He will raise them up on the last day.

Reflection:

In this passage, Jesus reassures us of His divine mission and the promise of eternal life for all who believe in Him. As the Bread of Life, Jesus not only sustains us in this life but also guarantees our resurrection and eternal life with Him. This promise invites us to trust deeply in Jesus, knowing that our ultimate fulfillment is found in Him alone. In a world full of uncertainties, His words offer us the assurance of God's unfailing love and the hope of everlasting life.

Prayer:

Lord Jesus, You are the Bread of Life who satisfies our every need and gives us the hope of eternal life. Strengthen our faith and help us to trust in Your promise of resurrection and eternal joy. May we always seek You and find our true fulfillment in Your love. Through Christ our Lord. Amen.

Thursday, May 8

❖ Thursday of the Third week of Easter

- First Reading: Acts 8: 26-40
- Responsorial Psalm: Psalms 66: 8-9, 16-17, 20
- Alleluia: John 6: 51
- Gospel: John 6: 44-51
- Lectionary: 276

Today's readings invite us to reflect on the openness and guidance of the Holy Spirit in leading us to deeper faith. The encounter between Philip and the Ethiopian eunuch, along with Jesus' continued teaching on the Bread of Life, reminds us that God's desire is to draw all people to Himself, nourishing them with His Word and His very life.

- First Reading: Acts 8: 26-40

Philip is directed by an angel of the Lord to go south to the road that goes from Jerusalem to Gaza. There, he meets an Ethiopian eunuch, a high official of the queen of the Ethiopians, who is reading from the prophet Isaiah. The Spirit tells Philip to approach the chariot, and Philip explains the Scriptures to the eunuch, pointing to Jesus as the fulfillment of Isaiah's prophecy. Moved by the explanation, the eunuch requests to be baptized when they come to some water. After the baptism, Philip is taken away by the Spirit, and the eunuch continues on his way rejoicing.

Reflection:
This encounter between Philip and the Ethiopian eunuch shows how God's Spirit actively leads and opens hearts to the truth of the Gospel. The eunuch's desire to understand the Scriptures and his immediate response in baptism highlight the importance of openness to God's Word and the transformative power of faith. Philip's readiness to follow the Spirit's guidance and his willingness to share the Good News remind us of our call to be attentive to God's promptings and to be ready to witness to our faith in everyday situations.

Prayer:
Holy Spirit, guide us as You guided Philip, that we may be attentive to Your promptings and ready to share the Good News of Jesus Christ. Open our hearts and the hearts of those we encounter to the truth of Your Word, and lead us all to a deeper faith and joy in You. Through Christ our Lord. Amen.

> Gospel: John 6: 44-51

Jesus continues His teaching on the Bread of Life, emphasizing that no one can come to Him unless drawn by the Father. He declares that He is the living bread that came down from heaven, and whoever eats of this bread will live forever. The bread that He will give for the life of the world is His flesh.

Reflection:

In this passage, Jesus makes it clear that our journey of faith is initiated by God's grace. The Father draws us to Jesus, the true Bread of Life, who offers Himself as the ultimate nourishment for our souls. This profound mystery of the Eucharist, where Jesus gives His very flesh for the life of the world, invites us to a deeper union with Him. As we receive the Bread of Life, we are called to live in His love and to share His life with others, becoming a source of life and blessing in the world.

Prayer:

Lord Jesus, You are the living Bread who came down from heaven to give us life. Draw us closer to You each day, and nourish us with Your presence in the Eucharist. May we be strengthened by Your love and become instruments of Your grace to those around us. Through Christ our Lord. Amen.

Friday, May 9

❖ Friday of the Third week of Easter

> First Reading: Acts 9: 1-20
> Responsorial Psalm: Psalms 117: 1, 2
> Alleluia: John 6: 56
> Gospel: John 6: 52-59
> Lectionary: 277

Today's readings reveal the transformative power of encountering Christ. Saul's dramatic conversion on the road to Damascus and Jesus' continued teaching on the Eucharist remind us that faith is both a gift and a call to a new way of life. In the Eucharist, we receive Christ fully, and like Saul, we are called to let this encounter change us profoundly.

> First Reading: Acts 9: 1-20

Saul, who is passionately persecuting the disciples of Jesus, experiences a life-changing encounter with Christ on the road to Damascus. A blinding light surrounds him, and he hears the voice of Jesus asking, "Saul, Saul, why are you persecuting me?" Struck blind, Saul is led into Damascus, where he fasts and prays for three days. Ananias, a disciple, is instructed by the Lord to go to Saul and lay hands on him so that he may regain his sight. Despite his initial fear, Ananias obeys, and Saul's sight is restored. He is baptized and begins to proclaim Jesus as the Son of God.

Reflection:
Saul's conversion is a powerful testament to the mercy and grace of God. Even those who seem farthest from faith can be radically transformed by an encounter with Christ. Saul's zeal, once directed against the followers of Jesus, becomes a fervent dedication to proclaiming the Gospel. This story reminds us that no one is beyond the reach of God's love and that each of us, too, is called to a continual conversion of heart, allowing Christ to transform us daily.

Prayer:
Lord Jesus, You transformed Saul from a persecutor to a great apostle. Grant us the grace of conversion, that we may turn away from sin and wholeheartedly follow You. Open our eyes to Your truth and guide us to live as faithful witnesses of Your love. Through Christ our Lord. Amen.

➢ Gospel: John 6: 52-59

In this passage, Jesus deepens His teaching on the Bread of Life, stating that His flesh is true food and His blood is true drink. He emphasizes that whoever eats His flesh and drinks His blood remains in Him, and He in them. This teaching causes dispute among the Jews, who struggle to understand how Jesus can give them His flesh to eat.

Reflection:
Jesus' words challenge us to move beyond a purely symbolic understanding of the Eucharist and to recognize the profound mystery of His Real Presence. In the Eucharist, Jesus gives us His very self, body, and blood, as true spiritual nourishment. This intimate union with Christ sustains us and draws us into a deeper relationship with Him. As we receive the Eucharist, we are called to remain in Christ, allowing His life to flow through us and transform us into His image.

Prayer:
Lord Jesus, in the Eucharist, You give us Your body and blood as true food and drink. Strengthen our faith in this mystery and help us to receive You with reverence and love. May our communion with You in the Eucharist deepen our union with You and empower us to live out Your love in the world. Through Christ our Lord. Amen.

Saturday, May 10

- ❖ Saturday of the Third week of Easter
- ❖ In the United States
- ❖ Saturday of the Third week of Easter
- ❖ Saint Damien de Veuster, Priest - Optional Memorial

> First Reading: Acts 9: 31-42

> Responsorial Psalm: Psalms 116: 12-13, 14-15, 16-17

> Alleluia: John 6: 63c, 68c

> Gospel: John 6: 60-69

> Lectionary: 278

Today's readings continue to explore the power of faith in action. We witness the early Church growing in peace and strength as it performs miracles in Christ's name. Jesus challenges His disciples to remain steadfast in their belief, even when His teachings are difficult to accept. On this day, we also remember Saint Damien de Veuster, whose life was a profound example of selfless service and unwavering faith.

> First Reading: Acts 9: 31-42

The Church in Judea, Galilee, and Samaria enjoys a period of peace and continues to grow as it lives in the fear of the Lord and is strengthened by the Holy Spirit. Peter, visiting the believers, performs miraculous healings: Aeneas, bedridden for eight years, is healed, and Tabitha (also known as Dorcas), a beloved disciple in Joppa who had died, is raised back to life. These miracles lead many to believe in the Lord.

Reflection:
The early Church's growth was fueled not just by preaching but by the tangible power of Christ working through the apostles. These miracles served as signs of God's Kingdom breaking into the world, bringing life and healing where there was death and despair. Peter's actions remind us that faith is not just about believing in words but also about living out that faith in deeds of love and mercy, trusting that God continues to work miracles through His Church.

Prayer:
Heavenly Father, just as You empowered Peter to bring healing and new life, empower us to be instruments of Your love in the world. Strengthen our faith so that we may live it out in action, bringing hope and healing to those in need. Through Christ our Lord. Amen.

➢ Gospel: John 6: 60-69

After hearing Jesus' discourse on the Bread of Life, many of His disciples find His teaching hard to accept and begin to leave Him. Jesus asks the Twelve if they too wish to leave, but Peter responds, "Lord, to whom shall we go? You have the words of eternal life. We have come to believe and to know that you are the Holy One of God."

Reflection:
The words of Jesus often challenge us, pushing us beyond our comfort zones and demanding a deeper commitment to Him. When confronted with teachings that are difficult to understand or accept, we may be tempted to turn away, as some of His disciples did. However, Peter's response invites us to place our trust in Jesus, even when we do not fully grasp His words. Faith is not merely an intellectual exercise but a relationship with the One who is the source of eternal life.

Prayer:
Lord Jesus, when Your teachings challenge us, give us the grace to remain steadfast in our faith. Help us to trust in Your words and to follow You, even when the path is difficult. Strengthen our belief in You as the Holy One of God, and guide us in our journey toward eternal life. Amen.

➢ Commemoration of Saint Damien de Veuster:

Saint Damien de Veuster, also known as Father Damien, was a Belgian missionary priest who dedicated his life to serving the lepers on the island of Molokai, Hawaii. His selfless service and compassion for the marginalized made him a powerful witness to the love of Christ. He ultimately contracted leprosy himself and died as a martyr of charity.

Prayer:
Saint Damien, you showed the love of Christ to those whom society had abandoned. Intercede for us, that we may have the courage to serve the most vulnerable among us with the same compassion and dedication. May we, like you, be witnesses of Christ's love in the world. Amen.

Sunday, May 11

❖ Fourth Sunday of Easter

- ➤ First Reading: Acts 13: 14, 43-52
- ➤ Responsorial Psalm: Psalms 100: 1-2, 3, 5
- ➤ Second Reading: Revelation 7: 9, 14b-17
- ➤ Alleluia: John 10: 14
- ➤ Gospel: John 10: 27-30
- ➤ Lectionary: 51

The Fourth Sunday of Easter, also known as Good Shepherd Sunday, invites us to reflect on Jesus as the Good Shepherd who knows His sheep and leads them to eternal life. The readings today emphasize the inclusive nature of God's love and the eternal security found in following Christ. We are reminded that, despite trials and opposition, those who follow the Shepherd are assured of His guidance and protection.

➤ First Reading: Acts 13: 14, 43-52

Paul and Barnabas continue their missionary journey, reaching Antioch in Pisidia. After preaching in the synagogue, they encounter both acceptance and rejection. While many Gentiles eagerly embrace the message of salvation, some Jewish leaders incite persecution against them, leading Paul and Barnabas to declare that they will now turn to the Gentiles. Despite the opposition, the disciples are filled with joy and the Holy Spirit.

Reflection:
The spread of the Gospel is marked by both acceptance and resistance. Paul and Barnabas encounter hostility, yet they remain resolute in their mission. This passage reminds us that the message of salvation is offered to all, regardless of their background. When faced with opposition or rejection, we are called to persist in our faith and continue sharing the love of Christ with others, trusting that God will guide and protect us.

Prayer:
Lord, give us the courage to proclaim Your Gospel even in the face of opposition. Fill us with Your Spirit so that, like Paul and Barnabas, we may remain joyful and steadfast in our mission. Help us to be instruments of Your love, bringing the message of salvation to all. Amen.

➢ Second Reading: Revelation 7: 9, 14b-17

John shares a vision of a great multitude from every nation, standing before the throne and the Lamb, dressed in white robes. These are the ones who have come through great tribulation and have washed their robes in the blood of the Lamb. The Lamb will shepherd them, leading them to springs of life-giving water, and God will wipe away every tear from their eyes.

Reflection:
This vision from Revelation offers a powerful image of hope and consolation. The multitude, representing all humanity, stands victorious before God, having endured trials and suffering. They are led by the Lamb, who is also their Shepherd, to the waters of eternal life. This passage reminds us that, despite the hardships we may face, we are destined for eternal joy and peace in God's presence. Jesus, our Good Shepherd, will guide us through all trials and lead us to everlasting life.

Prayer:
Lamb of God, You have redeemed us by Your blood and lead us to the springs of eternal life. Comfort us in our trials and wipe away every tear from our eyes. May we always remain close to You, our Shepherd, and find our ultimate rest in Your presence. Amen.

➢ Gospel: John 10: 27-30

Jesus speaks of His relationship with His followers, saying, "My sheep hear my voice; I know them, and they follow me. I give them eternal life, and they shall never perish. No one can take them out of my hand. My Father, who has given them to me, is greater than all, and no one can take them out of the Father's hand. The Father and I are one."

Reflection:
In this brief but profound passage, Jesus reassures us of the security and intimacy we have in Him. As the Good Shepherd, He knows each of us personally and calls us by name. Our response is to listen to His voice and follow Him. In doing so, we are promised the gift of eternal life, safe in the hands of the Father and the Son. This passage encourages us to trust in the unbreakable bond of love between us and God, a bond that nothing can sever.

Prayer:
Good Shepherd, help us to recognize Your voice and follow You with trust and confidence. Thank You for the gift of eternal life and the assurance that we are secure in Your hands. May we always remain close to You, finding our peace and protection in Your love. Amen.

Monday, May 12

- ❖ Monday of the Fourth week of Easter
- ❖ Saints Nereus and Achilleus, martyrs - Optional Memorial
- ❖ Saint Pancras, martyr - Optional Memorial

> First Reading: Acts 11: 1-18
> Responsorial Psalm: Psalms 42: 2-3; 43: 3-4
> Alleluia: John 10: 14
> Gospel: John 10: 1-10
> Lectionary: 279

Today's readings invite us to reflect on the inclusive nature of God's salvation and the role of Jesus as the true Shepherd. As we remember the martyrs Saints Nereus, Achilleus, and Pancras, we are inspired by their unwavering faith and witness to the Gospel. Their courage in the face of persecution encourages us to follow the voice of the Good Shepherd, trusting in His promise of abundant life.

> First Reading: Acts 11: 1-18

In this passage, Peter recounts his vision in which God reveals to him that the message of salvation is not limited to the Jews but is also for the Gentiles. Peter initially struggles with this revelation, as it challenges long-held beliefs about purity and God's chosen people. However, he comes to understand that God shows no partiality and that the Holy Spirit is poured out on all who believe, regardless of their background. This understanding leads to the acceptance of Gentile believers into the Christian community.

Reflection:
Peter's experience reminds us of the expansive and inclusive nature of God's love. Sometimes, our preconceived notions or biases can limit our understanding of whom God calls into His family. This reading challenges us to embrace the universality of the Gospel and to welcome all people into the fold of Christ, regardless of their background. We are called to be open to the work of the Holy Spirit, who leads us to new and sometimes unexpected understandings of God's will.

Prayer:
Lord, help us to recognize the boundless reach of Your love. Open our hearts to accept all people as Your children and to work for unity in the body of Christ. May we follow Your Spirit's leading in breaking down barriers and extending the message of salvation to all. Amen.

> Gospel: John 10: 1-10

In this passage, Jesus uses the metaphor of the Good Shepherd and the sheep. He contrasts Himself with those who are thieves and robbers, who come only to steal, kill, and destroy. Jesus, as the true Shepherd, enters through the gate, and His sheep recognize His voice and follow Him. He promises that those who enter through Him will be saved and will find abundant life.

Reflection:

Jesus, as the Good Shepherd, calls each of us by name, and He invites us to follow Him to safety and abundance. This passage reassures us that in a world where many voices compete for our attention, we can trust the voice of Jesus to lead us to true life. It also challenges us to discern the voices we listen to, ensuring that we are guided by Christ, who came so that we might have life in abundance.

Prayer:

Good Shepherd, guide us in recognizing Your voice amidst the noise of the world. Help us to follow You faithfully, trusting that You lead us to abundant life. Protect us from the thieves and robbers who seek to steal our peace and joy. May we always remain close to You, our true Shepherd. Amen.

Tuesday, May 13

❖ Tuesday of the Fourth week of Easter
❖ Our Lady of Fatima - Optional Memorial

> First Reading: Acts 11: 19-26
> Responsorial Psalm: Psalms 87: 1b-3, 4-5, 6-7
> Alleluia: John 10: 27
> Gospel: John 10: 22-30
> Lectionary: 280

On this day, the Church honors Our Lady of Fatima, commemorating the apparitions of the Blessed Virgin Mary to three shepherd children in Fatima, Portugal, in 1917. Her message of prayer, penance, and conversion is still relevant today. In the readings, we continue to explore the themes of discipleship and the guidance of the Good Shepherd, who leads His flock to eternal life.

> First Reading: Acts 11: 19-26

In this passage, we hear about the spread of the Gospel following the persecution of Christians after Stephen's martyrdom. The scattered believers preach the word to Jews and, eventually, to Greeks as well.

The church in Antioch grows significantly, and Barnabas is sent to encourage the new believers. He then seeks out Saul (Paul) to help with the work. The disciples are first called Christians in Antioch, marking a significant moment in the early Church's identity and mission.

Reflection:

The early Christians, despite facing persecution, did not shy away from spreading the Good News. Their mission extended beyond their immediate community, reaching out to those who were previously considered outsiders. This reading challenges us to embrace our identity as Christians and to be bold in sharing our faith, even in the face of adversity. Like Barnabas and Saul, we are called to support and encourage one another in our journey of faith, building up the body of Christ.

Prayer:

Heavenly Father, grant us the courage to live out our faith boldly and to spread the message of Your love to all people. Help us to be sources of encouragement to one another as we grow in our Christian identity. May we always seek to build up Your Church, following the example of the early disciples. Amen.

➢ Gospel: John 10: 22-30

In this passage, Jesus is in the temple during the Feast of Dedication (Hanukkah), and the people ask Him to clarify whether He is the Christ. Jesus responds by saying that His works testify to His identity, but they do not believe because they are not among His sheep. He reiterates that His sheep hear His voice, and He knows them, and they follow Him. He gives them eternal life, and no one can snatch them out of His hand, for He and the Father are one.

Reflection:

Jesus' words remind us of the deep relationship He desires with His followers. To be one of His sheep is to listen to His voice and follow His lead, trusting in the eternal life He offers. This passage assures us of the security we have in Christ—no one can take us from His hand. It also calls us to reflect on whether we are truly attentive to His voice in our lives and whether we are following Him with trust and fidelity.

Prayer:

Lord Jesus, help us to recognize Your voice in our lives and to follow You with unwavering trust. We thank You for the gift of eternal life and the assurance that nothing can separate us from Your love. Strengthen our faith so that we may remain faithful to You, our Good Shepherd, who leads us to the Father. Amen.

Wednesday, May 14

❖ Saint Matthias, apostle - Feast

- First Reading: Acts 1: 15-17, 20-26
- Responsorial Psalm: Psalms 113: 1-2, 3-4, 5-6, 7-8
- Alleluia: John 15: 16
- Gospel: John 15: 9-17
- Lectionary: 564

Today the Church celebrates Saint Matthias, who was chosen to replace Judas Iscariot as one of the Twelve Apostles. His selection is a testament to the importance of apostolic succession and the continuation of Jesus' mission through the apostles. The readings highlight the call to discipleship and the call to love one another as Jesus has loved us.

First Reading: Acts 1: 15-17, 20-26

In this reading, the apostles gather to select a replacement for Judas Iscariot. Peter addresses the group, explaining that the vacancy must be filled in accordance with Scripture. The criteria are that the new apostle must have been with them from the beginning of Jesus' ministry until His ascension. Two men are proposed: Joseph (Barsabbas) and Matthias. After praying for guidance, they cast lots, and Matthias is chosen to join the eleven apostles.

Reflection:
Saint Matthias' selection illustrates the early Church's commitment to fulfilling the mandate given by Jesus. His election reaffirms the importance of apostolic authority and the continuity of the Church's mission. It also reminds us of the importance of discernment and prayer in making decisions. Matthias' acceptance of the call reflects the readiness and obedience required to serve God's purposes. We are called to respond to God's call in our own lives with the same readiness and faithfulness.

Prayer:
Almighty God, who chose Saint Matthias to be numbered among the Twelve, grant us, through his intercession, that we may be firm in our faith and fervent in our service to You. Help us to respond with readiness to Your call and to live out our Christian vocation with dedication and joy. Through Christ our Lord. Amen.

➢ Gospel: John 15: 9-17

In this passage, Jesus speaks to His disciples about the nature of His love and the love they are called to have for one another. He explains that just as the Father has loved Him, He has loved them, and they are to remain in His love by keeping His commandments. Jesus calls them friends rather than servants, because He has made known to them everything He has learned from the Father. He commands them to love one another as He has loved them.

Reflection:
Jesus' command to love one another underscores the heart of His teaching and mission. The love He speaks of is not merely a feeling but a deep, sacrificial commitment to the well-being of others. By calling His disciples friends, Jesus highlights the intimacy of the relationship He desires with them and with us. This passage challenges us to live out our Christian vocation by loving others with the same self-giving love that Jesus has shown us.

Prayer:
Lord Jesus, thank You for calling us Your friends and for showing us the depth of Your love. Help us to remain in Your love by obeying Your commandments and to love one another as You have loved us. May our lives reflect the joy and peace that come from being Your friends and disciples. Amen.

Thursday, May 15

- ❖ Thursday of the Fourth week of Easter
- ❖ In the United States
- ❖ Thursday of the Fourth week of Easter
- ❖ Saint Isidore the Farmer - Optional Memorial

➢ First Reading: Acts 13: 13-25
➢ Responsorial Psalm: Psalms 89: 2-3, 21-22, 25 and 27
➢ Alleluia: Revelation 1: 5ab
➢ Gospel: John 13: 16-20
➢ Lectionary: 282

Today, the Church remembers Saint Isidore the Farmer, a patron saint of farmers and laborers. His life of humble work and piety exemplifies how ordinary work can be sanctified and made holy. The readings reflect themes of divine calling and the importance of faithfulness in one's vocation.

➢ First Reading: Acts 13: 13-25

In this passage, Paul and his companions arrive in Antioch in Pisidia, where Paul addresses the synagogue congregation. He recounts the history of Israel, highlighting God's faithfulness from the time of the Exodus to the establishment of King David. Paul emphasizes that Jesus is the fulfillment of God's promises made to the ancestors. He speaks of John the Baptist's role in preparing the way for Jesus and how Jesus' coming is the ultimate fulfillment of the promises made to Israel.

Reflection:
Paul's speech underscores the continuity of God's plan throughout history, culminating in Jesus. This historical perspective helps us see the broader picture of salvation history and understand the significance of Jesus' mission. It also reminds us that our own lives and vocations fit into a larger divine plan. As Saint Isidore lived his life faithfully in his simple vocation, we too are called to recognize and fulfill our role within God's grand design.

Prayer:
Heavenly Father, thank You for the example of Saint Isidore, who sanctified his work through his faith and devotion. Help us to recognize Your hand in our daily lives and to carry out our vocations with the same dedication and love. Strengthen us to be faithful in our own callings and to serve You in all that we do. Through Christ our Lord. Amen.

➢ Gospel: John 13: 16-20

In this passage, Jesus speaks about the servant's role and the significance of His actions. He explains that a servant is not greater than his master, and He is sending His disciples as His representatives. Jesus underscores that the one who accepts those He sends is accepting Him, and in turn, is accepting the One who sent Him.

Reflection:
Jesus' words remind us of the humility required in service and the interconnectedness of His mission with that of His followers. By serving others, we are serving Him and honoring the One who sent Him. This passage calls us to embrace a spirit of service and humility, reflecting Jesus' own example of love and sacrifice.

Prayer:
Lord Jesus, teach us to embrace the spirit of service that You modeled for us. Help us to live out our callings with humility and dedication, recognizing that in serving others, we serve You. May our lives be a reflection of Your love and grace, as we follow Your example and share Your message with the world. Amen.

Friday, May 16

❖ **Friday of the Fourth week of Easter**

- First Reading: Acts 13: 26-33
- Responsorial Psalm: Psalms 2: 6-7, 8-9, 10-11ab
- Alleluia: John 14: 6
- Gospel: John 14: 1-6
- Lectionary: 283

In today's readings, we reflect on the themes of divine promise and the way Jesus reveals the path to eternal life. These readings provide us with assurance of God's faithfulness and the promise of Christ as the way to the Father.

First Reading: Acts 13: 26-33

Paul continues his sermon in Antioch, recounting the fulfillment of God's promises through Jesus. He emphasizes that Jesus' resurrection is the culmination of the promise made to the ancestors. Paul explains that God has fulfilled His promises by raising Jesus from the dead, making Jesus the Savior who brings forgiveness and new life.

Reflection:
Paul's proclamation highlights the centrality of Jesus' resurrection in the Christian faith. It confirms that Jesus is the fulfillment of the ancient promises and that through Him, we find redemption and hope. This reading invites us to reflect on the significance of Jesus' resurrection in our own lives and how it assures us of God's steadfast love and faithfulness.

Prayer:
Lord God, we thank You for fulfilling Your promises through the resurrection of Jesus. Help us to live in the light of this great truth and to trust in Your promises for our own lives. May the hope of the resurrection strengthen us in our daily walk with You, and inspire us to share this hope with others. Through Christ our Lord. Amen.

Gospel: John 14: 1-6

In this passage, Jesus reassures His disciples not to be troubled, for He is going to prepare a place for them in His Father's house. He declares that He is the Way, the Truth, and the Life, and that no one comes to the Father except through Him. Jesus' words provide comfort and a clear direction for those seeking to follow Him.

Reflection:
Jesus' assurance that He is the Way, the Truth, and the Life offers profound comfort and guidance. His declaration that He is the only way to the Father emphasizes the centrality of His role in our journey of faith. This passage calls us to trust in Jesus as our guide and to follow Him faithfully, knowing that He leads us to the fullness of life with God.

Prayer:
Lord Jesus, we are grateful for Your promise to prepare a place for us and for being the Way, the Truth, and the Life. Help us to trust in Your guidance and to follow You with confidence. May Your presence be a source of comfort and strength in our journey, and may we always seek to deepen our relationship with You. Amen.

Saturday, May 17

❖ Saturday of the Fourth week of Easter

- First Reading: Acts 13: 44-52
- Responsorial Psalm: Psalms 98: 1, 2-3ab, 3cd-4
- Alleluia: John 8: 31b-32
- Gospel: John 14: 7-14
- Lectionary: 284

Today's readings invite us to reflect on the spread of the Gospel and the promises of Jesus. The Acts of the Apostles recounts the early church's mission and the response to the message of Christ, while the Gospel emphasizes Jesus' unity with the Father and the promise of answered prayer.

- First Reading: Acts 13: 44-52

In this passage, Paul and Barnabas encounter opposition from some Jewish leaders in Antioch, but they continue to boldly proclaim the message of salvation to the Gentiles. Their message is received with great joy by many, but the opposition leads to their expulsion from the region. The reading concludes with the disciples being filled with joy and the Holy Spirit, continuing their mission despite the challenges.

Reflection:
Paul and Barnabas' perseverance in the face of opposition is a powerful witness to their commitment to spreading the Gospel. Their experience reminds us that proclaiming the message of Christ may come with

difficulties, but the joy and fulfillment found in fulfilling God's mission far outweigh the challenges. It encourages us to remain steadfast in our own witness to the faith, trusting that God's Spirit will guide and sustain us.

Prayer:
Lord, we thank You for the example of Paul and Barnabas, who boldly proclaimed Your message despite opposition. Grant us the courage and strength to continue our own journey of faith, even when faced with challenges. Fill us with Your Spirit, and help us to be joyful witnesses to Your love and salvation. Through Christ our Lord. Amen.

> Gospel: John 14: 7-14

In this passage, Jesus assures His disciples that knowing Him is equivalent to knowing the Father. He emphasizes the unity between Himself and the Father, stating that anyone who has seen Him has seen the Father. Jesus also promises that whatever they ask in His name will be done, as this will glorify the Father through the Son.

Reflection:
Jesus' words affirm His divine unity with the Father and highlight the importance of recognizing Him as the revelation of God. His promise to answer prayers made in His name assures us of His presence and responsiveness to our needs. This passage calls us to deepen our relationship with Jesus, understanding that through Him, we come to know God more fully and experience His blessings.

Prayer:
Lord Jesus, thank You for revealing the Father to us and for Your promise to answer our prayers. Help us to grow in our relationship with You, knowing that through You, we come to know the fullness of God's love and grace. May our faith be strengthened, and may we always trust in Your promises as we seek to follow You more closely. Amen.

Sunday, May 18

❖ Fifth Sunday of Easter

> First Reading: Acts 14: 21-27
> Responsorial Psalm: Psalms 145: 8-9, 10-11, 12-13
> Second Reading: Revelation 21: 1-5a
> Alleluia: John 13: 34
> Gospel: John 13: 31-33a, 34-35
> Lectionary: 54

Today's liturgy focuses on the theme of renewal and the new commandment given by Jesus. The readings highlight the growth of the early Church, the promise of a new creation, and the call to love one another as a sign of discipleship.

➢ First Reading: Acts 14: 21-27

In this passage, Paul and Barnabas return to the cities where they had previously preached, strengthening the believers and appointing elders. They recount their journey and the many hardships they faced, emphasizing the importance of perseverance through trials. The church rejoices as they are welcomed back, and the missionaries report how God has opened the door of faith to the Gentiles.

Reflection:
Paul and Barnabas' journey reflects the challenges and joys of spreading the Gospel. Their perseverance despite adversity and their dedication to strengthening the early Church offer a model for us in our own struggles and efforts in living out our faith. Their experience underscores that the path of discipleship involves both trials and triumphs, and through it all, God is at work opening doors for faith.

Prayer:
Lord, we thank You for the faith and courage of Paul and Barnabas. As we face our own challenges in following You, grant us perseverance and joy in our journey. Help us to remain steadfast in our commitment to spreading Your message and to support one another as we grow in faith. Through Christ our Lord. Amen.

➢ Second Reading: Revelation 21: 1-5a

This passage from Revelation describes a vision of a new heaven and a new earth, where God will dwell with His people. The old order has passed away, and God makes all things new. The vision emphasizes the end of suffering and the promise of God's eternal presence among His people.

Reflection:
The vision of the new creation in Revelation offers hope and encouragement. It reminds us that despite the difficulties and imperfections of our current world, God is preparing a new and perfect reality where He will be with us forever. This promise calls us to live with hope and to anticipate the fulfillment of God's plan for a renewed world.

Prayer:
Heavenly Father, we rejoice in the promise of a new creation where You will dwell with Your people. Strengthen our hope and faith as we await the fulfillment of Your promises. Help us to live in a way that reflects the values of Your coming kingdom and to trust in Your plan for our lives. Through Christ our Lord. Amen.

> Gospel: John 13: 31-33a, 34-35

In this Gospel passage, Jesus speaks to His disciples about the new commandment He is giving them: to love one another as He has loved them. This commandment is a sign of their discipleship and a reflection of His own love for them. Jesus emphasizes that love is the mark of true discipleship.

Reflection:

Jesus' command to love one another as He has loved us is central to our identity as His disciples. It challenges us to live out His love in our relationships and interactions with others. This commandment is not just about loving in words but in action, reflecting the self-giving and sacrificial love that Jesus demonstrated. It is through this love that others will recognize us as His followers.

Prayer:

Lord Jesus, thank You for the gift of Your love and the new commandment You have given us. Help us to love one another with the same selfless and sacrificial love that You have shown us. May our love be a witness to Your presence in our lives and a sign of Your kingdom to others. Amen.

Monday, May 19

❖ Monday of the Fifth week of Easter

> First Reading: Acts 14: 5-18
> Responsorial Psalm: Psalms 115: 1-2, 3-4, 15-16
> Alleluia: John 14: 26
> Gospel: John 14: 21-26
> Lectionary: 285

Today's readings continue to emphasize the themes of faith and the work of the Holy Spirit. The early Church's mission and the promise of the Spirit's guidance are highlighted, encouraging us to live out our faith with confidence and reliance on God's presence.

> First Reading: Acts 14: 5-18

In this passage, Paul and Barnabas face opposition and are mistaken for gods in the city of Lystra. Despite the praise and offerings they receive, they direct the people's attention to the true God, emphasizing that they are mere servants. They continue their mission, speaking of the living God who made heaven and earth and urging the people to turn from false gods to the living God.

Reflection:

Paul and Barnabas' experience in Lystra shows the challenges of proclaiming the Gospel in a context filled with misunderstanding and opposition. Their response reminds us to stay focused on directing others to God rather than seeking personal glory. It also calls us to be bold in our witness while remaining humble and faithful to God's message.

Prayer:
Lord, we thank You for the boldness of Paul and Barnabas in proclaiming Your word. Help us to be courageous in our own witness, directing others to You and relying on Your guidance. Strengthen us to overcome misunderstandings and opposition as we share Your love and truth. Through Christ our Lord. Amen.

➢ **Gospel: John 14: 21-26**

In this passage, Jesus speaks about the relationship between love, obedience, and the presence of the Holy Spirit. He promises that those who love Him and keep His commandments will be loved by the Father and that He and the Father will come to dwell with them. Jesus also promises the Advocate, the Holy Spirit, who will teach and remind them of all that He has said.

Reflection:
Jesus' promise of the Holy Spirit is a source of great comfort and assurance. The Spirit's role is to teach and remind us of Jesus' words, guiding us in our relationship with Him and helping us to live out His commandments. This promise reinforces the connection between love, obedience, and divine guidance, encouraging us to remain faithful and receptive to the Spirit's presence in our lives.

Prayer:
Holy Spirit, we welcome Your presence and guidance in our lives. Help us to live in accordance with Jesus' teachings and to keep His commandments through Your strength. Remind us of His words and lead us in love and faithfulness as we seek to follow Him more closely. Through Christ our Lord. Amen.

Tuesday, May 20

❖ **Tuesday of the Fifth week of Easter**
❖ **Saint Bernardine of Siena, priest - Optional Memorial**

➢ First Reading: Acts 14: 19-28
➢ Responsorial Psalm: Psalms 145: 10-11, 12-13ab, 21
➢ Alleluia: Luke 24: 46, 26
➢ Gospel: John 14: 27-31a
➢ Lectionary: 286

Today's readings focus on the mission of the early Church and the peace that Jesus offers to His followers. Saint Bernardine of Siena, whom we remember today, was known for his passionate preaching and devotion to spreading the name of Jesus. His life exemplifies the call to bring the message of peace and salvation to all.

➢ First Reading: Acts 14: 19-28

Paul and Barnabas face persecution in Antioch and are even stoned in Lystra, yet they continue their mission. They return to the cities they had previously visited, encouraging the disciples and strengthening their faith. They appoint elders in each church and commend them to the Lord. Their journey demonstrates perseverance and commitment to building up the Church.

Reflection:
Paul and Barnabas' unwavering commitment, despite facing hardships, serves as an inspiration for us to persist in our own faith journey. Their example teaches us about the importance of community, support, and leadership in sustaining and nurturing the faith of others. It also reminds us of the challenges and sacrifices involved in evangelization.

Prayer:
Lord, we thank You for the example of Paul and Barnabas, who faced adversity with courage and perseverance. Grant us the strength to remain steadfast in our faith and to support one another in our spiritual journeys. May we, like them, build up Your Church and bring others closer to You. Through Christ our Lord. Amen.

➢ Gospel: John 14: 27-31a

In this passage, Jesus offers His peace to His disciples, a peace that is not like the world's but one that transcends all understanding. He assures them that He is leaving but will return, and He tells them to be not afraid or troubled. Jesus emphasizes His unity with the Father and the importance of obedience to His commands.

Reflection:
Jesus' gift of peace is profound and transformative, offering a stability and assurance that surpasses worldly concerns. His promise of returning and His call to obedience highlight the importance of trusting in His presence and teachings. This peace helps us to navigate our fears and uncertainties, grounding us in His love and commitment.

Prayer:
Lord Jesus, we receive Your gift of peace with gratitude and trust. Help us to remain calm and confident in Your promises, even amidst life's trials. Strengthen our faith and guide us in obedience to Your commands, so that we may live in the peace that only You can provide. Through Christ our Lord. Amen.

Wednesday, May 21

- **Wednesday of the Fifth week of Easter**
- **Saints Christopher Magallanes, priest and martyr, and Companions, martyrs - Optional Memorial**

> First Reading: Acts 15: 1-6
> Responsorial Psalm: Psalms 122: 1-2, 3-4ab, 4cd-5
> Alleluia: John 15: 4a, 5b
> Gospel: John 15: 1-8
> Lectionary: 287

Today, we honor Saints Christopher Magallanes and his companions, who were martyred for their faith in Mexico during a time of severe persecution. Their courage and steadfastness in proclaiming the Gospel inspire us to remain firm in our own faith. The readings today emphasize the importance of unity within the Church and the vital connection between Christ and His followers.

> First Reading: Acts 15: 1-6

The early Church faces a significant challenge as some members insist that Gentile converts must follow Jewish laws. The apostles and elders come together in Jerusalem to deliberate on this issue. Through discussion and discernment, they recognize that salvation comes through the grace of Jesus Christ, not adherence to the law. They affirm the importance of unity and decide to send a letter to the Gentile believers encouraging them to avoid certain practices but not to be burdened by the full Jewish law.

Reflection:
The Council of Jerusalem highlights the importance of resolving disputes with wisdom and seeking unity in the Church. The decision to focus on grace rather than law reflects the core of the Gospel message: that salvation is a gift from God, not earned by human effort. This reading calls us to embrace the grace of Christ and to promote unity within the Christian community.

Prayer:
Heavenly Father, we thank You for the wisdom and guidance of the early Church leaders who discerned Your will and maintained unity. Help us to follow their example in resolving conflicts with love and grace. Strengthen our faith and keep us united in our commitment to Your Gospel. Through Christ our Lord. Amen.

> Gospel: John 15: 1-8

In this passage, Jesus uses the metaphor of the vine and the branches to describe His relationship with His followers. He is the true vine, and His Father is the vine grower. Jesus emphasizes the necessity of remaining in Him to bear fruit. Those who do not remain in Him are like withered branches, while those who remain will bear much fruit and glorify the Father.

Reflection:
The imagery of the vine and branches underscores the importance of a deep, abiding relationship with Christ. To bear fruit in our spiritual lives, we must stay connected to Jesus, drawing our strength and nourishment from Him. This relationship not only sustains us but also enables us to contribute to the growth of God's kingdom.

Prayer:
Lord Jesus, You are the true vine, and we are the branches. Help us to remain in You, drawing our strength and vitality from Your presence. May our lives bear abundant fruit for Your glory, and may we always seek to live in close union with You. Through Christ our Lord. Amen.

Thursday, May 22

❖ Thursday of the Fifth week of Easter
❖ Saint Rita of Cascia, religious - Optional Memorial

> First Reading: Acts 15: 7-21
> Responsorial Psalm: Psalms 96: 1-2a, 2b-3, 10
> Alleluia: John 10: 27
> Gospel: John 15: 9-11
> Lectionary: 288

Today, we remember Saint Rita of Cascia, known for her extraordinary patience and perseverance in the face of suffering. Her life reflects a deep commitment to faith and forgiveness, embodying the teachings of Christ even in the midst of trials. The readings highlight the theme of God's grace and the joy that comes from remaining in Christ's love.

> First Reading: Acts 15: 7-21

During the Council of Jerusalem, Peter speaks out about the decision to welcome Gentile converts into the Christian community without requiring them to follow the Jewish law. He recounts how God gave the Holy Spirit to the Gentiles, affirming that salvation comes through the grace of Jesus Christ, not through the law. James supports this view and proposes a letter to be sent to the Gentile believers, advising them to avoid certain practices but not imposing the full Jewish law upon them.

Reflection:

This passage emphasizes the importance of embracing the inclusive nature of God's grace. The early Church's decision to welcome Gentiles without imposing the Jewish law underscores the universal scope of salvation. It reminds us that God's grace transcends boundaries and that the Church is called to be a place of inclusion and mercy.

Prayer:

Lord God, thank You for Your boundless grace and for the inclusive nature of Your salvation. Help us to reflect this grace in our own lives by welcoming others with open hearts. Guide us in following Your will and promoting unity within Your Church. Through Christ our Lord. Amen.

➢ Gospel: John 15: 9-11

In this passage, Jesus continues His teaching about the vine and branches, focusing on the love He has for His followers. He commands them to remain in His love by keeping His commandments, just as He has kept His Father's commandments and remains in His love. Jesus shares that His desire is for His followers to have His joy, which will be complete if they abide in His love.

Reflection:

Jesus' words highlight the connection between love, obedience, and joy. By remaining in His love and following His commandments, we experience true joy and fulfillment. This passage challenges us to live out our faith through love and obedience, reflecting the joy and peace that come from a deep relationship with Christ.

Prayer:

Lord Jesus, You have called us to remain in Your love and to find joy in our relationship with You. Help us to follow Your commandments and to live in a way that reflects Your love to others. May Your joy fill our hearts and guide us each day. Through Christ our Lord. Amen.

Friday, May 23

❖ **Friday of the Fifth week of Easter**

> First Reading: Acts 15: 22-31
> Responsorial Psalm: Psalms 57: 8-9, 10 and 12
> Alleluia: John 15: 15b
> Gospel: John 15: 12-17
> Lectionary: 289

Today's readings continue the themes of community and love that are central to the Easter season. We see the early Church's efforts to unify believers through the guidance of the Holy Spirit and Jesus' call to love one another. These readings invite us to reflect on our own commitment to the communal and loving aspects of our faith.

> **First Reading: Acts 15: 22-31**

In this passage, the apostles and elders in Jerusalem send a letter to the Gentile believers in Antioch, Syria, and Cilicia. The letter communicates the decision of the Council of Jerusalem, which includes not imposing burdensome requirements on the Gentiles but advising them to avoid certain practices. The letter is well-received, and the community rejoices at the encouragement and clarity it provides.

Reflection:
This reading highlights the importance of communication and unity within the Church. The decision to send a letter with clear guidelines demonstrates the Church's commitment to maintaining unity while respecting the diverse backgrounds of its members. It serves as a model for resolving conflicts and fostering a sense of community through mutual understanding and respect.

Prayer:
Heavenly Father, we thank You for the guidance and wisdom You provided to the early Church. Help us to embrace Your teachings and to foster unity within our communities. May we follow Your example of love and understanding in all our interactions. Through Christ our Lord. Amen.

> **Gospel: John 15: 12-17**

In this passage, Jesus commands His disciples to love one another as He has loved them. He explains that there is no greater love than to lay down one's life for one's friends and calls them friends rather than servants because He has shared everything He has learned from the Father with them. Jesus chooses them and appoints them to bear fruit that will last.

Reflection:
Jesus' command to love one another underscores the depth of His relationship with His followers. By calling them friends and revealing His intimate connection with the Father, He sets a high standard for love and sacrifice. This passage challenges us to embody Christ's love in our own lives, prioritizing selfless acts and fostering genuine relationships with others.

Prayer:
Lord Jesus, You have shown us the depth of Your love and called us to love one another as You have loved us. Help us to live out this command in our daily lives, making sacrifices for the good of others and bearing lasting fruit. Strengthen our bonds of friendship and community through Your love. Through Christ our Lord. Amen.

Saturday, May 24

❖ Saturday of the Fifth week of Easter

- First Reading: Acts 16: 1-10
- Responsorial Psalm: Psalms 100: 2, 3, 5
- Alleluia: Colossians 3: 1
- Gospel: John 15: 18-21
- Lectionary: 290

As we approach the end of the Easter season, today's readings reflect the challenges faced by the early Church and the call to persevere in faith despite opposition. The journey of the apostles and the teachings of Jesus remind us of the trials and triumphs of living out the Gospel message.

➤ First Reading: Acts 16: 1-10

In this passage, Paul and Silas travel through the region of Phrygia and Galatia. They meet Timothy, who joins them in their mission. The Holy Spirit guides them, preventing them from entering certain regions, and ultimately directs them to Macedonia. Paul receives a vision of a man from Macedonia urging them to come and help.

Reflection:
This reading illustrates the dynamic and guided nature of the apostolic mission. The Holy Spirit's direction and the vision of the Macedonian man highlight how God leads and prepares the way for the spread of

the Gospel. It serves as a reminder of the importance of being attentive to the Holy Spirit's guidance and open to new opportunities for evangelization.

Prayer:
Lord, we thank You for the guidance of the Holy Spirit in the lives of the apostles. Help us to be open to Your direction and attentive to the needs of those around us. Strengthen us in our mission to spread Your love and truth, and guide us in our journey of faith. Through Christ our Lord. Amen.

> Gospel: John 15: 18-21

In this passage, Jesus warns His disciples about the hatred and persecution they will face because of their association with Him. He explains that if the world hates them, it is because it has hated Him first. Jesus reminds them that they are chosen and not of the world, and that their suffering is a sign of their solidarity with Him.

Reflection:
Jesus' words prepare His disciples for the reality of persecution and opposition. His reassurance that their suffering is a result of their commitment to Him helps to frame adversity as a mark of true discipleship. This passage challenges us to remain steadfast in our faith, even in the face of difficulties and opposition, knowing that our suffering is united with Christ's.

Prayer:
Lord Jesus, You have warned us that following You will bring challenges and opposition. Give us the strength to remain steadfast in our faith and to bear witness to Your love despite adversity. May we find courage in Your words and comfort in the knowledge that we are united with You in our trials. Through Christ our Lord. Amen.

Sunday, May 25

❖ Sixth Sunday of Easter

> First Reading: Acts 15: 1-2, 22-29
> Responsorial Psalm: Psalms 67: 2-3, 5, 6 and 8
> Second Reading: Revelation 21: 10-14, 22-23
> Alleluia: John 14: 23
> Gospel: John 14: 23-29
> Lectionary: 57

On this Sixth Sunday of Easter, we reflect on the early Church's decisions and the promise of God's new creation. Today's readings offer insights into the unity of the Church and the transformative power of God's presence, as well as the peace that Jesus promises to His followers.

➤ First Reading: Acts 15: 1-2, 22-29

The reading describes the Council of Jerusalem, where the apostles and elders gather to resolve the controversy over whether Gentile converts must follow Jewish laws. They decide that imposing these laws is unnecessary and instead issue a decree with essential guidelines for the Gentiles, emphasizing the importance of grace and unity within the Church.

Reflection:
This decision marks a pivotal moment in the early Church, emphasizing the importance of inclusivity and the core principles of faith over cultural or ritualistic requirements. It highlights the Church's commitment to unity and the understanding that salvation is a gift of grace rather than human effort. It challenges us to focus on what truly matters in our faith and to work towards unity and understanding within our communities.

Prayer:
Lord, we thank You for the wisdom and guidance of the early Church leaders. Help us to embrace the unity and grace they championed and to live out our faith with humility and love. May we always seek to build up the body of Christ and to honor You in all that we do. Through Christ our Lord. Amen.

➤ Second Reading: Revelation 21: 10-14, 22-23

In this passage, John describes a vision of the New Jerusalem, coming down from heaven. The city is adorned with precious stones and has twelve gates, each named after the twelve tribes of Israel, and twelve foundations named after the apostles. There is no temple in the city, as God and the Lamb are its temple and its light.

Reflection:
This vision of the New Jerusalem symbolizes the ultimate fulfillment of God's promise and the perfection of His divine presence. The absence of a physical temple signifies that God's presence will be fully realized and experienced in the new creation. It invites us to anticipate the fulfillment of God's promises and to live in the light of His presence, looking forward to the eternal peace and unity He offers.

Prayer:
Heavenly Father, we are grateful for the promise of the New Jerusalem and the eternal presence of Your divine light. Help us to live in the hope of Your promises and to seek Your presence in our daily lives. May Your light guide us and Your peace dwell within us as we await the fulfillment of Your kingdom. Through Christ our Lord. Amen.

> Gospel: John 14: 23-29

In this passage, Jesus speaks of the coming of the Holy Spirit, who will teach and remind the disciples of all that He has said. He promises them peace, not as the world gives, but as a gift from Him. Jesus encourages them not to be troubled or afraid, assuring them of His continued presence and the coming of the Spirit.

Reflection:
Jesus' promise of the Holy Spirit and His peace provides comfort and assurance to His followers. The Holy Spirit's role as teacher and reminder reinforces the continuity of Jesus' teaching and presence. This passage calls us to trust in the peace that Jesus offers, which transcends worldly understanding and fear, and to rely on the Holy Spirit for guidance and strength.

Prayer:
Lord Jesus, we thank You for the gift of Your peace and the promise of the Holy Spirit. Help us to trust in Your guidance and to embrace the peace that surpasses all understanding. Strengthen us through the Holy Spirit and keep us steadfast in faith, even in times of trouble. Through Christ our Lord. Amen.

Monday, May 26

❖ Saint Philip Neri, priest - Memorial

> First Reading: Acts 16: 11-15
> Responsorial Psalm: Psalms 149: 1b-2, 3-4, 5-6a and 9b
> Alleluia: John 15: 26b, 27a
> Gospel: John 15: 26 – 16: 4
> Lectionary: 291

Today we celebrate Saint Philip Neri, known for his vibrant spirituality and joyful approach to faith. His life and work as a priest remind us of the importance of joy and the transformative power of the Holy Spirit in our lives. The readings highlight the role of the Spirit in guiding and empowering believers.

> First Reading: Acts 16: 11-15

In this passage, Paul and his companions arrive in Philippi, where they meet Lydia, a dealer in purple cloth. Lydia, moved by Paul's message, opens her heart to the gospel, and she and her household are baptized. Lydia then invites Paul and his companions to stay at her home, demonstrating hospitality and faith.

Reflection:
Lydia's response to the gospel is a testament to the power of the Holy Spirit working through Paul and the

early Church. Her open heart and hospitality reflect the welcoming nature of the Christian community and the transformative effect of encountering Christ. This reading calls us to be open to the Spirit's work in our lives and to extend hospitality and support to others as we live out our faith.

Prayer:
Lord, we thank You for the example of Saint Philip Neri and for Lydia's openness to Your message. Help us to welcome Your Spirit into our hearts and to be generous in our hospitality and support of others. May our lives reflect the joy and transformative power of Your presence. Through Christ our Lord. Amen.

➤ Gospel: John 15: 26 – 16: 4

In this passage, Jesus speaks of the coming of the Holy Spirit, who will be a witness to Him and will guide the disciples in truth. Jesus warns them that they will face challenges and persecution, but the Spirit will provide strength and comfort. He encourages them to remain steadfast despite the trials ahead.

Reflection:
Jesus' promise of the Holy Spirit as a witness and guide underscores the Spirit's role in sustaining and strengthening believers in the face of adversity. The assurance of the Spirit's support invites us to trust in God's guidance and to remain faithful, even when facing difficulties. This passage encourages us to rely on the Spirit for strength and to be witnesses of Christ in our own lives.

Prayer:
Lord Jesus, we are grateful for the gift of the Holy Spirit and for Your promise of guidance and strength. Help us to remain steadfast in our faith and to rely on the Spirit's support in times of trial. May we be faithful witnesses of Your love and grace. Through Christ our Lord. Amen.

Tuesday, May 27

❖ **Tuesday of the Sixth week of Easter**
❖ **Saint Augustine of Canterbury, bishop - Optional Memorial**

➤ First Reading: Acts 16: 22-34
➤ Responsorial Psalm: Psalms 138: 1-2ab, 2cde-3, 7c-8
➤ Alleluia: John 16: 7, 13
➤ Gospel: John 16: 5-11
➤ Lectionary: 292

Today we honor Saint Augustine of Canterbury, the missionary bishop who played a pivotal role in the conversion of the Anglo-Saxons and the revival of Christianity in England. His dedication and efforts in spreading the Gospel remind us of the importance of mission and evangelization in the life of the Church.

➢ First Reading: Acts 16: 22-34

In this passage, Paul and Silas are imprisoned after exorcising a spirit from a slave girl. Despite their imprisonment, they sing hymns and pray, leading to a miraculous earthquake that opens the prison doors. The jailer, fearing the prisoners have escaped, is about to take his own life, but Paul reassures him. Moved by the event, the jailer and his household are baptized.

Reflection:

This reading demonstrates the power of faith and prayer even in dire circumstances. Paul and Silas's unwavering faith and the subsequent miracle lead to the conversion of the jailer and his family. It illustrates how the presence of God can transform difficult situations into opportunities for witness and conversion. We are called to trust in God's power and to remain faithful, knowing that even in trials, God can bring about great good.

Prayer:

Lord, we thank You for the witness of Paul and Silas and for their faithfulness in adversity. Strengthen us in our own trials, and help us to trust in Your power to transform and bring about good. May we be instruments of Your grace, sharing the joy of the Gospel with those around us. Through Christ our Lord. Amen.

➢ Gospel: John 16: 5-11

In this passage, Jesus speaks of His departure and the coming of the Holy Spirit. He explains that it is to the disciples' advantage that He goes away, for the Spirit will come and convict the world concerning sin, righteousness, and judgment. The Spirit will guide the disciples into all truth and will glorify Jesus.

Reflection:

Jesus' teaching on the coming of the Holy Spirit emphasizes the transformative role of the Spirit in revealing truth and guiding believers. The Spirit's work in convicting the world of sin and righteousness is essential for the continued mission of the Church. This passage reassures us that even in Jesus' physical absence, the Spirit will continue to guide, comfort, and empower the faithful.

Prayer:

Lord Jesus, we are grateful for the promise of the Holy Spirit and for Your assurance of guidance and truth. Help us to be attentive to the Spirit's work in our lives and to rely on the Spirit for strength and wisdom. May we be faithful witnesses to Your truth and love. Through Christ our Lord. Amen.

Wednesday, May 28

❖ Wednesday of the Sixth week of Easter

- ➢ First Reading: Acts 17: 15, 22 – 18: 1
- ➢ Responsorial Psalm: Psalms 148: 1-2, 11-12, 13, 14
- ➢ Alleluia: John 14: 16
- ➢ Gospel: John 16: 12-15
- ➢ Lectionary: 293

➢ First Reading: Acts 17: 15, 22 – 18: 1

In this passage, Paul arrives in Athens and addresses the Areopagus, speaking to the Athenians about their altar to an unknown god. He proclaims that the unknown god is the one true God who created all things and calls people to repentance. Paul continues to reason with the Athenians about righteousness and judgment. After this, he leaves Athens and goes to Corinth.

Reflection:
Paul's sermon on Mars Hill illustrates his strategy of meeting people where they are, using their own cultural references to communicate the message of Christ. His approach reminds us of the importance of understanding and engaging with the culture in which we live, while remaining faithful to the Gospel. The call to repentance and the proclamation of God's sovereignty are central to Paul's message, encouraging us to reflect on how we can be effective witnesses in our own context.

Prayer:
Lord, we thank You for the example of Saint Paul and his dedication to spreading the Gospel. Help us to be courageous and thoughtful in sharing Your message, meeting people where they are and speaking with clarity and love. Guide us to be effective witnesses of Your truth in our own lives. Through Christ our Lord. Amen.

➢ Gospel: John 16: 12-15

In this passage, Jesus speaks to His disciples about the coming of the Holy Spirit. He tells them that there is much more He would like to tell them, but they cannot bear it now. The Spirit of truth will come, guiding them into all truth, speaking not on His own authority but on what He hears from Jesus. The Spirit will declare the things that are to come and will glorify Jesus.

Reflection:
Jesus' promise of the Holy Spirit as the Spirit of truth highlights the ongoing guidance and revelation that the Spirit will provide. This passage assures us that the Spirit will continue Jesus' work, leading us deeper

into the truth and helping us to understand and live out Jesus' teachings. The Holy Spirit's role in glorifying Jesus and revealing future things is a vital aspect of our faith journey.

Prayer:
Holy Spirit, we are grateful for Your role in guiding us into all truth and for Your continued presence in our lives. Help us to be open to Your guidance and to trust in Your wisdom as we seek to live according to the teachings of Christ. May we grow in our understanding and witness to Your truth. Through Christ our Lord. Amen.

Thursday, May 29

- ❖ Ascension of the Lord - Solemnity - * Holy Day of Obligation *
- ❖ In the archdioceses and dioceses of the US states of Alaska, California, Hawaii, Idaho, Montana, Nevada, Oregon, Utah, and Washington only
- ❖ Thursday of the Sixth week of Easter

> ➤ First Reading: Acts 18: 1-8
> ➤ Responsorial Psalm: Psalms 98: 1, 2-3ab, 3cd-4
> ➤ Alleluia: John 14: 18
> ➤ Gospel: John 16: 16-20
> ➤ Lectionary: 294

> ➤ First Reading: Acts 18: 1-8

In this passage, Paul arrives in Corinth and meets Aquila and Priscilla, fellow tentmakers. He stays with them and works while preaching in the synagogue every Sabbath. Many Corinthians believe in Jesus and are baptized. Paul's ministry in Corinth is marked by significant growth in the early Church, despite opposition from some Jews.

Reflection:
Paul's work in Corinth illustrates the importance of perseverance and collaboration in ministry. His dedication to preaching, even while working with his hands, highlights the integral role of both spiritual and practical efforts in the growth of the Church. The passage also demonstrates how God can bring fruitful results through the faithful efforts of His servants.

Prayer:
Lord, we thank You for the example of Saint Paul and his tireless efforts in spreading the Gospel. Help us to be diligent in our own calling, combining our work with our witness. May we be inspired by Paul's

commitment and collaboration, and trust in Your guidance as we strive to build Your Kingdom. Through Christ our Lord. Amen.

➤ Gospel: John 16: 16-20

In this passage, Jesus speaks to His disciples about His imminent departure and their future sorrow. He assures them that their grief will turn to joy, likening it to a woman in labor who forgets her pain once the child is born. Jesus promises that their sorrow will be replaced with joy that no one can take away.

Reflection:
Jesus' words offer comfort and hope in times of difficulty. His promise that sorrow will turn to joy reflects the transformative power of His resurrection and the ultimate fulfillment of His promises. This passage invites us to trust in Jesus' assurances and to find hope even in our moments of sorrow and struggle.

Prayer:
Lord Jesus, we rejoice in the promise of joy that You offer us, even amidst our sorrows. Help us to hold fast to Your assurances and find comfort in Your presence. As we celebrate Your Ascension, may we be filled with hope and joy, knowing that You are with us and guiding us always. Through Christ our Lord. Amen.

Friday, May 30

❖ Friday of the Sixth week of Easter

➤ First Reading: Acts 18: 9-18
➤ Responsorial Psalm: Psalms 47: 2-3, 4-5, 6-7
➤ Alleluia: Luke 24: 46, 26
➤ Gospel: John 16: 20-23
➤ Lectionary: 295

➤ First Reading: Acts 18: 9-18

In this reading, the Lord speaks to Paul in a vision, encouraging him not to be afraid and to continue speaking boldly, as He has many people in Corinth. Paul remains in Corinth for a year and a half, teaching the Word of God. Eventually, he faces opposition from some Jews who bring him before the Roman proconsul, Gallio, but the case is dismissed.

Reflection:
This passage demonstrates the importance of divine encouragement and the promise of God's protection in our mission. Paul's courage and persistence, despite opposition, reflect his deep trust in God's plan.

The reading reassures us that God is present and active in our efforts, providing support and protection as we fulfill our call to witness.

Prayer:
Lord, we thank You for Your encouragement and protection in our journey of faith. Like Paul, grant us the courage to speak boldly and the assurance of Your presence in our struggles. Help us to trust in Your promises and remain steadfast in our mission to share Your love with the world. Through Christ our Lord. Amen.

> Gospel: John 16: 20-23

In this passage, Jesus continues to speak to His disciples about His departure and the joy that will follow. He explains that their grief will turn into joy, using the analogy of a woman in labor whose pain is forgotten when she sees her child. Jesus assures them that their sorrow will be transformed into joy, and He encourages them to ask in His name and receive.

Reflection:
Jesus' promise of joy after sorrow underscores the transformative power of His resurrection and the new life He offers. This passage invites us to embrace the joy that comes from faith in Christ, even in our moments of suffering. It also emphasizes the power of prayer and asking in Jesus' name, assuring us that our requests will be heard and answered.

Prayer:
Lord Jesus, we rejoice in the promise of joy that follows our sorrows. Help us to trust in Your words and find peace in the knowledge that You are with us. Strengthen our faith and our prayer life, that we may experience the fullness of joy that comes from You. Through Christ our Lord. Amen.

Saturday, May 31

❖ Visitation of the Virgin Mary to Elizabeth - Feast

> First Reading: Zephaniah 3: 14-18a or Romans 12: 9-16
> Responsorial Psalm: Isaiah 12: 2-3, 4bcd, 5-6
> Alleluia: Luke 1: 45
> Gospel: Luke 1: 39-56
> Lectionary: 572

➢ First Reading: Zephaniah 3: 14-18a

This reading is a joyful proclamation of the restoration and redemption of Jerusalem. Zephaniah calls the people to rejoice and be glad because the Lord has removed judgment and exile from them. The Lord is in their midst, and He will gather the outcasts and bring them back.

Reflection:

Zephaniah's message of joy and restoration parallels the joy of the Visitation, where Mary and Elizabeth rejoice in the presence of the Lord. Both readings emphasize the theme of God's intervention in history, bringing healing and hope to His people. This reflection invites us to celebrate God's presence in our lives and His promises of restoration and peace.

Prayer:

Lord, we rejoice in Your promises of restoration and peace. Like the people of Jerusalem and the Virgin Mary, may we recognize Your presence in our lives and find joy in Your love and salvation. Guide us in our journey of faith and help us to be instruments of Your peace and grace. Through Christ our Lord. Amen.

➢ Gospel: Luke 1: 39-56

In this Gospel passage, Mary visits her cousin Elizabeth, and upon hearing Mary's greeting, Elizabeth's baby leaps in her womb. Elizabeth, filled with the Holy Spirit, praises Mary for her faith and the blessed fruit of her womb. Mary responds with her Magnificat, praising God for His greatness and His mercy.

Reflection:

The Visitation is a profound moment of shared joy and affirmation between Mary and Elizabeth. It highlights the mutual recognition of God's work in their lives and the fulfillment of His promises. Mary's Magnificat expresses her deep gratitude and acknowledges God's transformative power. This feast celebrates the humble yet powerful witness of Mary and Elizabeth, who respond with joy and praise to God's blessings.

Prayer:

Heavenly Father, we celebrate the joy of the Visitation and the powerful witness of Mary and Elizabeth. Fill us with the same spirit of gratitude and praise, and help us to recognize and respond to Your presence in our lives. May our hearts overflow with Your love and mercy, and may we be instruments of Your grace in the world. Through Christ our Lord. Amen.

June 2025

Sunday, June 1

- ❖ Seventh Sunday of Easter
- ❖ In the archdioceses and dioceses of the US states of Alaska, California, Hawaii, Idaho, Montana, Nevada, Oregon, Utah, and Washington only
- ❖ Ascension of the Lord - Solemnity

> First Reading: Acts 1: 1-11
> Responsorial Psalm: Psalms 47: 2-3, 6-7, 8-9
> Second Reading: Ephesians 1: 17-23 or Hebrews 9: 24-28; 10: 19-23
> Alleluia: Matthew 28: 19a, 20b
> Gospel: Luke 24: 46-53
> Lectionary: 58

> First Reading: Acts 1: 1-11

This passage recounts the events of the Ascension, where Jesus, after His resurrection, appears to His apostles over forty days, speaking about the Kingdom of God. He instructs them to wait in Jerusalem for the promise of the Holy Spirit. As He is taken up into heaven, two men in white robes appear and promise that Jesus will return in the same way He ascended.

Reflection:
The Ascension marks the end of Jesus' earthly ministry and the beginning of a new phase in the work of salvation. It emphasizes Jesus' divine authority and His exaltation at the right hand of the Father. The promise of the Holy Spirit signifies the continuation of His mission through the Church. The Ascension invites us to look forward with hope to Christ's return and to live in the light of His eternal reign.

Prayer:
Lord Jesus, as You ascended to the Father, we rejoice in the promise of the Holy Spirit and Your continued presence among us. Strengthen our faith and help us to live in anticipation of Your return. May Your ascension inspire us to carry out Your mission with courage and love, knowing that You are always with us. Through Christ our Lord. Amen.

➢ Second Reading: Ephesians 1: 17-23

Paul's letter to the Ephesians prays for the faithful to receive the Spirit of wisdom and revelation, so they may know the hope to which they have been called. He speaks of Christ's exaltation above all rule and authority and His headship over the Church, which is His body.

Reflection:

This reading highlights the significance of Christ's Ascension in the context of His ultimate authority and the Church's role as His body. It underscores the spiritual riches and the power available to believers through Christ, who reigns supreme. The reading calls us to recognize and embrace our place within the Church and to live according to the hope and authority given to us in Christ.

Prayer:

Heavenly Father, we give thanks for the exaltation of Christ and the rich blessings You have bestowed upon us. Open our hearts to the wisdom and revelation of Your Spirit, that we may fully understand and live out our calling as members of the body of Christ. May Your grace empower us to bear witness to Your Kingdom. Through Christ our Lord. Amen.

➢ Gospel: Luke 24: 46-53

In this passage, Jesus appears to His disciples and explains that the Scriptures foretold His suffering, death, and resurrection. He commissions them to preach repentance and forgiveness of sins to all nations, beginning in Jerusalem. He then blesses them and is taken up into heaven.

Reflection:

This Gospel passage captures the final instructions of Jesus to His disciples before His Ascension. It emphasizes the mission of the Church to proclaim repentance and forgiveness, rooted in the fulfillment of Scripture. The Ascension is portrayed as a blessing, affirming the disciples' mission and Jesus' divine authority. It calls us to continue the mission of spreading the Gospel with joy and confidence.

Prayer:

Lord Jesus, as You ascended into heaven, You commissioned Your disciples to spread the message of repentance and forgiveness. Empower us to carry out this mission with faith and zeal, and may Your blessing guide and sustain us as we witness to Your love and grace. Through Christ our Lord. Amen.

Monday, June 2

- ❖ Monday of the Seventh week of Easter
- ❖ Saints Marcellinus and Peter, martyrs - Optional Memorial

> First Reading: Acts 19: 1-8
> Responsorial Psalm: Psalms 68: 2-3ab, 4-5acd, 6-7ab
> Alleluia: Colossians 3: 1
> Gospel: John 16: 29-33
> Lectionary: 297

First Reading: Acts 19: 1-8

In this passage, Paul encounters some disciples in Ephesus who had only received the baptism of John. He explains the importance of receiving the Holy Spirit and baptizes them in the name of Jesus. They receive the Holy Spirit, speaking in tongues and prophesying. Paul continues to teach in the synagogue, speaking boldly for three months.

Reflection:
This reading highlights the essential role of the Holy Spirit in the Christian life. It demonstrates how the early Church understood the necessity of the full baptismal experience, including the reception of the Holy Spirit. It also underscores the importance of continued teaching and bold witness in the faith. The passage encourages us to seek a deeper relationship with the Holy Spirit and to be steadfast in our mission.

Prayer:
Holy Spirit, we thank You for Your presence and guidance in our lives. Help us to fully embrace the gifts You offer and to live out our faith with boldness and clarity. Strengthen us to be faithful witnesses of Christ in all we do. Through Christ our Lord. Amen.

Gospel: John 16: 29-33

In this passage, the disciples express their understanding of Jesus' teachings. Jesus assures them that a time is coming when they will be scattered, but He encourages them to find peace in Him despite their trials. He has overcome the world, and through Him, they will find true peace.

Reflection:
This Gospel reading offers a message of comfort and hope in the midst of difficulty. Jesus acknowledges the challenges the disciples will face but assures them of His victory over the world. His promise of peace

amidst tribulation is a reminder of His unwavering presence and strength. It encourages us to trust in Jesus' triumph and to seek peace in Him even when faced with adversity.

Prayer:
Lord Jesus, we find solace in Your promise of peace and victory over the world. Help us to trust in Your strength and to remain steadfast in our faith, even in times of trial. May Your peace dwell in our hearts and guide us through all challenges. Through Christ our Lord. Amen.

Tuesday, June 3

❖ Saints Charles Lwanga and companions, martyrs - Memorial

- ➢ First Reading: Acts 20: 17-27
- ➢ Responsorial Psalm: Psalms 68: 10-11, 20-21
- ➢ Alleluia: John 14: 16
- ➢ Gospel: John 17: 1-11a
- ➢ Lectionary: 298

➢ First Reading: Acts 20: 17-27

In this passage, Paul addresses the elders of the church in Ephesus, recounting his ministry among them. He speaks of his dedication to preaching the gospel and his impending departure, emphasizing his commitment to the truth and the importance of guarding the flock from false teachings. Paul expresses his determination to finish his course with faithfulness.

Reflection:
Paul's farewell to the Ephesian elders highlights his unwavering commitment to his mission and his deep concern for the spiritual well-being of his community. It serves as a powerful example of selfless leadership and dedication to the gospel. This passage encourages us to reflect on our own commitment to our faith and our responsibility to support and protect others in their spiritual journey.

Prayer:
Lord, we thank You for the example of Saint Paul and the dedication he showed in his ministry. Grant us the strength and courage to follow his example in our own lives, remaining faithful to Your calling and supporting others in their journey of faith. Through Christ our Lord. Amen.

➢ Gospel: John 17: 1-11a

In this passage, Jesus prays to the Father, acknowledging that His hour has come. He asks for glorification so that He may glorify the Father. Jesus speaks of the eternal life that comes through knowing the one true God and Jesus Christ, whom He has sent. He prays for His disciples, asking that they be protected and united as He and the Father are one.

Reflection:
Jesus' prayer in this passage reveals His deep concern for His disciples and His desire for their unity and protection. It also underscores the importance of knowing God and Jesus as the source of eternal life. This prayer invites us to reflect on our own relationship with God and our role in fostering unity within the Christian community.

Prayer:
Heavenly Father, we are grateful for the prayer of Jesus, which reminds us of Your deep love and concern for us. Help us to grow in our knowledge of You and Your Son, and grant us the grace to live in unity with one another as a reflection of Your love. Through Christ our Lord. Amen.

Wednesday, June 4

❖ Wednesday of the Seventh week of Easter

- First Reading: Acts 20: 28-38
- Responsorial Psalm: Psalms 68: 29-30, 33-35a, 35bc-36ab
- Alleluia: John 17: 17b, 17a
- Gospel: John 17: 11b-19
- Lectionary: 299

➢ First Reading: Acts 20: 28-38

In this passage, Paul continues his farewell to the Ephesian elders, urging them to be vigilant and shepherd the church with care. He warns them of the coming threats from within and outside the community. Paul emphasizes his own example of self-sacrificial service and devotion to the gospel. The passage concludes with an emotional farewell as Paul commends the elders to God and to the word of His grace.

Reflection:
Paul's words highlight the responsibilities of church leaders and the need for vigilance against threats to the faith. His example of dedication and humility serves as a model for all Christians. This passage encourages us to reflect on how we can support and protect our faith communities, following Paul's example of love and service.

Prayer:
Lord, we thank You for the example of Saint Paul and his commitment to shepherding Your flock. Grant us the wisdom and courage to protect and nurture our faith communities, and help us to follow his example of dedication and service. Through Christ our Lord. Amen.

> Gospel: John 17: 11b-19

In this passage, Jesus continues His prayer to the Father, asking for the protection of His disciples as He prepares to leave them. He prays that they may be one, just as He and the Father are one. Jesus also asks the Father to sanctify the disciples in the truth, indicating that He has given them the word of God. He expresses His concern for their well-being and mission in the world.

Reflection:
Jesus' prayer for His disciples reveals His deep concern for their unity and spiritual growth. He desires that they remain united in love and truth, reflecting His own relationship with the Father. This prayer calls us to consider our own role in fostering unity and holiness within the Church, and to seek God's guidance in our daily lives.

Prayer:
Heavenly Father, we thank You for Jesus' prayer for His disciples and for us. Help us to remain united in Your love and to live according to Your truth. Strengthen us in our mission and protect us from all harm, that we may bring Your light to the world. Through Christ our Lord. Amen.

Thursday, June 5

❖ Saint Boniface, bishop and martyr - Memorial

> First Reading: Acts 22: 30; 23: 6-11
> Responsorial Psalm: Psalms 16: 1-2a and 5, 7-8, 9-10, 11
> Alleluia: John 17: 21
> Gospel: John 17: 20-26
> Lectionary: 300

> First Reading: Acts 22: 30; 23: 6-11

In this reading, Paul stands before the Sanhedrin, having been brought before them to answer charges. Recognizing the division between the Pharisees and Sadducees, he strategically mentions his belief in the resurrection to create division among them. This act causes confusion and results in a violent dispute. The reading concludes with Paul being reassured by the Lord in a vision, telling him that he must continue to witness in Rome.

Reflection:
Paul's experience demonstrates the power of wisdom and the role of divine guidance in navigating difficult situations. His strategic thinking, coupled with his unwavering faith, highlights the importance of

relying on God's direction during times of trial. This reading invites us to trust in God's plan and seek His guidance in our own challenges.

Prayer:
Lord, we thank You for the example of Saint Paul and his courage in the face of adversity. Grant us the wisdom and strength to navigate our own challenges with faith and trust in Your guidance. Help us to rely on Your wisdom and to follow Your path with confidence. Through Christ our Lord. Amen.

> Gospel: John 17: 20-26

In this passage, Jesus prays not only for His immediate disciples but also for all who will come to believe in Him through their message. He prays for unity among believers, that they may be one as He and the Father are one. Jesus desires that the love He has from the Father be in His followers and that they may be brought to complete unity, so that the world may know that the Father has sent Him.

Reflection:
Jesus' prayer for unity among His followers underscores the importance of harmony and love in the Christian community. His desire for us to share in His relationship with the Father highlights the deep connection He seeks between Himself and His followers. This passage challenges us to work towards unity and reflect the love of Christ in our relationships with one another.

Prayer:
Heavenly Father, we thank You for the prayer of Jesus and His desire for our unity in love. Help us to overcome divisions and to live as one in Your Spirit. May Your love dwell in us and shine through our lives, so that the world may see and believe in Your Son. Through Christ our Lord. Amen.

Friday, June 6

- ❖ First Friday
- ❖ Friday of the Seventh week of Easter
- ❖ Saint Norbert, bishop - Optional Memorial

> First Reading: Acts 25: 13b-21
> Responsorial Psalm: Psalms 103: 1-2, 11-12, 19-20ab
> Alleluia: John 14: 26
> Gospel: John 21: 15-19
> Lectionary: 301

➢ First Reading: Acts 25: 13b-21

In this reading, Paul is brought before King Agrippa and Festus. Festus recounts Paul's case, emphasizing that Paul had been accused by the Jews and had appealed to Caesar. Festus is uncertain about the charges and seeks Agrippa's advice on how to frame Paul's case for Caesar. The passage highlights Paul's continued journey and his resolve to use every opportunity to witness to Christ.

Reflection:
Paul's determination to continue his mission despite the legal and political challenges reflects his deep commitment to his faith and mission. His appeal to Caesar underscores his trust in God's plan for him, even when faced with uncertainties. This passage encourages us to remain steadfast in our own commitments and trust that God's guidance will lead us through challenges.

Prayer:
Lord, we thank You for the example of Saint Paul and his perseverance in the face of adversity. Help us to trust in Your plan and to remain steadfast in our commitments, even when we face difficulties. Guide us with Your wisdom and strength, and let our actions reflect Your love and purpose. Through Christ our Lord. Amen.

➢ Gospel: John 21: 15-19

In this passage, Jesus asks Peter three times if he loves Him, and Peter affirms his love each time. Jesus then instructs Peter to "feed My sheep," symbolizing his role as the leader of the Church. Jesus also foretells the manner of Peter's death, indicating the depth of his commitment and sacrifice. The passage concludes with Jesus calling Peter to follow Him, reinforcing the call to discipleship and leadership.

Reflection:
Jesus' questions to Peter and His command to "feed My sheep" emphasize the importance of love and responsibility in leadership. Peter's affirmation of his love and Jesus' subsequent charge highlight the call to shepherd and care for others as an expression of true love for Christ. This passage invites us to reflect on our own call to serve and lead with love and dedication.

Prayer:
Lord Jesus, we are grateful for Your call to love and serve others. Help us to respond to Your invitation with the same commitment as Peter, and to lead and care for others with a heart full of love. Strengthen us in our discipleship and guide us to follow You faithfully. Through Christ our Lord. Amen.

Saturday, June 7

❖ First Saturday
❖ Saturday of the Seventh week of Easter

> First Reading: Acts 28: 16-20, 30-31
> Responsorial Psalm: Psalms 11: 4, 5 and 7
> Alleluia: John 16: 7, 13
> Gospel: John 21: 20-25
> Lectionary: 302

> First Reading: Acts 28: 16-20, 30-31

In this reading, Paul arrives in Rome and is allowed to live in his own rented house, though he is still under guard. He continues to preach the Gospel boldly and without hindrance. Paul's ministry in Rome is characterized by his dedication to sharing the message of Jesus Christ, demonstrating his unwavering commitment to his mission even while in confinement.

Reflection:
Paul's continued preaching in Rome, despite his imprisonment, reflects his deep conviction and resilience. His ability to share the message of Christ openly, even under restrictive conditions, serves as an inspiring example of faithfulness and dedication. This passage encourages us to remain committed to our own missions and to trust that God will work through us, regardless of the circumstances.

Prayer:
Lord, we thank You for the example of Saint Paul and his perseverance in spreading Your Word. Grant us the courage and strength to remain steadfast in our own callings, and to proclaim Your message with conviction and dedication. May our lives reflect Your grace and truth. Through Christ our Lord. Amen.

> Gospel: John 21: 20-25

In this passage, Peter turns to Jesus and asks about the fate of the beloved disciple. Jesus responds that what happens to the beloved disciple is not Peter's concern and instead focuses on the call to follow Him. The passage concludes with a note about the beloved disciple's role in bearing witness to these events, and a recognition of the vastness of Jesus' works, which cannot all be recorded.

Reflection:
Jesus' response to Peter highlights the personal nature of each disciple's journey and the importance of focusing on one's own path rather than comparing it with others. The beloved disciple's role in witnessing

to Jesus emphasizes the diversity of callings within the community of believers. This passage reminds us to concentrate on our own relationship with Christ and to trust that each person's path is part of God's greater plan.

Prayer:

Lord Jesus, help us to focus on our own journey of faith and to follow You with a sincere heart. Teach us to trust in Your plan for each of us and to support one another in our shared mission. May we be faithful witnesses to Your love and truth in all that we do. Through Christ our Lord. Amen.

Sunday, June 8

❖ Pentecost - Solemnity

- First Reading: Acts 2: 1-11
- Responsorial Psalm: Psalms 104: 1, 24, 29-30, 31, 34
- Second Reading: First Corinthians 12: 3b-7, 12-13 or Romans 8: 8-17
- Gospel: John 20: 19-23 or John 14: 15-16, 23b-26
- Lectionary: 63

- First Reading: Acts 2: 1-11

This reading describes the dramatic events of Pentecost, when the Holy Spirit descended upon the apostles in the form of tongues of fire. They began to speak in various languages, and people from many nations gathered, astonished by their ability to speak in their own tongues. This event marks the birth of the Church and the empowerment of the apostles to spread the Gospel to the entire world.

Reflection:

Pentecost represents a powerful manifestation of the Holy Spirit, marking the beginning of the Church's mission to evangelize and reach out to all nations. The diverse languages spoken symbolize the universality of the message of Jesus and the inclusiveness of the Christian community. This moment emphasizes the transformative power of the Holy Spirit in empowering and uniting believers for the mission of spreading God's love and truth.

Prayer:

Come, Holy Spirit, and fill our hearts with Your presence. Empower us to boldly proclaim the Gospel and to serve others with love and compassion. May Your gifts of wisdom, understanding, and courage guide us in our mission to bring Your light to all corners of the world. Through Christ our Lord. Amen.

➤ Second Reading: 1 Corinthians 12: 3b-7, 12-13

In this passage, Paul speaks about the gifts of the Holy Spirit and their role in the Church. He emphasizes that there are many gifts but one Spirit, and that all gifts are given for the common good. Paul explains that just as the body has many parts but is one body, so too are believers many but one in Christ. Through the Holy Spirit, we are baptized into one body and share in the same Spirit.

Reflection:
This reading highlights the unity and diversity within the Christian community. Each member is given unique gifts by the Holy Spirit, but these gifts work together to build up the Church and serve the common good. The metaphor of the body underscores the interdependence of believers and the importance of each person's contribution to the whole. It calls us to recognize and appreciate the diverse gifts within the Church and to use them for the greater good.

Prayer:
Lord, we thank You for the many gifts You bestow upon us through Your Holy Spirit. Help us to recognize and use these gifts for the benefit of the Church and the service of others. May we work together in unity and love, building up the Body of Christ and furthering Your mission on earth. Through Christ our Lord. Amen.

➤ Gospel: John 20: 19-23

In this Gospel passage, Jesus appears to His disciples after His resurrection and breathes on them, saying, "Receive the Holy Spirit." He then gives them the authority to forgive sins. This event is often seen as the moment of the Church's commissioning and the giving of the Holy Spirit to the disciples, empowering them for their mission.

Reflection:
Jesus' appearance and His gift of the Holy Spirit signify the beginning of the Church's mission and the authority to forgive sins. The Holy Spirit's role is crucial in guiding, empowering, and sanctifying the Church and its members. This passage underscores the importance of the Holy Spirit in the life of the Church and the continuation of Jesus' work on earth through the disciples and their successors.

Prayer:
Lord Jesus, we are grateful for the gift of the Holy Spirit and the authority You have given to Your Church. Strengthen us with Your Spirit and guide us as we continue Your mission in the world. Help us to forgive others as You have forgiven us and to be witnesses of Your love and grace. Through Christ our Lord. Amen.

➤ Alternative Gospel: John 14: 15-16, 23b-26

In this Gospel, Jesus promises to send the Holy Spirit, the Advocate, to teach and remind the disciples of all He has said. He emphasizes that the Holy Spirit will dwell with them and in them, guiding them in truth and reminding them of His teachings.

Reflection:
Jesus' promise of the Holy Spirit assures the disciples that they will not be left alone. The Spirit's role is to

teach and remind them of Jesus' words, providing guidance and support. This passage reassures us of the continual presence of the Holy Spirit in our lives, helping us to understand and live out the teachings of Christ.

Prayer:
Lord Jesus, we thank You for the gift of the Holy Spirit, our Advocate and Guide. May Your Spirit dwell in us and help us to live according to Your teachings. Teach us and remind us of Your ways, and strengthen us to follow You with faith and conviction. Through Christ our Lord. Amen.

Monday, June 9

- ❖ Monday of the Tenth week in Ordinary Time
- ❖ Saint Ephrem, deacon and doctor - Optional Memorial

> - ➢ First Reading: Second Corinthians 1: 1-7
> - ➢ Responsorial Psalm: Psalms 34: 2-3, 4-5, 6-7, 8-9
> - ➢ Alleluia: Matthew 5: 12a
> - ➢ Gospel: Matthew 5: 1-12
> - ➢ Lectionary: 359

> ➢ First Reading: 2 Corinthians 1: 1-7

In this passage, Paul opens his letter to the Corinthians by expressing gratitude for God's comfort and consolation. He reflects on the suffering endured by himself and others, emphasizing that their comfort comes from God, who is the source of all comfort. Paul explains that the suffering they experience is meant to help them comfort others in their struggles.

Reflection:
This reading highlights the theme of divine comfort in times of suffering. Paul's words remind us that God's comfort is not only for us but is also intended to be shared with others. The experiences of suffering and consolation can deepen our empathy and compassion, enabling us to offer support and encouragement to those who are hurting. It underscores the communal aspect of faith, where our personal experiences contribute to the broader support network within the Church.

Prayer:
Lord God, we thank You for Your comforting presence in our times of trouble. Help us to extend the comfort we receive from You to others who are in need. May we be instruments of Your peace and solace, reflecting Your love and compassion in our interactions with those who suffer. Through Christ our Lord. Amen.

> ➤ Gospel: Matthew 5: 1-12

This Gospel passage presents the Beatitudes, which are part of Jesus' Sermon on the Mount. Jesus describes the blessedness of those who exhibit certain virtues, such as poverty of spirit, meekness, and mercy. He also speaks about the rewards that await those who suffer for righteousness and face persecution for His sake.

Reflection:
The Beatitudes offer a radical vision of blessedness that contrasts with worldly values. They highlight the virtues that are valued in the Kingdom of Heaven and promise divine blessings and rewards to those who live according to these values. Jesus' words call us to embrace humility, compassion, and righteousness, and to find joy and fulfillment even in the face of adversity. The Beatitudes invite us to reassess our values and priorities in light of God's Kingdom.

Prayer:
Lord Jesus, Your Beatitudes reveal the true path to blessedness and fulfillment. Help us to live according to these values, embracing humility, mercy, and righteousness. Strengthen us to remain steadfast in faith, especially when facing trials and persecution. May our lives reflect the joy and peace of Your Kingdom. Through Christ our Lord. Amen.

Tuesday, June 10

❖ Tuesday of the Tenth week in Ordinary Time

- ➤ First Reading: Second Corinthians 1: 18-22
- ➤ Responsorial Psalm: Psalms 119: 129, 130, 131, 132, 133, 135
- ➤ Alleluia: Matthew 5: 16
- ➤ Gospel: Matthew 5: 13-16
- ➤ Lectionary: 360

➤ First Reading: 2 Corinthians 1: 18-22

In this passage, Paul affirms the faithfulness of God and his own reliability in preaching the gospel. He explains that the promises of God are always fulfilled in Christ, who is the "yes" to all of God's promises. Paul also speaks about the anointing and sealing of believers by the Holy Spirit, emphasizing that their faith is secure in Christ.

Reflection:
This reading reassures us of the certainty of God's promises and the steadfastness of His love. Paul's assurance that Christ is the fulfillment of God's promises offers hope and confidence to believers. The

mention of the Holy Spirit's anointing and sealing highlights the divine guarantee of our relationship with God. It is a reminder that, despite any uncertainties or challenges, God's promises remain true and His Spirit is a constant source of strength and assurance.

Prayer:

Lord God, we thank You for the certainty of Your promises fulfilled in Christ. Strengthen our faith and trust in Your Word, and let the presence of Your Holy Spirit guide and reassure us. Help us to live confidently in the knowledge of Your promises and to share the hope we have in You with others. Through Christ our Lord. Amen.

> ➤ Gospel: Matthew 5: 13-16

In this passage, Jesus uses the metaphors of salt and light to describe the role of His followers. He explains that just as salt preserves and enhances flavor, and light illuminates and dispels darkness, His disciples are to impact the world by living out their faith. Jesus calls them to be visible witnesses of His teachings and to let their good works shine before others, thereby glorifying God.

Reflection:

Jesus' metaphors of salt and light emphasize the transformative role of Christians in the world. As salt, believers are called to preserve and enrich the moral and spiritual fabric of society. As light, they are to reveal the truth of God's love and teachings, dispelling ignorance and darkness. This passage challenges us to live authentically and visibly as followers of Christ, demonstrating our faith through actions that reflect God's love and righteousness.

Prayer:

Lord Jesus, You call us to be the salt of the earth and the light of the world. Help us to live our faith boldly and authentically, making a positive impact on those around us. May our lives reflect Your love and truth, and may our good works bring glory to You. Through Christ our Lord. Amen.

Wednesday, June 11

❖ Saint Barnabas, apostle - Memorial

> ➤ First Reading: Acts 11: 21b-26; 13: 1-3
> ➤ Responsorial Psalm: Psalms 98: 1, 2-3ab, 3cd-4, 5-6
> ➤ Alleluia: Psalms 25: 4b, 5a
> ➤ Gospel: Matthew 5: 17-19
> ➤ Lectionary: 580/361

➢ First Reading: Acts 11: 21b-26; 13: 1-3

In this passage, we see the early Church's growth and the role of Barnabas in nurturing and guiding it. Barnabas, known for his encouragement and generosity, is instrumental in teaching and strengthening the Christian community in Antioch. He later goes on to travel with Paul on missionary journeys. The reading highlights the importance of community and mission in the early Church, as well as Barnabas' significant contribution to spreading the gospel.

Reflection:
Barnabas' role as an encourager and a missionary demonstrates the power of support and collaboration in the Church's mission. His work in Antioch and his partnership with Paul illustrate the importance of nurturing faith communities and actively participating in the spread of the Gospel. This passage invites us to reflect on how we can support and uplift others in their faith journeys and contribute to the Church's mission through our own gifts and actions.

Prayer:
Lord God, we thank You for the example of Saint Barnabas, whose encouragement and dedication to the mission of the Church inspired many. Grant us the grace to support and uplift one another in faith, and to actively participate in the spreading of Your Gospel. May we follow Barnabas' example in our own lives. Through Christ our Lord. Amen.

➢ Gospel: Matthew 5: 17-19

In this passage, Jesus emphasizes His fulfillment of the Law and the Prophets. He states that He has come not to abolish the Law, but to fulfill it. Jesus stresses the importance of following and teaching even the smallest commands of the Law, as this will lead to greatness in the Kingdom of Heaven.

Reflection:
Jesus' affirmation of the Law underscores its continuing relevance and His role in bringing its full meaning to light. By fulfilling the Law, Jesus shows that His teachings are in continuity with the Old Testament, not in opposition to it. This passage challenges us to respect and uphold the commandments, recognizing their role in guiding our relationship with God and others. It calls us to live out our faith by embracing the spirit of the Law as taught by Jesus.

Prayer:
Lord Jesus, You came to fulfill the Law and the Prophets. Help us to understand and embrace Your teachings fully, living according to the spirit of Your commandments. Guide us in our journey of faith so that we may be true to Your Word and reflect Your love and righteousness in our lives. Through Christ our Lord. Amen.

Thursday, June 12

❖ Thursday of the Tenth week in Ordinary Time

- First Reading: Second Corinthians 3: 15 – 4: 1, 3-6
- Responsorial Psalm: Psalms 85: 9ab and 10, 11-12, 13-14
- Alleluia: John 13: 34
- Gospel: Matthew 5: 20-26
- Lectionary: 362

First Reading: 2 Corinthians 3: 15 – 4: 1, 3-6

In this passage, Paul speaks of the transformation that comes through Christ, lifting the veil that covers hearts. He contrasts the fading glory of the old covenant with the enduring glory of the new covenant in Christ. The passage emphasizes that through Christ, the veil is removed, and we can behold God's glory with unveiled faces, being transformed into His image. Paul reminds us that this ministry is by God's mercy, and therefore, we should not lose heart. He also speaks of the light of the gospel that reveals the glory of Christ, who is the image of God.

Reflection:
Paul's words remind us of the transformative power of the gospel, which enables us to see and reflect the glory of God. The veil that once covered our understanding is lifted in Christ, allowing us to experience a deep and abiding relationship with God. This passage encourages us to be steadfast in our faith, recognizing the mercy that underpins our ministry and the light of Christ that shines through us. As we are transformed into His likeness, we are called to bear this light to others, revealing God's glory in our lives.

Prayer:
Heavenly Father, thank You for the light of the gospel that reveals the glory of Christ. Help us to be steadfast in our faith, allowing Your light to shine through us as we are transformed into the image of Your Son. May we not lose heart in our ministry but continue to serve You with joy and confidence. Through Christ our Lord. Amen.

Gospel: Matthew 5: 20-26

In this passage, Jesus teaches about the righteousness required to enter the Kingdom of Heaven, emphasizing that it must surpass that of the scribes and Pharisees. He expands on the commandment against murder, teaching that even anger and insults toward others can lead to judgment. Jesus calls for reconciliation with others before offering gifts at the altar, highlighting the importance of right relationships and resolving conflicts quickly.

Reflection:
Jesus challenges us to go beyond mere external observance of the law, urging us to cultivate a deeper righteousness that transforms our hearts. The call to reconcile with others before offering gifts to God underscores the importance of love and harmony in our relationships. This passage invites us to examine our attitudes toward others, seeking to resolve conflicts and extend forgiveness, knowing that our relationship with God is deeply connected to our relationships with others.

Prayer:
Lord Jesus, You call us to a righteousness that goes beyond outward appearances, touching the depths of our hearts. Help us to be mindful of our relationships, seeking reconciliation and peace with others. May we live out Your command to love, forgiving as we have been forgiven, and striving for harmony in all our interactions. Through Christ our Lord. Amen.

Friday, June 13

❖ Saint Anthony of Padua, priest and doctor - Memorial

- First Reading: Second Corinthians 4: 7-15
- Responsorial Psalm: Psalms 116: 10-11, 15-16, 17-18
- Alleluia: Philippians 2: 15d, 16a
- Gospel: Matthew 5: 27-32
- Lectionary: 363

- First Reading: 2 Corinthians 4: 7-15

Paul describes how, as followers of Christ, we carry the treasure of the gospel in "jars of clay," highlighting our human frailty. Despite being afflicted, perplexed, persecuted, and struck down, we are not crushed, despairing, abandoned, or destroyed. This resilience is a testament to the life of Jesus being manifested in our mortal bodies, even as we share in His sufferings. Paul also emphasizes that this suffering is for the sake of others, so that grace may extend to more and more people, increasing thanksgiving to the glory of God.

Reflection:
This passage reminds us of the paradox of Christian life: through our weakness, God's strength is revealed. The image of "jars of clay" speaks to our vulnerability, yet within us lies the priceless treasure of the gospel. As we endure trials, we share in Christ's sufferings, but we also share in His life and resurrection power. Paul's words encourage us to persevere, knowing that our suffering can lead others to experience God's grace and that it ultimately brings glory to God.

Prayer:
Lord, thank You for the treasure of the gospel that You have entrusted to us, despite our frailty. Help us to remain steadfast in trials, confident that Your strength is made perfect in our weakness. May our lives reflect Your glory, and may our endurance lead others to give thanks to You. Through Christ our Lord. Amen.

> Gospel: Matthew 5: 27-32

In this passage, Jesus teaches about the seriousness of sin, particularly in the context of adultery. He expands the understanding of the commandment against adultery to include even lustful thoughts, highlighting the need for purity not only in actions but also in the heart. Jesus uses hyperbolic language, suggesting that if a part of the body causes one to sin, it should be removed, emphasizing the importance of avoiding sin at all costs. He also addresses the issue of divorce, reinforcing the sanctity of marriage.

Reflection:
Jesus calls us to a deeper understanding of righteousness, one that begins in the heart. His teachings on adultery and divorce challenge us to uphold the sanctity of marriage and to strive for purity in our thoughts and intentions. This passage reminds us that sin begins in the heart and that we must be vigilant in guarding against anything that could lead us away from God's will. Jesus' words also underscore the seriousness of our commitments, particularly in marriage, and the need to approach these with reverence and fidelity.

Prayer:
Lord Jesus, You call us to purity of heart and faithfulness in our commitments. Help us to guard our thoughts and actions, seeking to honor You in all that we do. Strengthen us to uphold the sanctity of marriage and to resist anything that would lead us into sin. May we always strive to live according to Your will. Through Christ our Lord. Amen.

Saturday, June 14

❖ Saturday of the Tenth week in Ordinary Time
❖ Blessed Virgin Mary - Optional Memorial

> First Reading: Second Corinthians 5: 14-21
> Responsorial Psalm: Psalms 103: 1-2, 3-4, 9-10, 11-12
> Alleluia: Psalms 119: 36a, 29b
> Gospel: Matthew 5: 33-37
> Lectionary: 364

➢ First Reading: 2 Corinthians 5: 14-21

Paul speaks of the love of Christ as a compelling force in the lives of believers. He explains that Christ died for all, so that those who live might live no longer for themselves but for Him. Through Christ, we are a new creation; the old has passed away, and the new has come. Paul emphasizes that all this is from God, who reconciled us to Himself through Christ and gave us the ministry of reconciliation. He calls us to be ambassadors for Christ, urging others to be reconciled to God. Christ, who knew no sin, was made to be sin for our sake, so that we might become the righteousness of God.

Reflection:

This passage beautifully captures the transformative power of Christ's love and sacrifice. As Christians, we are called to live not for ourselves, but for Christ, who died and was raised for our salvation. Through Him, we are made new, and our lives should reflect this profound change. Paul's call to be ambassadors for Christ reminds us of our responsibility to share the message of reconciliation with others, inviting them to experience the same transformation and renewal that we have received.

Prayer:

Loving Father, thank You for the gift of reconciliation through Your Son, Jesus Christ. Help us to live as new creations, no longer for ourselves but for Him who died and rose again for us. Empower us to be faithful ambassadors of Your love and grace, sharing the message of reconciliation with those around us. Through Christ our Lord. Amen.

➢ Gospel: Matthew 5: 33-37

In this passage, Jesus addresses the issue of oaths, urging His followers to be people of integrity. He teaches that we should not swear oaths at all, whether by heaven, earth, or any other thing, because our words should be truthful in themselves. Instead of swearing by various things, Jesus instructs that our "yes" should mean "yes," and our "no" should mean "no." Anything more than this, He says, comes from evil.

Reflection:

Jesus calls us to a standard of honesty and integrity in our speech. His teaching on oaths challenges us to be people whose words are trustworthy and true, without the need for elaborate promises or vows. In a world where truth can often be compromised, Jesus invites us to let our simple words be enough, reflecting the truthfulness of our hearts. This passage encourages us to examine the integrity of our speech and to strive for honesty in all our communications.

Prayer:

Lord Jesus, You call us to be people of truth and integrity. Help us to let our words be simple and honest, reflecting the truth of our hearts. May our "yes" always mean "yes," and our "no" always mean "no." Guide us to speak with sincerity, that our words may honor You and build trust with others. Through Christ our Lord. Amen.

Sunday, June 15

❖ The Holy Trinity - Solemnity

- First Reading: Proverbs 8: 22-31
- Responsorial Psalm: Psalms 8: 4-5, 6-7, 8-9
- Second Reading: Romans 5: 1-5
- Alleluia: Revelation 1: 8
- Gospel: John 16: 12-15
- Lectionary: 166

First Reading: Proverbs 8: 22-31

In this passage, Wisdom is personified and speaks of its presence with God from the beginning of creation. Wisdom was established before the earth, before the mountains and the hills, before the heavens were set in place. Wisdom was there when God marked out the foundations of the earth, delighting in the creation and rejoicing in the human race. This passage highlights the deep connection between God, creation, and Wisdom, portraying Wisdom as a master craftsman at God's side.

Reflection:
The reading from Proverbs offers us a glimpse into the mystery of God's creative power and the role of divine Wisdom in the world. Wisdom's joy in creation reflects the delight God takes in His works, especially in humanity. As we celebrate the Holy Trinity, we are reminded of the harmonious relationship within the Godhead—Father, Son, and Holy Spirit—and how divine Wisdom permeates all of creation. This invites us to contemplate the beauty of the world around us and the wisdom that underlies it, recognizing the divine hand in all things.

Prayer:
O God of all Wisdom, as we marvel at the wonders of Your creation, help us to see Your wisdom at work in the world around us. May we grow in reverence for all that You have made and seek to live in harmony with Your divine will. Through Christ our Lord. Amen.

Second Reading: Romans 5: 1-5

Paul speaks of the peace we have with God through our Lord Jesus Christ. Justified by faith, we rejoice in the hope of sharing in God's glory. Paul also notes that we rejoice in our sufferings, knowing that suffering produces endurance, endurance produces character, and character produces hope. This hope does not disappoint us, because God's love has been poured into our hearts through the Holy Spirit who has been given to us.

Reflection:

This passage from Romans beautifully illustrates the work of the Holy Trinity in our lives. We are justified by faith in Jesus Christ, and this brings us peace with God. The Holy Spirit, poured into our hearts, fills us with God's love and sustains us in our journey, even through suffering. The hope that comes from this divine love is unshakeable, because it is rooted in the very nature of God. As we celebrate the Holy Trinity, we are invited to reflect on the deep relationship between the Father, Son, and Holy Spirit, and how this relationship shapes our own spiritual journey.

Prayer:

Heavenly Father, thank You for the gift of peace and hope that comes through faith in Jesus Christ. Fill our hearts with Your love through the Holy Spirit, and strengthen us in times of suffering, that we may always trust in Your unfailing promise. Through Christ our Lord. Amen.

➤ Gospel: John 16: 12-15

In this Gospel passage, Jesus speaks to His disciples about the coming of the Holy Spirit, the Spirit of truth. He tells them that there is much more He wants to say, but they cannot bear it now. However, when the Spirit of truth comes, He will guide them into all truth. The Spirit will not speak on His own, but will speak what He hears and declare what is to come. The Spirit will glorify Jesus by taking what is His and declaring it to the disciples. Jesus emphasizes that all the Father has is His, and that the Spirit will take what belongs to Him and make it known to the disciples.

Reflection:

This passage reveals the intimate relationship within the Holy Trinity. Jesus speaks of the unity between Himself, the Father, and the Holy Spirit, emphasizing that the Spirit will continue the work of revelation, guiding the disciples into all truth. The Spirit's role is to glorify Jesus and to make known the deep mysteries of God to those who follow Christ. As we celebrate the Solemnity of the Holy Trinity, we are invited to deepen our understanding of this divine relationship and to open our hearts to the guidance of the Holy Spirit, who leads us into the fullness of truth.

Prayer:

O Holy Spirit, Spirit of truth, guide us into the fullness of Your divine truth. Help us to understand the mysteries of God and to live in the light of Your wisdom. May our lives glorify Jesus, and may we always be open to the voice of the Spirit, leading us closer to the heart of the Father. Through Christ our Lord. Amen.

Monday, June 16

❖ Monday of the Eleventh week in Ordinary Time

> ➢ First Reading: Second Corinthians 6: 1-10
> ➢ Responsorial Psalm: Psalms 98: 1, 2b, 3ab, 3cd-4
> ➢ Alleluia: Psalms 119: 105
> ➢ Gospel: Matthew 5: 38-42
> ➢ Lectionary: 365

➢ First Reading: 2 Corinthians 6: 1-10

In this passage, Paul urges the Corinthians not to receive God's grace in vain. He reminds them that now is the acceptable time and the day of salvation. Paul speaks of the hardships he and his companions have endured as servants of God—afflictions, hardships, calamities, beatings, imprisonments, riots, labors, sleepless nights, and hunger. Despite these challenges, they demonstrate patience, kindness, genuine love, and the power of God. They are seen as having nothing, yet possessing everything, and being sorrowful, yet always rejoicing.

Reflection:
Paul's message is one of perseverance and faithfulness in the face of adversity. He encourages us to embrace our calling as servants of God, even when it leads to difficulties. The paradoxes he presents—having nothing, yet possessing everything; being sorrowful, yet always rejoicing—speak to the deep spiritual riches that come from a life rooted in Christ. As followers of Christ, we are called to endure with patience and to allow God's grace to work in us, transforming our sufferings into opportunities for growth and witness.

Prayer:
Lord, grant us the strength to remain faithful in the face of trials and to live out Your grace with patience and love. Help us to embrace the hardships that come our way, knowing that in You, we find true joy and fulfillment. Through Christ our Lord. Amen.

➢ Gospel: Matthew 5: 38-42

In this Gospel passage, Jesus challenges the traditional notion of retribution by teaching the principle of non-retaliation. He instructs His followers not to resist an evil person: if someone strikes you on the right cheek, turn the other as well; if someone wants to take your tunic, let him have your cloak too; if someone forces you to go one mile, go with him two miles. Jesus calls for a radical response to injustice, one that goes beyond the letter of the law and reflects the generosity and mercy of God.

Reflection:
Jesus' teaching in this passage is both challenging and transformative. He calls us to respond to wrongs not with vengeance, but with a spirit of love and forgiveness. This radical approach to justice and mercy reflects the heart of the Gospel—loving others as God loves us, even in difficult situations. By turning the other cheek, giving more than is asked, and going the extra mile, we break the cycle of retaliation and open the door to reconciliation and peace. This way of living invites us to trust in God's justice and to embody His mercy in our interactions with others.

Prayer:
Merciful Father, help us to follow the example of Your Son, responding to wrongs with love and forgiveness. Teach us to live out the radical call to mercy, trusting in Your justice and reflecting Your grace in all we do. Through Christ our Lord. Amen.

Tuesday, June 17

❖ Tuesday of the Eleventh week in Ordinary Time

- First Reading: Second Corinthians 8: 1-9
- Responsorial Psalm: Psalms 146: 2, 5-6ab, 6c-7, 8-9a
- Alleluia: John 13: 34
- Gospel: Matthew 5: 43-48
- Lectionary: 366

➢ First Reading: 2 Corinthians 8:1-9

In this passage, Paul commends the churches of Macedonia for their generosity despite their poverty. Even though they were experiencing severe trials, they gave joyfully and generously beyond their means. Paul uses their example to encourage the Corinthians to excel in the grace of giving. He reminds them that Christ, who was rich, became poor for their sake, so that through His poverty, they might become rich.

Reflection:
The Macedonian churches serve as a powerful example of what it means to give with a generous heart. Their willingness to give beyond their means, even in the face of trials, reflects a deep trust in God's provision and a heart transformed by grace. Paul's reminder that Christ became poor for our sake challenges us to consider our own generosity. How do we respond to the needs of others? Are we willing to give sacrificially, as Christ did for us? True generosity stems not from abundance, but from a heart filled with love and gratitude for all that God has given us.

Prayer:
Lord, fill our hearts with the spirit of generosity. Help us to give joyfully and sacrificially, trusting in Your

provision and following the example of Christ, who gave everything for our sake. May our giving reflect Your love and grace in our lives. Amen.

➢ Gospel: Matthew 5: 43-48

In this Gospel passage, Jesus continues His teaching on love by challenging His followers to love their enemies and pray for those who persecute them. He reminds them that loving only those who love you is not enough, for even tax collectors do the same. Jesus calls His followers to be perfect, just as their heavenly Father is perfect, by extending love and kindness to everyone, including those who oppose them.

Reflection:
Jesus' call to love our enemies and pray for those who persecute us is one of the most challenging aspects of the Christian life. It goes against our natural instincts and societal norms, yet it is central to the message of the Gospel. By loving our enemies, we reflect the perfect love of God, who shows kindness to both the just and the unjust. This kind of love is transformative—it has the power to break down barriers, heal wounds, and bring about reconciliation. It invites us to step out of our comfort zones and extend the love of Christ to all, even those who may not seem deserving in our eyes.

Prayer:
Heavenly Father, help us to love as You love, extending kindness and compassion even to our enemies. Give us the grace to pray for those who hurt us, and to seek reconciliation and peace in all our relationships. May we strive for the perfection of love, as You have called us to do. Through Christ our Lord. Amen.

Wednesday, June 18

❖ Wednesday of the Eleventh week in Ordinary Time

- ➢ First Reading: Second Corinthians 9: 6-11
- ➢ Responsorial Psalm: Psalms 112: 1bc-2, 3-4, 9
- ➢ Alleluia: John 14: 23
- ➢ Gospel: Matthew 6: 1-6, 16-18
- ➢ Lectionary: 367

➢ First Reading: 2 Corinthians 9:6-11

In this passage, Paul teaches the Corinthians about the principles of generosity. He emphasizes that whoever sows sparingly will also reap sparingly, and whoever sows generously will reap generously. God loves a cheerful giver and is able to provide abundantly for all their needs, enabling them to be generous on every occasion. Paul reassures them that their generosity will result in thanksgiving to God.

Reflection:

Paul's words remind us that our generosity is a reflection of our trust in God's provision. When we give freely and joyfully, we acknowledge that everything we have comes from God, and that He is able to supply all our needs. Our giving is not just about meeting the needs of others, but also about participating in God's work of grace and bringing glory to Him. Generosity is an act of faith, and through it, we experience the joy of being a blessing to others and the satisfaction of knowing that we are contributing to the Kingdom of God.

Prayer:

Lord, grant us the grace to give generously and joyfully, trusting in Your abundant provision. Help us to be channels of Your love and blessings to others, so that our generosity may result in thanksgiving and praise to You. Amen.

➢ Gospel: Matthew 6:1-6, 16-18

In this passage, Jesus teaches about the proper attitude toward almsgiving, prayer, and fasting. He warns against practicing righteousness in order to be seen by others, and instead encourages His followers to do these things in secret, where only the Father sees. Jesus emphasizes that our acts of piety should not be done for the approval of people, but out of a genuine desire to honor and please God.

Reflection:

Jesus calls us to examine our motives when it comes to spiritual practices. Are we seeking the praise of others, or are we truly focused on our relationship with God? The challenge of this passage is to live our faith authentically, without the need for external recognition. When we give, pray, and fast in secret, we shift our focus from ourselves to God, who sees what is done in secret and rewards us accordingly. This passage invites us to cultivate a heart of humility, seeking to please God rather than impress others.

Prayer:

Heavenly Father, purify our hearts and motives as we seek to live out our faith. Help us to give, pray, and fast with sincerity, not for the approval of others, but for Your glory alone. May our lives be a true reflection of our love and devotion to You. Amen.

Thursday, June 19

- ❖ The Body and Blood of Christ (Corpus Christi) - Solemnity
- ❖ In the United States- Thursday of the Eleventh week in Ordinary Time

> First Reading: Second Corinthians 11: 1-11
> Responsorial Psalm: Psalms 111: 1b-2, 3-4, 7-8
> Alleluia: Romans 8: 15bc
> Gospel: Matthew 6: 7-15
> Lectionary: 368

> First Reading: 2 Corinthians 11:1-11

In this passage, Paul expresses concern for the Corinthians, worried that they might be led astray from their sincere devotion to Christ. He fears that, just as Eve was deceived by the serpent, they may be deceived by false teachings. Paul defends his apostleship, reminding them that, although he may not be a skilled speaker, he has shared the true Gospel with them out of love and without seeking any material gain.

Reflection:
Paul's words remind us of the importance of remaining faithful to the true Gospel. In a world filled with many voices and teachings, it can be easy to be swayed by what sounds appealing. However, we must be discerning and hold fast to the truth that has been revealed to us through Christ. Paul's example of selfless ministry encourages us to focus on serving others and sharing the Gospel with sincerity and love, without seeking personal gain or recognition.

Prayer:
Lord, keep us steadfast in our devotion to You and protect us from the deceptions of the world. Help us to discern Your truth and to share it with others in love and humility, just as Paul did. May we always seek to glorify You in all that we do. Amen.

> Gospel: Matthew 6:7-15

In this passage, Jesus teaches His disciples about prayer, urging them not to use empty phrases or many words, as the pagans do, thinking that they will be heard for their many words. Instead, Jesus provides them with the Lord's Prayer, a model of simplicity and sincerity in prayer. He emphasizes the importance of forgiveness, stating that our forgiveness from God is tied to our willingness to forgive others.

Reflection:
The Lord's Prayer is a profound yet simple guide to our relationship with God. It teaches us to approach God with humility, seeking His will above all else and relying on Him for our daily needs. The call to forgive others as we seek God's forgiveness is a powerful reminder of the interconnectedness of our relationships with God and with others. True prayer is not about impressing God with our words but about aligning our hearts with His will and extending the same grace to others that we have received.

Prayer:
Our Father, teach us to pray with sincerity and humility. Help us to forgive others as You have forgiven us, and may our prayers reflect a deep trust in Your goodness and a desire to see Your will done in our lives. Amen.

Friday, June 20

❖ Friday of the Eleventh week in Ordinary Time

- First Reading: Second Corinthians 11: 18, 21-30
- Responsorial Psalm: Psalms 34: 2-3, 4-5, 6-7
- Alleluia: Matthew 5: 3
- Gospel: Matthew 6: 19-23
- Lectionary: 369

➢ First Reading: 2 Corinthians 11:18, 21-30

In this passage, Paul reluctantly engages in boasting, a practice he normally condemns, to highlight the trials and hardships he has endured for the sake of the Gospel. He lists the many sufferings he has faced: imprisonments, beatings, shipwrecks, and constant dangers. Paul shares these experiences not to boast of his strength, but to demonstrate his weaknesses, through which God's power is made evident. His suffering underscores the depth of his commitment to Christ and the Gospel.

Reflection:
Paul's words challenge us to reflect on what we consider as marks of true discipleship. It's not about our accomplishments or strength, but about our willingness to endure hardships for the sake of the Gospel. Paul's life was a testimony to the power of God working through human weakness. In our own lives, we may face difficulties and challenges in following Christ, but it is in these moments that God's grace becomes most apparent. Our weaknesses and struggles are opportunities for God's strength to shine through.

Prayer:
Lord, in our weaknesses, may Your strength be made perfect. Help us to endure the trials and challenges

of life with the same faith and perseverance that Paul displayed. May our lives testify to Your power and grace at work within us. Amen.

➢ Gospel: Matthew 6:19-23

In this passage, Jesus instructs His disciples to store up treasures in heaven rather than on earth. Earthly treasures are vulnerable to decay and theft, but heavenly treasures are eternal and secure. Jesus also teaches that where our treasure is, there our hearts will be also. He emphasizes the importance of spiritual vision, urging His followers to keep their eyes focused on the light, which symbolizes truth and righteousness, rather than on darkness, which represents sin and materialism.

Reflection:
Jesus calls us to examine where we place our values and what we treasure most in life. Earthly possessions and achievements can easily become idols, distracting us from our true purpose and relationship with God. By focusing on heavenly treasures—acts of love, kindness, and service to others—we align our hearts with God's will. The condition of our spiritual vision determines the direction of our lives. If our eyes are fixed on God, our lives will be filled with His light and purpose.

Prayer:
Heavenly Father, help us to seek treasures that are eternal and to keep our eyes fixed on You. Guide us in living lives that reflect Your light and love, and protect us from the distractions and temptations of worldly wealth. May our hearts always be drawn to what truly matters—Your kingdom and righteousness. Amen.

Saturday, June 21

❖ Saint Aloysius Gonzaga, religious - Memorial

➢ First Reading: Second Corinthians 12: 1-10

➢ Responsorial Psalm: Psalms 34: 8-9, 10-11, 12-13

➢ Alleluia: Second Corinthians 8: 9

➢ Gospel: Matthew 6: 24-34

➢ Lectionary: 370

➢ First Reading: 2 Corinthians 12:1-10

In this passage, Paul speaks about a vision he received and a thorn in the flesh that he was given to prevent him from becoming conceited. Despite pleading with the Lord three times to remove this affliction, Paul was told, "My grace is sufficient for you, for power is made perfect in weakness." Paul then embraces his weaknesses, insults, hardships, persecutions, and difficulties for Christ's sake, recognizing that when he is weak, then he is strong.

Reflection:
Paul's experience teaches us a profound spiritual truth: God's power is most evident in our weaknesses. We often desire to be strong and self-sufficient, but God sometimes allows us to face challenges and limitations to remind us of our dependence on Him. By accepting our weaknesses and trusting in God's grace, we open ourselves to His transforming power. Saint Aloysius Gonzaga, whose memorial we celebrate today, embraced a life of humility and service despite his noble background, showing that true strength lies in surrendering to God's will.

Prayer:
Lord, in our moments of weakness and struggle, remind us that Your grace is sufficient. Help us to rely on Your strength rather than our own, and to find joy in knowing that Your power is made perfect in our frailty. May we follow the example of Saint Aloysius Gonzaga in living lives of humility and trust in You. Amen.

➢ Gospel: Matthew 6:24-34

In this Gospel passage, Jesus teaches about the futility of worrying. He reminds His disciples that they cannot serve both God and wealth, and encourages them to trust in God's providence for their needs. Jesus points to the birds of the air and the lilies of the field as examples of God's care, emphasizing that if God cares for them, how much more will He care for His children? He concludes by instructing His followers to seek first the kingdom of God and His righteousness, and all their needs will be provided for.

Reflection:
Worry is a natural human response to uncertainty, but Jesus calls us to a higher level of trust in God. He invites us to let go of our anxieties about material needs and to focus instead on seeking God's kingdom and righteousness. When we prioritize our relationship with God and His purposes, we can rest in the assurance that He will take care of our needs. Saint Aloysius Gonzaga exemplified this trust by dedicating his life to serving others and living out his faith with unwavering commitment, even in the face of personal sacrifice.

Prayer:
Heavenly Father, help us to cast aside our worries and trust in Your loving care. Teach us to seek Your kingdom and righteousness above all else, knowing that You will provide for our every need. May we follow Saint Aloysius Gonzaga's example of deep faith and reliance on Your providence. Amen.

Sunday, June 22

- ❖ Twelfth Sunday in Ordinary Time
- ❖ In the United States
- ❖ The Body and Blood of Christ (Corpus Christi) - Solemnity

---

- ➢ First Reading: Genesis 14: 18-20
- ➢ Responsorial Psalm: Psalms 110: 1, 2, 3, 4
- ➢ Second Reading: First Corinthians 11: 23-26
- ➢ Alleluia: John 6: 51
- ➢ Gospel: Luke 9: 11b-17
- ➢ Lectionary: 169

➢ First Reading: Genesis 14:18-20

In this passage, Melchizedek, king of Salem and priest of God Most High, meets Abram and offers him bread and wine. Melchizedek blesses Abram, and Abram gives him a tenth of everything he has. This encounter is significant as it prefigures the Eucharistic offering of bread and wine that will be fulfilled in the New Testament with the institution of the Eucharist by Jesus.

Reflection:
Melchizedek's offering of bread and wine symbolizes the divine nourishment and blessing that will find its full expression in the Eucharist. His role as both king and priest highlights the prefiguration of Christ, who would later establish the New Covenant through His own body and blood. This early Biblical account connects to the Eucharist, which is central to Christian worship, reminding us of God's continuous provision and blessing throughout history.

Prayer:
Heavenly Father, we thank You for the gift of the Eucharist, which continues to nourish and sustain us. Help us to recognize the profound connection between the offering of Melchizedek and the sacrifice of Your Son. May we approach the altar with hearts full of gratitude and reverence, always mindful of Your eternal presence in our lives. Amen.

➢ Second Reading: 1 Corinthians 11:23-26

In this reading, Paul recounts the institution of the Eucharist, which he received from the Lord. He describes how Jesus, on the night He was betrayed, took bread, broke it, and gave it to His disciples, saying, "This is My body, which is for you; do this in remembrance of Me." Similarly, He took the cup after supper, declaring it as the new covenant in His blood. Paul emphasizes that whenever we eat the bread and drink the cup, we proclaim the Lord's death until He comes.

Reflection:
This passage is a central text for understanding the Eucharist. Paul emphasizes its significance as a memorial of Christ's sacrifice and a proclamation of His death and resurrection. The Eucharist is not merely a symbolic act but a profound participation in the sacrificial love of Christ. Celebrating this feast invites us to reflect on the depth of Christ's love and His continual presence among us.

Prayer:
Lord Jesus, we celebrate Your presence in the Eucharist with joy and thanksgiving. As we partake of Your body and blood, help us to remember Your sacrifice and to live out the reality of Your love in our daily lives. Strengthen our faith and unity through this sacred meal, and keep us ever mindful of Your promise to return. Amen.

Gospel: Luke 9:11b-17

In this Gospel passage, Jesus performs the miracle of feeding the five thousand. After a day of teaching and healing, Jesus' disciples suggest sending the crowd away to find food, but Jesus instructs them to give the people something to eat. With only five loaves and two fish, Jesus gives thanks, breaks the bread, and distributes it through the disciples. Everyone eats and is satisfied, and there are twelve baskets of leftovers.

Reflection:
The feeding of the five thousand is a powerful demonstration of Jesus' compassion and ability to provide abundantly. It prefigures the Eucharist, where Jesus offers Himself as the Bread of Life. The miracle shows that even with limited resources, God can provide more than we need. It also reflects the call to share and trust in God's provision, reinforcing the theme of divine nourishment present in the Solemnity of Corpus Christi.

Prayer:
Lord Jesus, we marvel at Your generosity in feeding the multitude and at Your continued provision for us in the Eucharist. Help us to trust in Your ability to provide for our needs and to share Your blessings with others. May our participation in this Holy Communion strengthen our faith and inspire us to live in love and service. Amen.

Monday, June 23

❖ **Monday of the Twelfth week in Ordinary Time**

> First Reading: Genesis 12: 1-9
> Responsorial Psalm: Psalms 33: 12-13, 18-19, 20 and 22
> Alleluia: Hebrews 4: 12
> Gospel: Matthew 7: 1-5
> Lectionary: 371

> **First Reading: Genesis 12:1-9**

In this passage, God calls Abram to leave his country, kindred, and father's house to go to a land that God will show him. God promises to make Abram a great nation, bless him, and make his name great. Abram obeys and travels to Canaan with his wife Sarai and nephew Lot. Upon arriving, God appears to Abram and reaffirms His promise to give the land to his descendants. Abram builds altars and worships the Lord as he journeys through the land.

Reflection:
This passage marks the beginning of God's covenant with Abram, who becomes Abraham. God's call to leave everything behind and trust in His promise exemplifies faith and obedience. Abram's journey is a profound example of trust in divine providence and the willingness to follow God's plan even when the destination is uncertain. It invites us to reflect on our own trust in God's promises and our readiness to follow His guidance.

Prayer:
Lord, we thank You for calling us to follow You and for Your promises that guide us through life's uncertainties. Help us to trust in Your plan as Abram did and to follow Your call with faith and obedience. Strengthen our resolve to leave behind what holds us back and to journey toward the fulfillment of Your promises. Amen.

> **Gospel: Matthew 7:1-5**

In this Gospel passage, Jesus teaches about judgment and hypocrisy. He advises against judging others, emphasizing that the measure we use to judge others will be used to judge us. Jesus uses the metaphor of a speck in someone's eye and a log in one's own eye to illustrate the importance of addressing our own faults before correcting others. He calls for self-examination and humility in our interactions with others.

Reflection:
Jesus' teaching on judgment highlights the importance of humility and self-awareness. Before pointing

out the flaws in others, we must first address our own shortcomings. This passage challenges us to practice mercy and compassion, recognizing our own imperfections while striving to support and guide others with understanding and patience.

Prayer:
Lord Jesus, help us to examine our own hearts and actions before passing judgment on others. Grant us the humility to recognize our own faults and the grace to approach others with kindness and compassion. May we be instruments of Your love and understanding in our relationships with others. Amen.

Tuesday, June 24

❖ Birth of Saint John the Baptist - Solemnity

- First Reading: Isaiah 49: 1-6
- Responsorial Psalm: Psalms 139: 1b-3, 13-14ab, 14c-15
- Second Reading: Acts 13: 22-26
- Alleluia: Luke 1: 76
- Gospel: Luke 1: 57-66, 80
- Lectionary: 587

➤ First Reading: Isaiah 49:1-6

In this passage from Isaiah, the prophet speaks of the servant of the Lord who is called from the womb and appointed to bring Israel back to God. This servant is chosen to be a light to the nations and to restore the tribes of Jacob. The reading emphasizes the servant's mission to be a beacon of hope and salvation for both Israel and the Gentiles.

Reflection:
Isaiah's prophecy about the servant is often seen as a foreshadowing of John the Baptist's role in the New Testament. John's mission was to prepare the way for the Lord and to announce the coming of the Messiah. This passage reminds us of the divine calling and purpose in each person's life and the importance of fulfilling our God-given mission with dedication and faithfulness.

Prayer:
Lord, we thank You for the prophetic vision of Isaiah and the calling of John the Baptist. Help us to recognize our own divine calling and to live our lives with purpose and dedication. May we be instruments of Your light and grace, preparing the way for Your presence in the world. Amen.

➢ Second Reading: Acts 13:22-26

In this passage from Acts, Paul recounts how God raised up David as king and how He promised that a Savior would come from David's lineage. Paul highlights John the Baptist's role in proclaiming the coming of Jesus and preparing the way for Him. The reading emphasizes the continuity between the Old Testament promises and their fulfillment in Jesus Christ.

Reflection:
This reading underscores the important link between the Old Testament prophecies and their fulfillment in the New Testament through Jesus Christ. John the Baptist's role as the forerunner of Christ connects the prophetic tradition with the new covenant. It invites us to reflect on how we can be faithful witnesses to the promises of God and contribute to the unfolding of His plan in our lives.

Prayer:
Heavenly Father, we thank You for the fulfillment of Your promises through Jesus Christ and the role of John the Baptist in preparing the way. Strengthen our faith and resolve to be witnesses of Your truth and grace in our own time. Help us to live in accordance with Your will and to share the message of salvation with others. Amen.

➢ Gospel: Luke 1:57-66, 80

This Gospel passage narrates the birth of John the Baptist. Elizabeth, his mother, gives birth to him, and neighbors and relatives rejoice at the miracle of his birth. When Zechariah, his father, confirms that the child's name is to be John, his speech is restored. The passage concludes with John growing up and becoming strong in spirit, preparing the way for the Lord.

Reflection:
The birth of John the Baptist is celebrated as a significant event in salvation history. His arrival, marked by the fulfillment of divine promises, signals the beginning of a new era. John's growth and preparation for his mission highlight the importance of readiness and spiritual strength in fulfilling God's purposes. This passage encourages us to embrace our roles in God's plan with faith and dedication.

Prayer:
Lord God, we celebrate the birth of Saint John the Baptist and his role in preparing the way for Your Son. Help us to be inspired by his example and to live with the same faithfulness and zeal in our own lives. Guide us in fulfilling the tasks You have set before us and strengthen us in our journey of faith. Amen.

Wednesday, June 25

❖ Wednesday of the Twelfth week in Ordinary Time

- First Reading: Genesis 15: 1-12, 17-18
- Responsorial Psalm: Psalms 105: 1-2, 3-4, 6-7, 8-9
- Alleluia: John 15: 4a, 5b
- Gospel: Matthew 7: 15-20
- Lectionary: 373

First Reading: Genesis 15:1-12, 17-18

In this passage from Genesis, God makes a covenant with Abram, promising him countless descendants and the land of Canaan. Abram is assured that despite his current childless state, he will be the father of a great nation. The reading also describes a dramatic ritual in which God seals this covenant with Abram, symbolized by a firepot and a torch passing between divided animals.

Reflection:
This reading highlights the foundational moment of God's covenant with Abram, a promise that will shape the future of the Israelite people. The covenant is a testament to God's faithfulness and the deep trust that Abram placed in Him. It calls us to reflect on our own relationship with God and the promises He has made to us, encouraging us to live in faith and trust, even when the fulfillment of His promises seems distant.

Prayer:
Lord, we thank You for the covenant You made with Abram and for Your enduring faithfulness to Your promises. Strengthen our trust in Your plans for us and help us to walk in faith as we await the fulfillment of Your promises. May we be steadfast in our relationship with You and ever faithful to Your word. Amen.

Gospel: Matthew 7:15-20

In this Gospel passage, Jesus warns against false prophets, comparing them to bad trees that bear bad fruit. He teaches that one can recognize a false prophet by their fruits, meaning their actions and the outcomes of their teachings. The passage emphasizes the importance of discernment and the need to evaluate others by their deeds.

Reflection:
Jesus' teaching on recognizing false prophets underscores the need for vigilance and discernment in our spiritual lives. The metaphor of trees and fruits illustrates that the true character of a person or teaching

is revealed through their actions and results. This passage encourages us to be discerning in our judgments and to ensure that our own lives bear good fruit, reflecting the teachings and love of Christ.

Prayer:
Lord Jesus, guide us in discerning true from false teachings and help us to recognize and avoid those who lead us astray. Grant us wisdom to evaluate others by their fruits and to live our own lives in a manner that bears witness to Your love and truth. May our actions reflect Your teachings and bring glory to Your name. Amen.

Thursday, June 26

❖ Thursday of the Twelfth week in Ordinary Time

- First Reading: Genesis 16: 1-12, 15-16 or 16: 6b-12, 15-16
- Responsorial Psalm: Psalms 106: 1b-2, 3-4a, 4b-5
- Alleluia: John 14: 23
- Gospel: Matthew 7: 21-29
- Lectionary: 374

- First Reading: Genesis 16:1-12, 15-16

This passage recounts the story of Hagar, Sarah's maidservant. Sarah, unable to conceive, suggests that Abram have a child with Hagar to build a family. Hagar becomes pregnant, and tensions rise between her and Sarah. Hagar flees, but an angel of the Lord finds her, promises her a multitude of descendants, and instructs her to return and submit to Sarah. The chapter concludes with the birth of Ishmael, and Abram is 86 years old at this time.

Reflection:
The story of Hagar and Abram's child with her reveals the complexity of human actions and their consequences. It underscores themes of impatience and human attempts to control situations outside of God's timing. Yet, even in this difficult situation, God's mercy and promises are evident. Hagar's encounter with the angel shows that God sees and cares for those who are in distress and offers hope and assurance even in challenging circumstances.

Prayer:
Lord, we recognize that Your plans are often beyond our understanding and that our attempts to control our situations can lead to unforeseen complications. Help us to trust in Your timing and to seek Your guidance in our decisions. May we find comfort in knowing that You see and care for us in every situation, and may Your will be done in our lives. Amen.

> ➤ **Gospel: Matthew 7:21-29**

In this Gospel passage, Jesus teaches about the true nature of discipleship. He explains that not everyone who calls Him "Lord" will enter the Kingdom of Heaven, but only those who do the will of His Father. Jesus contrasts those who hear His words and act on them with those who hear but do not act, likening the former to a wise man who builds his house on rock and the latter to a foolish man who builds on sand. The passage concludes with the crowds marveling at Jesus' authority, as He taught with authority and not like the scribes.

Reflection:

Jesus emphasizes the importance of aligning our actions with His teachings. True discipleship involves more than verbal affirmation; it requires living out the teachings of Christ and putting them into practice. The metaphor of building on rock versus sand illustrates the stability and reliability of following Jesus' teachings versus the instability of ignoring them. This passage challenges us to examine whether our faith is reflected in our actions and to build our lives on the solid foundation of His word.

Prayer:

Lord Jesus, we ask for the strength and wisdom to be doers of Your word, not merely hearers. Help us to build our lives on the solid rock of Your teachings and to act in accordance with Your will. May our faith be evident in our actions, and may we live as true disciples of Your love and truth. Amen.

Friday, June 27

❖ Sacred Heart of Jesus - Solemnity

- ➤ First Reading: Ezekiel 34: 11-16
- ➤ Responsorial Psalm: Psalms 23: 1-3a, 3b-4, 5, 6
- ➤ Second Reading: Romans 5: 5b-11
- ➤ Alleluia: Matthew 11: 29ab or John 10: 14
- ➤ Gospel: Luke 15: 3-7
- ➤ Lectionary: 172

> ➤ **First Reading: Ezekiel 34:11-16**

In this passage, God speaks through the prophet Ezekiel, promising to shepherd His people Himself. He describes how He will search for His sheep, rescue them from where they are scattered, bring them back to their own land, and provide for them. The Lord will care for the weak and injured and will bring them to rest, emphasizing His loving and attentive care for each one of His flock.

Reflection:

The image of God as the Good Shepherd in this reading is a powerful reminder of His deep love and care for us. God does not abandon His people but actively seeks out the lost and the broken, tending to their needs with compassion and mercy. On this Solemnity of the Sacred Heart, we are called to reflect on the boundless love of Christ, who came to seek and save us, offering us rest and healing in His embrace.

Prayer:
O Sacred Heart of Jesus, You are the Good Shepherd who seeks out the lost and brings us back to the fold. We thank You for Your unfailing love and care for us. Help us to trust in Your guidance and to rest in the knowledge that You are always with us, tending to our needs with compassion and mercy. Amen.

➢ Second Reading: Romans 5:5b-11

Paul writes about the love of God poured into our hearts through the Holy Spirit. He speaks of how Christ died for us while we were still sinners, demonstrating the depth of God's love. Through Christ's death and resurrection, we have been reconciled to God and saved from wrath. Paul encourages us to rejoice in God through our Lord Jesus Christ, who has brought us this reconciliation.

Reflection:
This passage from Romans highlights the transformative power of God's love, made manifest in the death and resurrection of Christ. Even in our sinfulness, God's love is poured out for us, offering us reconciliation and salvation. The Sacred Heart of Jesus is a symbol of this divine love, which overflows into our lives, bringing us peace, joy, and the assurance of our redemption.

Prayer:
Lord Jesus, we marvel at the depth of Your love, which led You to lay down Your life for us while we were still sinners. Fill our hearts with gratitude and joy as we contemplate the Sacred Heart, the source of our salvation. May we live each day in the light of this love, sharing it with others and rejoicing in the gift of reconciliation You have given us. Amen.

➢ Gospel: Luke 15:3-7

In this Gospel passage, Jesus tells the parable of the lost sheep. A shepherd who has 100 sheep loses one and leaves the 99 to search for the lost one. When he finds it, he rejoices and carries it back on his shoulders. Jesus concludes by saying that there is more joy in heaven over one sinner who repents than over 99 righteous people who have no need of repentance.

Reflection:
The parable of the lost sheep is a beautiful illustration of the Sacred Heart of Jesus, full of mercy and compassion. Jesus seeks out the lost with a relentless love, rejoicing when they are found and brought back to the fold. This parable reminds us of the immense value that each person holds in the eyes of God. No one is beyond the reach of His love, and there is great joy in heaven when we return to Him.

Prayer:
Sacred Heart of Jesus, You rejoice over each one of us, especially when we turn back to You in repentance. We thank You for Your boundless mercy and the joy You take in finding us when we are lost. Help us to always trust in Your love and to seek out others with the same compassion You show to us. Amen.

Saturday, June 28

❖ Saint Irenaeus, bishop and martyr - Memorial

> ➢ First Reading: Genesis 18: 1-15
> ➢ Responsorial Psalm: Luke 1: 46-47, 48-49, 50 and 53, 54-55
> ➢ Alleluia: Luke 2: 19
> ➢ Gospel: Luke 2: 41-51
> ➢ Lectionary: 376/573

➢ First Reading: Genesis 18:1-15

In this reading, the Lord appears to Abraham by the oaks of Mamre in the form of three men. Abraham shows them great hospitality, providing them with food and rest. One of the visitors, speaking for the Lord, tells Abraham that his wife Sarah will have a son. Sarah, overhearing this, laughs because of her old age, but the Lord questions why she laughed, reaffirming that nothing is too hard for Him.

Reflection:
The story of Abraham and Sarah is a powerful reminder of God's faithfulness and the fulfillment of His promises, even when they seem impossible by human standards. Saint Irenaeus, whose feast we celebrate today, was a defender of the faith who proclaimed the truth of God's promises in the face of heresy. Just as Sarah doubted but later saw the fulfillment of God's promise, we are called to trust in God's word, knowing that He is always faithful.

Prayer:
Lord, You are the God of the impossible, and Your promises are always fulfilled in Your perfect time. Strengthen our faith, especially in moments of doubt, and help us to trust in Your unfailing word. Through the intercession of Saint Irenaeus, may we always hold fast to the truth of Your promises. Amen.

➢ Gospel: Luke 2:41-51

This Gospel passage recounts the story of Jesus being lost and then found in the temple when He was twelve years old. Mary and Joseph search for Him anxiously and finally find Him sitting among the teachers, listening and asking questions. When His mother asks why He stayed behind, Jesus responds that He must be in His Father's house, but they do not understand. Despite this, Jesus returns to Nazareth with them and is obedient to them, and His mother keeps all these things in her heart.

Reflection:
The finding of Jesus in the temple is a moment of both anxiety and revelation for Mary and Joseph. It highlights Jesus' awareness of His divine mission, even at a young age, and His deep connection to His

Heavenly Father. For Saint Irenaeus, understanding the mystery of Christ was central to his teaching. This Gospel reminds us that God's ways are sometimes beyond our understanding, but like Mary, we are called to ponder these mysteries in our hearts and trust in His divine plan.

Prayer:
Heavenly Father, like Mary and Joseph, we sometimes struggle to understand Your ways. Help us to trust in Your wisdom and to seek You with all our hearts. Through the intercession of Saint Irenaeus, may we grow in our understanding of the mysteries of faith and remain steadfast in our devotion to You. Amen.

Sunday, June 29

❖ Saints Peter and Paul, apostles - Solemnity

- First Reading: Acts 12: 1-11
- Responsorial Psalm: Psalms 34: 2-3, 4-5, 6-7, 8-9
- Second Reading: Second Timothy 4: 6-8, 17-18
- Alleluia: Matthew 16: 18
- Gospel: Matthew 16: 13-19
- Lectionary: 591

First Reading: Acts 12:1-11

In this passage, we read about Peter's miraculous escape from prison. King Herod had arrested Peter and planned to bring him out for public trial. However, an angel of the Lord appeared to Peter while he was in chains, causing the chains to fall off and leading him out of the prison. Peter thought he was seeing a vision, but once he was safely outside, he realized that God had indeed delivered him from Herod's grasp.

Reflection:
Peter's escape from prison demonstrates God's providence and protection over His chosen ones. Despite the dire circumstances, God intervened in a miraculous way to save Peter. As we celebrate the feast of Saints Peter and Paul, we are reminded of their unwavering faith and the powerful ways in which God worked through them. Peter's deliverance encourages us to trust in God's ability to rescue us from any situation, no matter how hopeless it may seem.

Prayer:
Lord, just as You delivered Peter from his chains, deliver us from the things that bind us and keep us from living fully in Your light. Strengthen our faith so that we may trust in Your saving power, even in the darkest of times. Through the intercession of Saints Peter and Paul, may we have the courage to follow You without fear. Amen.

➢ Second Reading: 2 Timothy 4:6-8, 17-18

In this reading, Saint Paul reflects on his life as he approaches the end of his earthly journey. He speaks of having "fought the good fight" and "finished the race," confident that a "crown of righteousness" awaits him. Paul also acknowledges how the Lord stood by him and gave him strength, delivering him from all dangers and enabling him to continue proclaiming the Gospel.

Reflection:
Paul's words resonate as a testament to a life lived in total dedication to Christ. His journey was fraught with hardships, yet he remained faithful, knowing that the Lord was with him every step of the way. As we honor both Peter and Paul today, we are called to emulate their commitment and perseverance in the face of trials. Their example inspires us to remain steadfast in our faith, trusting that God will sustain us in our own race toward eternal life.

Prayer:
Gracious God, as we reflect on the lives of Peter and Paul, we are inspired by their faithfulness and courage. Help us to fight the good fight and to finish our race with the same perseverance, knowing that You are with us every step of the way. May we always be mindful of the crown of righteousness that awaits those who remain true to You. Amen.

➢ Gospel: Matthew 16:13-19

In this Gospel passage, Jesus asks His disciples, "Who do people say that the Son of Man is?" After hearing their responses, He asks them directly, "But who do you say that I am?" Peter boldly declares, "You are the Messiah, the Son of the living God." Jesus blesses Peter for this revelation, telling him that this truth was revealed to him by the Father. He then declares that Peter is the rock on which He will build His Church, and gives him the keys to the kingdom of heaven, granting him the authority to bind and loose on earth and in heaven.

Reflection:
Peter's confession of faith is a pivotal moment in the Gospels. It marks the beginning of his role as the leader of the early Church. Jesus' declaration that Peter is the rock upon which the Church will be built underscores the importance of faith in Christ as the foundation of our lives. As we celebrate the feast of Saints Peter and Paul, we are reminded of the essential role of faith in our journey and the trust that Jesus places in each of us to be His witnesses in the world.

Prayer:
Lord Jesus, You chose Peter to be the rock upon which You built Your Church. Strengthen our faith so that we may boldly confess You as the Messiah, the Son of the living God. Help us to live out this faith with the same zeal and dedication as Peter and Paul, bringing others closer to You. Through their intercession, may we grow in our commitment to Your mission and always seek to build up Your Church on earth. Amen.

Monday, June 30

- ❖ Monday of the Thirteenth week in Ordinary Time
- ❖ First Martyrs of the Church of Rome - Optional Memorial

- ➤ First Reading: Genesis 18: 16-33
- ➤ Responsorial Psalm: Psalms 103: 1b-2, 3-4, 8-9, 10-11
- ➤ Alleluia: Psalms 95: 8
- ➤ Gospel: Matthew 8: 18-22
- ➤ Lectionary: 377

➤ First Reading: Genesis 18:16-33

In this passage from Genesis, Abraham engages in a profound conversation with God about the fate of Sodom. As God reveals His intention to destroy the city due to its grave sins, Abraham pleads on behalf of the righteous who might live there. He begins by asking if God would spare the city if fifty righteous people were found, and gradually lowers the number until God agrees to spare the city if only ten righteous people are found. This dialogue highlights Abraham's deep sense of justice and compassion, as well as God's willingness to listen and be merciful.

Reflection:
Abraham's intercession for Sodom reflects the power of prayer and the importance of advocating for mercy, even when faced with seemingly insurmountable evil. It teaches us about the heart of God, who is both just and merciful. Abraham's persistence in prayer is an example for us to continually bring our concerns before God, trusting in His goodness and compassion. In a world often filled with injustice, we are called to be intercessors, praying for God's mercy and working toward justice.

Prayer:
Lord, teach us to pray with the same persistence and compassion as Abraham. May we never cease to intercede for those in need, trusting in Your infinite mercy. Help us to be advocates for justice and instruments of Your peace in a world that so desperately needs it. Amen.

➤ Gospel: Matthew 8:18-22

In this Gospel passage, Jesus encounters two would-be disciples. The first expresses his willingness to follow Jesus wherever He goes, but Jesus warns him that following Him means embracing a life without earthly security, saying, "Foxes have dens and birds of the air have nests, but the Son of Man has nowhere to lay His head." The second man asks for time to bury his father before following Jesus, but Jesus responds, "Follow me, and let the dead bury their own dead," emphasizing the urgency and total commitment required to be His disciple.

Reflection:

This passage challenges us to consider the cost of discipleship. Following Jesus requires a willingness to let go of earthly attachments and embrace a life of uncertainty and sacrifice. Jesus' words may seem harsh, but they underscore the urgency and radical nature of His call. To follow Him is to prioritize the Kingdom of God above all else, even above the most sacred duties and comforts. As we reflect on this, we are invited to examine our own lives and ask what we might need to let go of in order to follow Jesus more fully.

Prayer:

Jesus, help us to respond to Your call with wholehearted commitment. Grant us the courage to let go of anything that holds us back from following You. May we be willing to embrace the sacrifices required of discipleship, trusting that in You, we find our true home and ultimate security. Amen.

Manufactured by Amazon.ca
Bolton, ON